# Alfred

# Alfred

A fictionalized biography of my father
based on journals, letters, and experience

## Piers Anthony

**To order additional copies of this book, contact:**
Xlibris Corporation
1-888-795-4274
www.Xlibris.com
Orders@Xlibris.com
43950

# CONTENTS

# CONTENTS

# MARION

Marion held on to her books and stepped down off the train. She had a fifteen minute walk to the high school. It was a pleasant day, June 16, 1924, and school would soon be out for the summer.

As she left the station, a boy intercepted her. He was her age, fifteen, short and active, the son of rich Edward J the mushroom grower. In fact, said to be the largest mushroom grower in the world. "Hello, Alfred."

He fell in beside her. "I saw the train come in. We live close by."

She knew that. She was flattered by his evident interest in her, though he was by no means high on her list of prospects. Still, his family had several automobiles, and that was not something a girl just ignored. So she made conversation. "You went to the Commencement Dance."

"With my sister Elinor," he agreed quickly. "She's old, seventeen, but she's great when she gets started. She can really dance."

Still, he had had to take his sister, instead of some other girl. That spoke volumes. She changed the subject. "What is your outlook on life?" Her purpose was to get him talking, so that she wouldn't have to.

It worked. "I'm out for a good time. I have six years before I need to get serious. I can't imagine being a bachelor like Uncle Joe."

Was he trying to steer the dialogue to romance? That needed to be defused. "I mean your ambitions for accomplishment."

He thought for a moment, a mannerism of his. It was as if he had never considered this matter before, though she was sure he had. *Everyone* had. "Two things I want to be: a good man, and a good musician. The first is an ideal."

Marion wasn't musical, but knew he practiced with several instruments, such as the saxophone and bassoon. His family could afford those, too. She was not in a position to judge whether he was good with them, so she focused on the more general ideal. "That seems worthy."

"I know I'm not there yet. Sometimes I wonder why I have such a strong adverseness to displeasure."

"Adverseness?" That was a new word to her.

"I haven't the least pity for suffering people in general, unless they suffer at another person's desire."

"I suppose it is their own problem."

"I also dislike anything that isn't quite clean. Not believing in a deity, I can turn only to the fact that uncleanliness hasn't killed me thus far."

She laughed. Alfred had such odd thoughts! "No Deity? But what about when someone dies? Where does she go?"

"I don't know. Last week my grandmother Mary died. I hardly knew her, though she lived only half a mile away. I sent her a nice card for her birthday in April; I put a lot of thought into it. Father says I must attend the funeral, though I don't see the point. Why go to see her after she is dead? Everyone will say good things about her, how wonderful she was, what a great person, when really she was just an ordinary person like the rest of us. Why should we have to stifle things after a person's death that were okay to think during her life?"

This was getting uncomfortable, so she changed the subject again. "What was the blowout you had with your teacher last week?"

He grimaced. "Miss Hunt. I seem to be making an enemy of her. She keeps sending me out into the hall."

"The hall? Why?"

"I don't know. Several days ago she sent Bill out for talking. I said I had been talking more than he had, but she didn't send me out. Then some time later she sent me out Then another day I looked at her, because she was looking at me, and I could do it as long as she could, and she said 'You evidently haven't any studying to do, so you might as well go out in the hall.' She sends me out and I have nothing to do except to meditate about the wrong she has done me."

There was surely reason, probably his arrogance in trying to stare down the teacher, but he might not consider that to be bad behavior. Students were not supposed to be too assertive. "I suppose she's a character."

"Character," he repeated thoughtfully. "I judge character by the nose and the shape of the head, but feel I know very little about myself."

"I'm glad I have a good head of hair covering my head," she said lightly. "But I can't do anything about my nose."

"It's a good nose."

She felt foolishly flattered. But now they had arrived at the school, and had to go to their separate home rooms.

The day was unfortunately ordinary. Marion was not an apt student; the studies that seemed easy for others were not so for her.

The following day she walked to school with her mother. She chafed under the restrictions her parents put on her. They would not let her smoke cigarettes or go out with the boy she liked, so she had to sneak these things. Often she just had to sit on her porch alone, wishing she were not alone. To make it worse, one of her friends was suffering a cruel turn of fate, and there was nothing she could do

Alfred intercepted her as she arrived on the train, any day she was alone. There could be no doubt of his interest in her, but she did not encourage him in that respect; he was not the one who turned her on. Yet his company was convenient; he carried her books and made conversation that distracted her temporarily from her problems. "But my grandmother's funeral was pretty," he admitted.

Then it was summer. She no longer went to school. Alfred went to the shore for three weeks with his family. Seaside Park, New Jersey—how she wished she could have that kind of diversion! But her family was not wealthy.

She pondered that, and wrote Alfred a letter. She phrased it carefully so as not to seem too eager to travel, but mentioning it seemingly incidentally, putting the notion in his mind. "Oh, Alfred," she said three times, getting a bit carried away, and signed it simply, informally, Marion. They had known each other four years, but contacts had been incidental until this year. In her loneliness she was finding him increasingly appealing. Maybe nothing would come of it, but how exciting it would be to get away from home for a while. With anyone!

A few days later she had his reply. "I dreamed of you," it said in part. "I was at the shore, and you were in the town of Toms River, not far from Seaside Park, so I went over. Later you came over to join me at the shore, and all we did was talk. I was entirely at ease and natural with you. We talked as if we were comrades or friends."

This was progress.

The letter continued with his concern for his mother, Edith, who was seriously ill with cancer on the face. "Things are not the same since Mother came home. I can't play the piano or phonograph. I feel guilty because I don't want to be near her. I hate illness; it's unclean."

All that money, and his mother was dying. What kind of trade-off was that? Surely he hated the fact that she was so ill, and that translated to an aversion to everything associated with it. Marion wasn't sure how she would feel if her mother were dying; probably she would be no better able to cope.

She responded sympathetically. She hadn't cared much when Alfred walked her to the school, but now that she had no daily contact with him, she missed him. The letters brought her closer, and as she wrote, it was as if she were with him.

His next delighted her: he had dreamed of her again. The constraints of family and culture limited their association, but in dreams anything could happen. It was a way to be foolishly daring, without evil consequence. His dreams were bolder than hers, and she relished them.

"I had a wonderful dream last night. In it I was happier than I ever remember being. I hope I won't describe it in a poor way, because it was beautiful, however impractical. I must have married you, Marion, or something, for we were sleeping together—on the beach. I was supremely happy. I hugged you with all my ardent fervor, giving vent to my feelings, and you liked it. It felt wonderful, wonderful, to be able to do that which has been my waking dream for so long."

She pictured it as she read, and soon felt as if it were her own dream. There was the warm beach, and the surging sea. There she was with Alfred. He embraced her with all his strength, without hurting her, and all their thoughts were of their happiness and devotion. "The feel of your soft body against mine is enchanting. I am in a supreme moment. All my hopes of years are embodied in this embrace. I am almost drunk with happiness."

Whew! She felt guilty for being thrilled. It was wonderful to be such a dream for a man. She knew herself to be a pretty girl, but that was potential, while this was achievement. "Go on," she murmured.

"You are such a beautiful creature, clasped tight against my breast." She smiled, liking the naughty proximity. "We are united in love."

"Yes we are," she breathed. She looked around, hearing the wash of the sea as it advanced on them. "I think we should move." So they went to a higher bank on the beach. Looking down they saw the water entering the place where they had been. A wave came and trickled in to their second abode, so they moved again, this time to a wooden platform. Standing there, out of reach of the sea, they continued their embrace. She felt his strong hands on her back, pressing her girlish form close to him. They could hug to their heart's content without thinking of the world or its people.

The letter ended, and she came out of it. Of course they couldn't do that in real life, and not just because they did not live near the sea. She wasn't even sure she wanted to do it. They were fifteen, too young to be allowed serious adult pleasures. It would be six more years before they completed their education and could marry, if they wanted to. A lot could happen in six years, and there were other boys on her horizon. It was fun sharing Alfred's dream, but it was only a dream, to be appreciated but not taken too seriously. Still, what an experience!

Their correspondence continued, but Alfred's letters lacked the flair of the dream letter. His mother seemed to be nearing the end; the consensus was that she would die within a month. Surgeons tried to ameliorate her condition, but that only disfigured her eye and face. Alfred didn't say much about it, but it had to be weighing him down. Meanwhile his family kept him busy with chores, such as painting their boat. Yes, they had a boat as well as all the cars.

He reported having a blowout with his Aunt Louisa. He said that he thought religion had grown out of superstition, and she flared. Like many older folk, she was more religious than was seemly. Marion wasn't sure where she stood on religion, but she followed the forms so as not to get into trouble. Alfred was sometimes too intellectually pushy for his own good. He hadn't, as he explained in a letter, decried religion itself; he had merely assessed its likely derivation. In the time of primitive man, such things as storms with severe thunder and lighting, or earthquakes, or tidal waves, or floods, could not be understood. So they formed theories. They conjectured some superior being who was beyond the comprehension of ordinary men, with enormous power. He might watch over human beings, but also send the thunder. He had to have a reason. So people tried to bribe him to be good to them. But what value would presents have to an invisible being with infinite power? Well, maybe the best they had to offer: the choicest cattle, treasure, the most attractive maidens. So they lived under the shadow of fear. They worshiped what they didn't understand.

It went farther, Alfred said. Someone wrote a book telling his idea of this super-being. Other people wrote their versions, and together they made the Bible. Thus civilized people came to worship a book! Bah, he concluded. People were deceiving themselves. He wanted none of it. It was as likely that mankind was the product of some higher civilization, created and set adrift to see what the baby human minds could think of. After a while they might get tired and throw it on the dump. Why take it so seriously?

That kind of talk made Marion nervous, not because it was necessarily wrong, but because it could get him in trouble. His aunt wasn't the only one who could react.

Then came September, the end of summer. He spied her walking to school—by her green sweater—and joined her. He was disturbed about something that had happened the prior week. Everyone had given up hope for his mother except himself and his sister Elinor. Perhaps his mother knew that. She called him into her room and dictated a telegram to one Mrs. Batten. He sent it with nobody else in the family knowing; it was a private matter. The following day the reply came. He didn't know whether to give the sealed telegram directly to her or to his father, so he asked his Aunt Louisa. She opened it, read it, and gave it to his father to read, then returned it to Alfred to read. Then they gave it to the nurse, who took it in to Mrs. J. She said she wanted it brought to her unopened, and wanted Alfred to read it to her. He had to make a pretense of opening it, and read it to her.

"The affair between mother and me was a secret," he concluded. "Now it is not. I thought Louisa could be trusted, but guess she could open anybody's private and personal correspondence without missing a heartbeat. I'd like to let this meddler go to hell!"

Marion realized that he was speaking in the heat of the moment and didn't really mean it. Still, he had a case. She expressed her sympathy, as much to calm him as from any real agreement.

Three days later she was the one doing most of the talking, as was generally the case now, as Alfred was less of a conversationalist than she. She described her ideal for a companion. He must wear a cagy sweater, gray flannels, wide belt, and no hat. His hair should be straight back, he should have a fairly dark complexion, and had to have a car.

What she didn't say was that Alfred really didn't qualify, except that he had a rich father, so had access to a car. But perhaps he understood.

So why was this talented, intellectual, rich boy attracted to her? She was none of these things, as he had to know. There were many other girls who were smarter or more athletic. She had only one thing going for her: her appearance. She was pretty. That worked magic.

It also gave her a wider choice than just Alfred. The problem was that the kind of man she liked was not the kind her parents approved of. They approved of Alfred, deeming him safe and of good (i.e. wealthy) family. So it was easy to go along with him for now.

Thursday, the second day of October, as they walked to school, she told him of her trouble with Liz. Later that day she learned that Liz had asked him about her. The next day Alfred told her about the condition of his mother: at any point she could sleep and not wake again. "It is piteous to see such a good woman, thin, weak, helpless on a bed, her head wrapped in bandages, unable to take nourishment, even water, and hard for her to speak," he said. "She used to do everything. Now, nothing."

"It must be fate," Marion said, unable to come up with anything appropriate, but needing to respond.

"I think she married a man she did not love, and that's why she is fading. Yet she has accomplished much. She should be an inspiration."

"Of course." Marion was sure the woman was good, and did not deserve this awful fate. Why had God decreed it for her?

It got worse. On October 13 he reported that his father said his mother had been given just two more days to live. "It's too bad to see how a once robust woman is now a poor little frail piece of humanity. It makes me wonder *Why?*"

She couldn't answer. It did seem unfair.

Two days later Edith died. She was 44. She told the nurse that the fight was over, and died about 7:30 in the morning. Alfred did not say much, and was away from school Friday, for the funeral, which was an elaborate one. Marion did not attend, not being an official friend of the family, but understood that the casket was hidden behind a great bank of flowers, that Mr. Lloyd performed a very nice service, and that Alfred's older brother Edward and older sister Elinor played Shubert's serenade. The casket was buried at Birmingham in the little family plot, and her infant son David was put beside her. David had died years before when Edward Senior's deafness prevented him from hearing a train, and there was a collision that killed the baby. It seemed fitting.

Another day, Alfred spoke with greater feeling. "I wasn't fooled. It was only her body that they hid in the ground. She was not covered by earth. What she gave us, we still have. We have her good advice, her love for us, her unselfishness. The great spirit which she showed us, we still retain. Matter is matter, but what she gave us can never change. We have all gained. She left her sickness in her poor old body, which lies out in the country now. She is happy. We remember her teachings, we know her ideals, we are men enough to stick to the good, as she has shown it to us. To be sure she can't say 'Put on a clean shirt,' as she used to, but nevertheless, if she thinks I need one, I shall put one on. All that we don't have is her body. That's a trifle. It just helped us to get used to her. Now we don't need it. She is with us. She will comfort Father in the night, and help him to know that nothing real has left us. She will be proud of her children. Yes. 'Lo, I am with you always.'"

"That's beautiful," Marion said. Of course she had sent a note of sympathy, and knew that many others had done so too. It was the thing to do.

Another day he telephoned and told her of a dream he had had of her while at the shore in summer; he had encountered his note about it, reminding him. Again, she entered it, as if it were her own experience; it was fun being a dream girl.

She was a princess, living in a beautiful white palace on the side of a steep green hill. She was always dressed in white, matching the palace. She had a strict aunt who did not wear white and wouldn't let Alfred in to see her, but sometimes he was able to climb to a hidden balcony where they could talk. Once when he arrived and was climbing up she took a ring from her finger and threw it to him. But her aim wasn't good, and it went past him and rolled down the roof. He crawled down after it, but it rolled off the roof to the ground below, and he couldn't see it.

"Don't go after it now," she said. "You can look for it when you go back down. It's just a bauble."

He resumed his climb to the balcony, and they talked about how he could more readily get to see her, or somehow get her away from her aunt. "Maybe you could climb up the other side of the hill, and get above the palace, and let a string down to my window so I could climb up," she suggested. But she knew that wouldn't work, because she lacked the strength to climb such a rope.

She asked him to go into town to get some books and an ice cream cone for her, as she was not allowed such simple un-princessly pleasures. He agreed, and took his eldest brother John's Ford for the drive. But he couldn't figure out how to hold the cone and the books while steering and working the gas lever all at once. So that didn't work.

Finally she realized that she was the princess, and was of age, and made her aunt back off. She invited Alfred to come in regardless.

That was the end of his dream. She liked it. "We can make that much come true, Alfred," she said. "You must come to visit me here on Green Hill." For his dream was based on reality: Marion lived on Green Hill, named after the family, and her parents were unconscionably strict about whom she could visit with. It was time to stand up to them.

"That's wonderful," he said, sounding truly thrilled. "You must come with me to the symphony concert in Coatsville next month." She agreed, but wasn't sure her parents would allow it.

Friday, he walked with her again, and told her of another dream, this one a bit naughty. It was that she lived at his house, and in the morning when he got up she was standing before the bathroom window in her underwear. She had wide hips, being highly feminine.

"Hello," he said.

"Oh!" she replied, startled. "I can't take my shower here, with you watching." It wasn't clear why she didn't simply close the bathroom door.

So she went down into the front yard, where there was a shower stall. Alfred's cousin Ellis wanted to watch her do it, but Alfred did his best to stop him. That was just as well. While they were distracted she was able to complete her shower and enter the house again.

Then her train was due. Alfred walked to the corner with her, happy for her company.

"I like your dreams, Alfred, even the naughty ones," she said. Because in them she was a princess or creature of delight, in contrast to her dreary reality. Naughtiness could be contemplated in dreams far more safely than in real life. Thus she encouraged him to tell them, and he obliged. It seemed he had been making notes of his dreams of her for several months, and could refresh his memory.

Thus a melange of assorted dreams or fragments, tricky to integrate into any cohesive narrative, but in her fancy she tried. Alfred was riding his bicycle out of town, completed his mission, and started back by a different route. Before long he came across what he thought was Lenape Park. He rode his bicycle into the buildings and out, and after a while came upon John's Ford. Just for fun he cranked it, and it started. Marion was standing near, in that magic manner of dreams. He said "It's a wonder it started."

She saw no reason to waste such an opportunity. "Let's go for a drive."

So they got in, and he drove around the area. It was delightful. Then they returned, parked the car, sat in the back seat, and began spooning. He put his arm around her and spoke endearingly, and she responded affectionately, but they didn't actually kiss. Then it was time to leave.

Another time he walked up the street to where the Ford was parked. Marion saw him, ran up, and then back to a stand where there were bananas, and gave him one. Then she took a big bunch and gave them to passers by. "I hope I remembered to pay for them," she murmured.

Alfred was walking through a hurrying throng in a large station, when he came out on a platform. There was Marion, dressed in her bridal clothes. He didn't know what was happening, but it looked as though he was going to get married, so, as she was the one he loved, he did. He had on his everyday clothes, shirt open at the neck, but she didn't mind, so they were married. He wasn't sure whether he gave her the final kiss or how it occurred.

Well. If it had been *her* dream, she would have kissed him at the appropriate time, in the proper manner. And made sure he was properly dressed for the occasion. She was merely being polite in his dream, so as not to make a scene. Informal clothing was definitely out.

Alfred's whole family, except for his brother John, in another dream, visited Marion's family. Her father was an old man with a thin sprinkling of white hairs on his head. He was tall and deaf, but a nice old chap. Their house was in good order. They sat in the living room and talked for a while. Then Alfred noticed that Marion wasn't there. Where was she? They were served refreshments. They ate at the table; Mr. G sat at the head, with his back to the hearth. Creamed veal on toast, and Alfred had two helpings. Then Marion came down. She acted as if Alfred had to be put up with, because his father was somebody.

The G's left, and the J's sat around until half past ten in the evening. Then they left, and he noticed the town of Green Hill beyond the house. It was a row of buildings: first a few ramshackle one story houses, then a big fine hall, and at the other end a large white stone building. There were some stores.

Marion shook her head. That wasn't much of a dream. The house and town were all wrong, and nothing interesting happened. But the next one was better.

Marion was stranded off the trolley at Gay and High Streets. He was on his bicycle, and offered her a ride to wherever she might want to go. She accepted, and he found that she lived somewhere near the fair grounds. She sat on the bar of the bike, and he pushed up the hill. He dropped her off, then pedaled on until the dream stopped.

Then Alfred came to see her in reality. It was somewhat awkward, but it surely set him straight about the actual nature of her house and parents. He put on a record, and she wanted to dance, but didn't say so, and he didn't think to ask her. He was socially imperfect, and evidently realized it. He said he thought he needed to learn to be more entertaining, rather than let her be bored. She told him she was bored all the time. It was true; he might not be her perfect man, but his company relieved the boredom.

Then he had another dream. He was up in something like a school room, except that the seats were beds. Marion was up in front, drawing on the blackboard. The teacher was smoking a big long Turkish cigarette. Alfred remembered that Marion had smoked out at Sharpless's. Would he give himself away if he took a puff or two? She came around and gave him one puff: very mild taste.

There were others there, but they didn't matter. Marion came and stood by his bed. "You are all so slow," she said, and threw herself down across him. He was determined to show her that he wasn't slow, so he put his arms around her and hugged her very closely, twice. She seemed to be wearing an Egyptian two piece costume, leaving her waist with nothing on it. So she was bare where he clasped her. Then they sat up, still embracing. He forgot the position, and she began blowing at him. Her breath was as lean and nice as the purest open air, but warm. She wanted him to blow at her, but he wasn't sure of his breath.

Then they began kissing. He kissed her on the chin and on the lower lip, but couldn't seem to get a good full-mouth kiss. Through it all she retained a kind of condescending air, not very superior, but tolerant, as if she had done it before and he was only one more. So though it meant everything to him, it seemed to mean little to her.

Marion thought about that. Obviously he wanted to kiss her, but didn't quite dare; even in his dreams he shied away some. Yet he was correct in one sense: she had kissed elsewhere, despite her parents' best efforts to prevent it. She did know something about kissing, and one day she might show Alfred how to do it right.

At the beginning of November, Alfred said his father wanted him to go next year to either Westtown School, or George School. Those were the two leading Quaker schools in the Philadelphia area. The Quakers were the Religious Society of Friends, and of course Pennsylvania was Quaker country, because of William Penn. All Alfred's family was Quaker. They went to silent Meetings instead of church, and didn't like war. Alfred didn't really want to go to either school, he told her, because he didn't want to be away from her for a year. But he was in a poor position to oppose his father's wish.

A week later he went out to visit her. Marion wore a red dress. They went riding in his family's car—and ran out of gasoline. That was apt to make them the butt of jokes. They went into a nearby farmhouse to wait. There was a fire on the hearth.

After a moment she realized he was looking at her. "What is it?"

"In that flickering light, you look prettier than ever," he said.

"Thank you." Actually it was no coincidence; she had done her best to look good tonight.

They finally got gasoline and drove back to her house. There was Carroll B waiting for her. Her heart skipped a beat; she very much wanted to be with him. But he wouldn't stay. He had a nice new Buick. He must have wanted to take her for a ride in it, and she wanted to go, but Alfred's presence interfered. Darn it!

Alfred belatedly picked up on that. "I should have left sooner."

"It's all right," she reassured him, though it wasn't. "It doesn't make any difference."

He wasn't fooled. Whatever else Alfred was or was not, he wasn't stupid. "If I see him, I'll chase him back here," he said as he departed.

"I wish you would," she agreed longingly. She didn't want to be unkind to Alfred, but there was just something about Carroll that turned her on, and she didn't care to be a hypocrite about it.

Two days later Alfred asked her mother for permission to take Marion to the Pavlova performance, and got immediate approval. A quality event with a safe rich boy. Too bad Carroll didn't have money or care for ballet.

On November 19 they went to the ballet. Alfred came for her, and they boarded the train to Philadelphia. She was pensive, thinking of Carroll. She would rather have gone out with him, but of course her mother prevented that. She stared out the window, imagining that he was the one beside her.

"What are you looking at?" Alfred asked.

She gave a guilty start. "I was looking at you. At your reflection." She indicated the window.

"Carroll's an interesting man."

Was he reading her mind? "Please don't talk about him."

When the train arrived, Marion was eager to leave, but Alfred sat until all the other passengers had cleared. They caught a taxi from the train station to the academy.

The ballet turned out to be good. They had balcony seats. "The Swan" dance was pretty. The last dance had an oriental atmosphere. The three wise men were dressed rather scantily. One had a huge plate, shiny on one side. Another had a large tray of fruit. The third had a large and vivid cloth. He was naked from the waist up, and his feet were bare. He had a wonderful physique. He was moving all the time, especially his shoulders, head, and hands. The maiden came on later; she wore a very thin and filmy dress. The entire form of her body showed under it. Her legs seemed to be tattooed all the way up. It was really quite a dance, and it pleased the audience; the two were called out again and again.

It was late when they got back to her house. She ran up the steps and her mother opened the door. Then she turned back. Alfred was on the ground, she on the porch. She leaned over till she could look right into his eyes, gave him a serious gaze, and said "I enjoyed every minute of it."

"Marion!" he breathed.

She didn't see Alfred for a while after that, but did see Carroll. He fascinated her, yet she knew her mother was right: he was not a good match for her. She also pondered nursing as a career, yet knew that it had its disadvantages.

Alfred phoned, and they talked for some time about the Thanksgiving holiday, happiness, and friendship. It was a nice dialogue.

Monday, the first of December, she told Alfred in school that she wanted to see him. But there was time only for passing fragments, no serious talk. He said there was something to tell her, but when she invited him to do that, he declined. Something was bothering him.

Finally, as he was walking her to school, he was more forthcoming. "I wanted to thank you for writing the letters last summer. They really helped me during my mother's illness."

"I would have written more letters, if I had realized."

"And thank you for not asking about her, then."

"I thought of it, but realized you would not want to talk about it."

"You have really helped me get through."

"I'm glad."

Still, she wanted to be honest with him, conscious that he was more serious about her than she was about him. How could she convey that without hurting him?

She tried. "Suppose you liked a girl, and you know she liked you a lot, but you liked another girl better? Wouldn't you wish that the first girl didn't like you as much?"

"I suppose I would," he said. "But there's only one girl for me."

She wasn't sure he understood, but didn't care to be more direct. Then her mother told her to change her dress, and she went upstairs to put on her nice red dress. She wanted to get out of the house, which stifled her, but her mother would not hear of it. Finally, dutifully, she said "All right," and went down the stairs to rejoin Alfred.

She learned that Alfred kept a record of his thoughts each day in a book. "Don't write them in your book," she said. "Tell them to me. I can answer, and a book can't."

"I can make my book answer what I want."

"I'll answer what you want." But she didn't convince him.

He told her how his father was insisting that he go next year to Westtown or George School. "Don't go away to school," she said.

"I have to."

"But *don't* go." But of course he would do his father's will. "You'll come to see me sometimes, won't you? Oh—you don't make promises."

"I try not to."

"Oh, I wish you would. But you'll come out to see me—in your vacation, won't you?"

"If I can. I can't promise."

She sighed. "That's too bad."

"Marion, I'll tell you something at the risk of cooling the house. You remember, I think I told you, that I felt at home at the shore?"

"Yes."

"And the second place I felt at home was on the soccer field?"

"Yes."

"This is the third place I feel at home."

"I'm glad. That's so sweet. I want you to look on me as your friend, though I doubt I really have done anything to deserve it."

They were close together. She considered kissing him, but did not want to be too forward. Had he kissed her, she would have accepted it, but he did not. He was perhaps too shy.

A few days later she received a letter from a female friend, but three words were not in English: *Yo tu amo*. What could they mean? She wasn't proficient at languages. So when she saw Alfred in the fifth period class she called out to him: "Oh, Alfred, come here a minute." She dug out the letter as he came to her. "What does this mean? Yow tue ammo" But she couldn't pronounce it, so she wrote it out: YO TU AMO.

He read it, hesitating. She was sure he understood it; he knew languages. Then he wrote the translation below the words: I you love.

Oh. Of course he hadn't wanted to speak those words aloud; the rest of the class would find them hilarious. "Thank you."

"I wonder who could be writing that to you?"

"Oh, it doesn't matter. You wouldn't know her anyway." Thus she reassured him that it wasn't a secret boyfriend. He knew about Carroll; that wasn't secret, and of course Carroll wouldn't be writing a letter.

Later, during play rehearsal, she was feeling blue. Alfred came back and sat by her. "Good night."

There was a pause. "Good night," she murmured from the depths of her blues.

"I'm talking to you. Good night."

"Good night," she said more firmly.

"See you in the morning."

"Sure." It was ludicrous to suppose that a mere exchange of partings could lift her out of her mood, yet it did help.

Next day the play rehearsal ran late. Marion was worried that she would miss her train home. "What's the time?"

"Four fifteen," Alfred replied.

Later she asked again, and it was 4:25. Still the play practice dragged on. She looked at the office clock, and it was 4:50. She didn't know what to do. She didn't want to miss her train, but the play wasn't nearly finished. "What shall I do?" she asked desperately.

"Why *don't* you miss your train?" he asked.

"But I can't! Mother would have a fit."

"Not if you got home another way. I could get a car and take you home. Your folks wouldn't know the difference."

She wavered. "Should I tell mother?"

"You couldn't do anything better."

Finally she decided. "All right, Alfred, if you can do it."

"I'll phone immediately." He did so. His father, returning from the office, obligingly parked his car in front of the Senior steps. Another girl in the play, Dot, also needed a lift home, so she joined them.

Marion whispered "You'll take Dot home first, won't you?"

They went out to meet the man, and after a somewhat difficult introduction, piled into the car. Marion wasn't usually unduly shy, but Mr. J was probably the richest man in the county, and she was awed to meet him. He was perfectly polite, but she had to talk loudly so he could hear her.

First they took Alfred's father home, then Dot. Then, alone together, they drove to Green Hill. That gave them a chance to talk.

"Whenever you can I wish you'd come out, because I always like to see you."

"You've played with balloons, surely you have. Well, suppose you blow one up, a big one, a watermelon balloon. You blow it up pretty far, and it looks nice, and you say 'That's good enough, I don't want to break it.' But after a while you'd like to have it a little bigger, so you blow it up, and then still bigger, and bigger, until it's the size of a watermelon, and you say 'That's enough. I'll let it go at that.' But then you'd like it a little bigger, and you blow it until you are forced to stop of necessity, because there's nothing left to blow."

"I think I understand." She smiled. "And you're comparing me to a balloon."

"No. But each visit to your house has been so enjoyable, and each so much more so than the one before, that I'm almost afraid to come out."

"Oo! Come out anyway."

They reached her house, and she got out. "Don't go yet," she whispered as she hurried up the walk.

Both her father and her mother were worried, because she was late returning; they came out to meet her. "The play ran late," she explained breathlessly. "I couldn't catch the train. So Alfred phoned his father, and Mr. J came to pick us up. We took Dot home too."

"The Mushroom King?" her father asked, impressed. "*He* picked you up?"

"Yes, and I met him. He's a nice man, but a bit deaf. He let Alfred take the car. So I was all right. Now let me go thank Alfred."

Her mother nodded, not fooled. It was always fun to sit in a car. Her parents returned to the house, and Marion went to the car and got back in beside Alfred. "I explained," she said.

"That's good." He looked as if he wanted to put his arm around her, and she would have acquiesced, but he didn't. Sometimes he was so darned proper! But of course that was one reason why her parents approved of him. He wasn't the tallest or handsomest man, but he was smart and talented and had access to a car. She was coming to like him better as she came to know him better.

She left the car, and he drove slowly off. It had been an interesting afternoon.

Next day she reported a detail to Alfred: "I told mother last night, about us being alone together in the car."

"I hoped you would. Thank you."

"I did it for you."

"Thank you again." He paused thoughtfully. "You should have done it because it's right."

"The things *you* say are always right."

The next day, Friday, was the school party, with dancing. Marion loved dancing! She knew she was good at it, and she liked dressing up and being pretty. Alfred was there, to play his saxophone. She spoke to him only briefly. He needed a music stand, so went out to hunt one up. In due course he returned with one, then sought her out again. "Carroll is out there. We shook hands. He asked whether you were here, and I said yes. He wanted you to come out, but I explained that you couldn't, because they wouldn't let you in again. So he said to tell you that he's here, and has been for two and a half hours. He's going to take you home."

"Thank you, Alfred," she said. "You're such a gentleman."

He shrugged. "I'm just doing what I said I would."

"I like Carroll an awful lot," she confided, barely audibly.

Sunday she received a call form Carroll. "I had an accident," he said, sounding awful. "I broke up the Dodge so bad it can't be repaired."

"That's terrible," she said sympathetically.

"My head is getting infected, but my father won't let me go to a doctor."

"That's even worse."

After the dialogue she sat down and did some serious thinking. She liked Carroll, maybe in part because her parents didn't, but there was no getting around the fact that he could be wild. He had wrecked his car! Probably she ought to give him up until she was sixteen, then give him a date on her sixteenth birthday. Her mother said she would be better able to decide for herself then.

But when she told Alfred, he was negative. "It's none of my business."

"Well, *make* it your business."

"I know, but I can't interfere with your family's business."

"You know, I thought I'd hang up a nice little stocking for Mother, and in it I'd put a nice little note saying that I'd give up Carroll, for her Christmas present."

"You have to do what you believe is right, not what anyone else thinks is right."

"I know it." But she also knew that she couldn't stay away from Carroll. He was just so—so *manly*.

Alfred sat beside her for the play. She leaned toward him. "Oh, I almost called you up last night," she confided. "I was feeling so blue, and stayed around until half past eight." Then it was time for her part. She jumped up and ran to the door.

When they were together again, Alfred said he wanted to have a picture of her. "But I don't have any to give," she said with regret.

"At least I have two very pretty mental pictures of you."

"Oh, you must describe them for me!" But she was surprised by their nature and detail.

"In a farmhouse in the country sits the farm family, but also two travelers who have been caught without gasoline. The girl sits in a chair to the right of the fireplace, and the man to the left in back of her. He is in a place where he can see her profile, and is in an ideal position to gaze at her without her knowing it. The fire is burning merrily in the hearth, casting a warm glow, which flickers on the objects in the room. She is gazing into the fire, and the firelight plays on her face. She is wearing a dark red dress with black trimming, and the firelight plays on it. She has pretty light hair, slightly curly, and the firelight plays on that too. She sits there leaning forward toward the fire, the red dress and the firelight bringing out the colors of her skin, which is flushed from the cold. Her beauty is remarkable; she is so young, so poised, so unaffected, and so pensive."

"Oh, Alfred," she breathed. "I remember!"

"The second picture is in a room of a house in the country where a man and a girl stand. A mahogany table stands close to a light colored wall, and on the table are two burning red candles. She stands on the right of the table, facing it, and leaning closely against the wall. She is playing with the tiny flame, and when she asks a question, she looks at him with her eyes, the lights flickering on her countenance. She is in the red dress, and is pretty—never more so than when she is serious."

What could she say? This was love in vision.

Then the Christmas holiday cut off their contact; both of them had family obligations. Later Alfred expressed his private opinions: there was the exchange of gifts, and he thanked his siblings for them, but saw little real purpose in it. "I must thank and be thanked, but what is thanks? Words of gratitude. When the words are said, the thanking is done." His eldest brother John took a girl to a show, and she was pretty affectionate, but he didn't like her very much. "It seems that he doesn't like anybody much, and wishes he did," Alfred remarked. The brothers were set against their sister Elinor, who didn't make or keep friends, didn't fit in socially, and was wrapped up in herself. John recommended that Alfred go to Westtown School, while Edward thought he should get into Hill School. His father said that if he went to Westtown he could come home often and bring his friends. "What's he sending me away for, then?"

Then he went with Edward to Trenton, New Jersey, where he met his brother's girlfriends, who were sisters but quite different: "Ramona was small, assertive, changeable from glee to sadness, and seems to have to have her own way. Eliza is tall, quiet, with potential; she took a little longer to get acquainted, but was a downright nice girl." He rode home in the back seat with Eliza, who wasn't talkative. However, she went to George School, one of the ones he was considering, and they stopped there for a while. "I liked it, and shouldn't mind going there."

"But it's far away," Marion protested.

"Everything is far away," he said gloomily. "I'd much rather stay here." But it seemed that was not an option.

It happened that Edward invited a crowd for the evening. Alfred stayed around, running the gramophone, feeling out of place. However, he danced with Elinor, who was being a very good hostess, and she said he did well enough not to be afraid to try.

"Dance with me," Marion said.

"I'd like that."

But contact remained too rare and fleeting. He sent her a Christmas card, which was a little four page booklet with the usual Christmas greetings, and added: "Is there any service which I may render which will help you to be happier or more content?"

She took that seriously. She wrote a careful letter in response:

Dec 26, 1924

Dear Alfred,

First, I want to thank you for your beautiful Christmas greeting. It was very thoughtful of you and I appreciate it.

Can you understand this writing? I have just gotten home from the city and I'm so tired I can't see straight.

Well, to continue, I liked the little booklet so much but I didn't quite understand the message on the back. However, if you mean just exactly what that said, I'll tell you. There are things, too numerous to mention, that you and only you can do for me, but—well, it's useless to speak of them, and if I do I'll only be very, very blue, so why do it? It was very sweet of you to offer to help me be more happy and content but I know that if I really try hard enough I can be content, for I have almost everything I want including a wonderful Mother and Father, so why shouldn't I be happy?

At any rate, Alfred, *if you really want to*, I'd love to have you come out and see me. Please notice that I underscored "if you want to," I don't want you to come out if you have other plans or would rather not, but please remember you are welcome here at any time.

With all good wishes for a happy and prosperous New Year

I remain as ever

Marion

But they still couldn't get together. She saw the New Year in with Carroll, and loved it, but knew that this couldn't last. They agreed to see each other next New Year, no matter what happened.

Alfred came to see her Sunday, January 4th, 1925. It had been almost two weeks since they had been together, and it seemed like an eternity. They couldn't speak freely, because her parents would be able to overhear if they wanted to. She read him her compositions, and he didn't comment. She talked of various people and parties, hoping she wasn't being too catty in her remarks.

"Suppose I like banana salad," he asked. "Should I eat banana salad all the time?"

"Why yes, I mean you might—well, suppose you like lemon meringue pie, you might start out with one piece, and then the next time take two pieces, and the next time three, and then when you're sure you like it, take all you want of it."

"Suppose I like banana salad, but the maids only make enough so that each person may have only one banana at each meal. I enjoy it each time and I'm always glad to see it on the table. Well, suppose I was going around the world after seven months and two days, and I was going to keep going around the world all my life, and I knew that they didn't serve banana salad on the boat and that after I got on the boat I'd never have any more banana salad. Suppose then that I should keep on with one banana each day and keep liking banana salad, and on the last day, eat all I want, because it wouldn't make any difference after that."

"Oh, no. Why don't you eat all you want and enjoy it?"

"Suppose I should eat one banana on the last day?"

They talked further, but she concluded that she didn't really understand his point. He was saying he liked her, but somehow didn't think he should continue liking her? This did not make a lot of sense to her.

Later, unfortunately, it did.

Meanwhile, life continued. Saturday evening, January 10, she went riding with Carroll, and they saw someone walking beside the road. "That's Alfred!" she exclaimed as they passed him.

"That so? Let's see." Carroll stopped the car, then backed up until he could put the lights directly on the figure. Indeed, it was Alfred, looking embarrassed to be discovered.

They got out and approached him. "Hello," Carroll said.

"Hello," Alfred said.

"Who were you speaking to?" Marion asked.

"Hello, Marion."

"What are you doing out here?"

"Wasting time. Wiling away the hours till Lopez begins. I was jogging but I got a side stitch."

"Won't you come in?"

"No, I'm not coming in tonight. I'll go for a walk with you."

"I don't have shoes." They talked further, and she cautioned him about not thinking of banana salad. Then he went on, and she returned her attention to Carroll.

"Alfred's funny sometimes," she said.

"He likes you."

"Shouldn't he?"

Carroll laughed. "Of course he should. So do I. Everyone likes you. You're a beautiful woman."

"Oh, you're just saying that." But it was a good thing the darkness concealed her flush of pleasure.

Monday Alfred called her and invited himself over, though she wasn't enthusiastic. She had been ill more than one day the past week, and wasn't fully recovered. But she greeted him politely. "If you're going to stay, you might as well hang up you coat and hat."

"Are you coming riding with me?"

"Do you want me to?"

"Yes, I want you to. Are you coming?"

"All right. Wait till I ask Mother. Excuse me while I ask her?"

"No, of course not."

"Oh, you're horrid!"

Soon they went out to the car. She got snow in her shoe while getting in. That was a bad start. They rode around, but she soon got cold. He remarked how the back window was rattling.

As if it were shivering, she thought. "Well, I'm not going to sit here and freeze."

So they returned to the house, and she lit the lights while he fetched records from the car. They listened to them and talked, and it was good.

Wednesday she found her chemistry intolerably difficult; she just didn't have the head for it. Alfred was glad to go over it with her. He drove to her house and spent a solid hour on it, and she began to catch on. Then he had to go for his orchestra practice. She was satisfied; now she would not be afraid to go to chemistry class.

On Sunday the 17th Alfred called, and she asked him to come over. She had had a row with her father and was not in an ideal mood. Then she quarreled briefly with Alfred, pointlessly. But she made up for it by copying out a poem he wanted:

Mother
It's a wonderful thing, a mother—
Other folks can love you,
But only your mother can understand you.
She works for you,
Looks after you,

Loves you.
Forgives you anything you may do.
Understands you, and then
The only thing bad she ever does to you is to die and leave you.

She realized that this poem had special meaning to him because that was what his mother had done. But they didn't talk about that. They talked about religion, the Bible, her dress, her mother, brothers, the two sisters aged 18 and 17 she could have had, and how she cried all Sunday and Monday morning when she thought it was Alfred instead of David who had been killed in that collision his father had with a train.

Next day he called her, and talked about everything under the sun for an hour, a horribly, wonderfully long call. Alfred was considering George School more seriously; it had good recommendations, among them, it seemed, that his brothers hadn't gone there.

Meanwhile she had known Carroll for five months, but wasn't speaking to him now.

Sunday the first of February was a bad day: Carroll had agreed to take her to church, but he got drunk and her mother wouldn't let her go with him. She argued, not seeing why she couldn't go where she pleased, when she pleased, as she pleased, but did not prevail. She talked with Alfred, and learned he had problems of his own: his father had announced that he was engaged to marry Emma Taylor. Alfred didn't know how he felt about that, as he didn't know her, but was uncomfortable about another woman taking his mother's place in the family. His father planned to put away his pictures of his first wife. And Alfred had made a mistake: he told his father that he had been writing about him. Naturally the man wanted to know what; in fact he wanted to read Alfred's Journal. Alfred demurred; he held it sacred. But now he feared that his father would at some point read it; Alfred really could not prevent him.

Then, it seemed, they had a long talk—an hour and a half. It was about Emma Taylor, of their various brothers and sisters, of love and marriage, of children's love and its course. Alfred requested the story of his father's proposal to his mother. Marion listened, picturing them as herself and Alfred; this was bound to be romantic.

Edward met Edith when she was sixteen. He liked her originality and companionship. Of course he was a handsome young man, and she a pretty young woman. He would call on her, and thought she didn't mind him, though sometimes she wouldn't come down to see him or go out with him. He never thought much of marriage; he just liked being with her. But once when he went to the corundum mines in Georgia, expecting to stay six months, he felt so lonely that he realized how much she meant to him. At the same time he thought of her popularity, and of the possibility of her being engaged to someone else by the time he got back. He wrote and told her just how he felt, and asked her to become his wife.

She, taken aback, wrote that his letter was quite unexpected, and that she couldn't think of marrying him. She explained that she didn't think she could make him happy, and there were many nicer girls than she. That gave him a chance to write again, and they corresponded. Oh, yes, Marion knew exactly how that was.

When he came back she was at "the Breakers," a seven spring lake. He used to take her riding, walked with her, talked with her, and they sat and watched the water, but still she wouldn't marry him. After a while he had to go south, and she made a kind of agreement that if he should return alive, she would consider herself engaged to him. Unsurprisingly, he was anxious to get back, and did return alive. She accepted him, and had he not been sent on another trip to Georgia, they would have been married on April 16, 1902, her birthday; instead they made it April 15th, one day before. She was 21, he 31. Edward said that a man shouldn't think of marriage until he was between 22 and 30 and had sufficient income for them both and a thousand dollars beside.

And of course he succeeded in amassing more than that amount, and the marriage was successful. If only she hadn't fallen ill with the dreadful cancer and died. Would she, Marion, fall ill like that, if she married Alfred? What a horrible notion!

She walked with Carroll, but was sad all day. She had first met Carroll Baldwin last fall, and the very first night poured out her heart to him. They had dates several nights a week. November 2, 1924, he had taken a bunch of people, including her, to Wilmington, and she had missed an afternoon of school. When her parents found out, they forbade her to see him any more. But she saw him anyway, and after a while things wore off, and Carroll was allowed to visit the house and take her out. She watched the New Year in with him. Then came the drunk episode, and her parents cracked down, and she cried herself to sleep.

Yet she realized that her parents were right: Carroll was not ideal. Alfred was really better. It was just that Carroll had that magic appeal that so turned her on; she liked being with him. Alfred was relatively staid, safe, all right, just not magic. And he was clearly devoted to her, while Carroll had other girls. So her heart was foolish, and she needed to get over it.

She studied herself in the mirror. She had blond hair, parted down the middle, usually in a bob, with a ribbon. Hair style made such a difference, but she had to be practical. Her face had a straight profile, straight nose, medium lips, a good throat, but maybe too prominent a chin. Her shoulders were small, and so were her hands and feet, and she was slender overall. So she was pretty rather than smart; was that enough? She kept her voice soft, melodious if she could manage it. Alfred had first written to her when they were in ninth grade, and of course she had answered, but he had been too shy to speak to her directly.

But Carroll was far bolder, and she liked him better, though she knew this wasn't wise. If he asked her to run away with him, she would probably do it, though that might owe as much to her frustration with her restrictive parents as to any real merit on his part.

Sunday, March 8, Alfred told her of another dream he had had. The two of them went riding with their friend Bill's Dodge, and stopped at a nice place, like Eagle. Marion spoke a word of resignation about her fate, then passionately threw herself on Alfred and embraced him with the love that had been restrained for months. How soft her skin! Her lips! He returned such loving kisses as never before. Joy! Rapture! Bliss! Ecstasy! Two young people, untouched by the cares of the world, reveling in the adoration of each other. A subject not fit for the finest poet to sing of, for the love of children was pure with a child's natural purity. Such tender endearing kisses on her beautiful face, and how gently she reclined in his arms. But finally she said he should get more gasoline for the car. How they hated to break that ethereal embrace! He turned the car around, got gas and returned to the same place, and got a kiss on the nose, which he returned.

He also told her of a briefer dream he had had of seeing her with Carroll in the firelight, a nice looking couple. He was clearly trying not to be jealous. "Oh, Alfred," she said. "You made me cry."

Yet, oddly, Alfred's sister Elinor thought their relationship was fading. "Greenie, you and Alfred aren't nearly so thick as you use to be, are you? And you've let him slip like all the rest. You couldn't even hold *him*, could you, Greenie?" Maybe Elinor was speaking more to her hope than to reality.

Meanwhile Alfred was going to accompany his father on a trip to California the next month. He said he didn't really want to go, to be away from her that long, but he didn't have a choice. "Why do you have to go?" she asked rhetorically. "Rather than Carroll or Bud."

"Life on a steamer is luxury," he said. "I wish you could share it."

"Why don't we drive around until half past nine tomorrow morning," she suggested. "Then you'd miss your boat and wouldn't have to go."

"Actually it's the train we catch," he said. "That will take us to New York, where we'll board the boat in the afternoon."

"Maybe you could just put me in your pocket and take me along."

"I'd like that."

They both laughed at the ridiculously nice idea. "I wonder what the expression on your father's face would be when he found you had me with you."

"I guess he is happy when I am."

"I know I ought to be happy because you're going to have such a wonderful time and all that, but I'm *not*, and I wish you didn't have to go away."

They shared a sweet embrace, and he remarked how nice her hair smelled. "But all of you is nice," he said.

Nevertheless, he did have to go, and he and his father caught the train to New York. She spent the day in school feeling lonely. True, she knew other boys, but Alfred was the absent one, and she thought about him a lot.

A week later she received a five page letter from him, which she read avidly. He detailed their arrival in New York, what a huge place the Pennsylvania Station was, very clean. Boarding the huge ship, which was very nice, and he felt at home there. Their stateroom was small but good. "But I thought mostly of you, Marion. I'm thrilled by the memory of our last embrace." So was she.

"Marion, this life is luxury. I think if I stay here I'd like it better than home. I just bathed. I went in and there was every single thing ready! Hot water in the tub, cold water in the basin, a little stool, a towel, a bath rug, just as if some nice mother had been there 2 seconds before. Now if I could only know that you were somewhere on the boat—but I can't."

It did make her feel as if she were on the boat, at least while she was reading the letter. She shared his stateroom, his bathroom (naughty thought!), and walked the deck with him as he explored the craft. But it could not change the fact that he would be gone for six endless weeks.

Other letters traced their arrival in Cuba, where they went through Havana by auto, and had problems because of his father's deafness; Alfred had to be alert. Then back to sea, occasionally passing islands that showed that land still existed. Wednesday the 8th his father gave him a poem that touched him, about a sailor who dreamed of his home, father, mother, and his "Marion." Then a storm blew up and he was killed. Reading that poignant story brought a tear to her eye. He played with the ship's orchestra several times, and liked it, but then was not allowed: he was playing the horn out of tune.

And he remembered her birthday, April 13. She was sixteen. "I wonder what you're doing while I'm away, and what you will be like when I return. Remember the turtle you picked up in the road when you were out with Ellis and me last spring on a Sunday afternoon?" Oh, yes!

He saw the Panama Canal, and dolphins jumping high out of the water, maybe six feet.

And on the twentieth they arrived in California, and he found three of her letters waiting for him. "Marion, I can't hold it in. I love you! You are adorable, divine."

She realized that she could live with this sort of exaggeration. But she worried about him being so far away; anything could happen to prevent his return.

Then she had an awful dream. It was like the poem he had described, with the sailor remembering his family and girlfriend, before a storm came up and sank the ship. But in her dream, it was Alfred on the ship. She saw his face as he struggled to get out of the cabin, but it was too late, and the ship filled with water and went down. She knew with a horrible certainty that he was dead.

She woke, and knew it was a dream, and that it wasn't true. If the ship had gone down, there would have been headlines galore. Alfred had made it safely to land; she knew it. Yet the dream had captured her belief, on some persuasive level; its horror remained.

What could she do? She couldn't tell him. Yet neither could she ignore it. It could be a premonition. So she compromised. She wrote to him with a masked reference to it. "Alfred, it is one thing to be insulted, it is one thing to be misunderstood, it is one thing to be hated, but it is another thing to be hurt deeply. I have been hurt dreadfully about something concerning you. You haven't done it and you don't know what it is, perhaps some day I'll tell you about it." That might confuse him, but at least she had been honest to the degree she could manage. She mailed the letter.

She followed him via letters across the country. Then at long last he was back, and they were together again. It was wonderful. Her dream-fear faded; nothing had happened.

Thereafter their relationship progressed to embracing even some kissing; there was no doubt in her mind now that Alfred was the one.

As summer came they spent more time together, and kissing became regular. Sometimes Alfred needed guidance. Once they were at the car, her parents were on the porch and she was standing on the running board. Alfred was about to kiss her hand, but she bent down close to him and gave him a long, sweet, tender kiss on the lips. He looked dazed; indeed, it was a good one.

Another time they went swimming together, and she knew he was admiring her body in the tight suit. But of course he wasn't obvious about it, and she pretended not to be aware. That was after all much of the point of bathing suits. That evening when he arrived she was sitting, reading a paper. Then they went out to a pot of chrysanthemums on top of a stump in the yard, and she picked one for him. She knew her blouse fell away from her body as she bent forward over the flowers. He was standing facing her, and thus had a view all the way down to her waist; she wasn't wearing a corset or brassiere, so everything showed. Again, they both pretended otherwise. It was a silent game they played, surely as old as mankind: show and don't tell.

He got summer work as an assistant plumber; it was expected by his family. Boys had to get experience in trades. She understood, but it meant that they couldn't be together as much. Still, they had a number of nice evenings.

In July Alfred's family spent a few days at the cottage in Seaside Park, on the New Jersey shore. She cried when she learned he would be away. Her mother thought she was spending too much time with Alfred, but she just wanted to spend more.

Then came one of the most marvelous experiences of her life. Alfred lent her a volume of his Journal! His private personal record of his thoughts, his most precious possession. He allowed her to read it, and even to make entries in it! In this manner he demonstrated his love and trust. He wouldn't even let his father read it. She was utterly thrilled.

"It's raining," she wrote in green ink. Green was her color, after all. "Raining! Raining! It's rather cold and sticky too, and it really seems an ideal night (not knight) to write. There isn't anyone at home and Alfred has just left, so I shall proceed." Oh, glorious! It was Thursday, July 15, 1925, 8:15 PM. Never had she been so delighted in a rainy night.

Alfred's last entry was Friday the 9th, so she filled in the missing time. That evening he had called and asked to speak with mother: he wanted Marion to go to the city with him. Mother agreed, and he took her to his place, where she met his big brother John and little brother Philip, and his father Edward. "(Oh, I mean Mr. J. I'm making a horrible mess of this blessed book.)" Then she, Alfred, and Philip drove to the city of Brotherly Love, Philadelphia, where they met his other older brother Edward and his friends. They came home in the Franklin, but she had left her coat in the other car, which was by this time on its way to the shore. They tried to catch it, but didn't. Oh, bother!

Alfred was rather blue about it, and she tried to console him. Still, it was a great minor adventure.

"I wish I could write down some of my personal feelings. However, this isn't my book and I can't." So she detailed the week, concluding "Dear Alfred J, I have written in your dear old book. The old saying is 'One line is sufficient for memory.' I have written many lines but here is one that I hope you shall always remember. When you are happy or sad, wherever you may be or whatever you may be doing, always remember that Marion loves you."

She made another entry next day. Alfred had other business and didn't come to see her. "At any rate, I am here—waiting."

She returned the Journal after that, and normal life resumed. Unfortunately Alfred could be moody at times, for no seeming reason, and sometimes sarcastic. She didn't like him when he was like that. But she didn't have much choice; she loved him.

It got worse. Someone circulated a cruel story about her and Bud Bicking, and maybe Alfred believed it. She had been on a date with Bud, and he had wanted to neck, but she had demurred. He had held on to her and hurt her wrist before going. He had been really angry, and maybe after that pretended he had got what he hadn't.

Alfred didn't say anything about it to her, but she felt his emotional withdrawal. She hated that, but what could she do? Still, they continued to associate, and slowly his seeming alienation passed and he was as affectionate as before. On August 15 they went to the club and danced, and he had evidently been working on it, because he was improving. His brother Edward cut in on them and danced with her, and then the eldest brother cut in. They were better dancers, and she was mildly flattered. But her shoes weren't tight, so she had to dance closer than she was accustomed to.

Then Alfred took her home, and they embraced, kissed, and parted. Two weeks later he let her borrow the Journal again, and she looked up that day in it, and read "I love her." What wonderful words! She also read how when she had worn her soft white dress he had seen down her front to the the hint of her breasts. He liked that dress. No wonder! But he liked her filmy green dress too. She did think she looked good in green, as befitted her name.

Then he told her that they might be breaking up in October, when he was away at George School. Not because he wanted to, but because it seemed that that was the way it normally happened. His father thought they were too close, and forbade him use of the car because of it. She was hurt that he could think it could happen that way with them. In fact she was more than hurt; she was furious, crushed, and bruised. A picture of the near future came to her, of Alfred at George School meeting new people, and finally caring for another girl as he had cared for Marion. Then he might see her, Marion, as young and even childish. She went to her room, threw herself on the bed, and wept. She made a beautiful circle of tears in the middle of the bed. Then she got into bed and cried herself to sleep.

Well, she had only two more days to be with him. She would try to make herself agreeable. She would put their beautiful little romance down in her heart, buried as a sacred memory. But it only covered over the fact that she had been unbearably hurt.

And she wrote that in Alfred's Journal, finishing one of its volumes. At least now he know how she felt.

He phoned her on Thursday. She was still hurting, and couldn't help letting it show. He came out to her house and she let him have it: "Men are such beasts. They're all right until they get what they want, and then they're terrible."

He, of course, was typically dense. Did she think he wasn't sincere in his attentions? Not a word about his threat to leave her when he went to George School. Then they got into a discussion about love, marriage, and children. She expressed her ideal of married life—and he told her how the second, or possibly the third girl he should treat as he had her would become his wife. Here he was with her, and he was talking of her successors! He had won her, so was already moving on, in his fancy. And had no idea how she felt about it, though she had pretty well told him.

But she was determined not to let her anguish show. They played, and embraced, and kissed, and it all seemed fine for the moment. Yet beneath the pleasant surface lurked that hurt.

Saturday he was at Sea Side Park again. How she wished she could go there; it sounded like so much fun. At least he had left the early volumes of his journal with her to read, and they were fascinating, full of references to her. He had been aware of her since they were ten, though at first only as a girl in his class. Then he got more interested, and dreamed of her. He had told her some of those dreams, but there were many more. She loved being his dream object!

Another night he left her the fourth volume. When the visit got late, her mother was about to go to bed. "Mother, come back," Marion called.

Her mother turned. "Yes?"

"Kiss me good night."

"Oh, of course." She did.

"Kiss Alfred."

Mother hesitated, confused.

"Kiss Alfred," Marion repeated, feeling giddy.

Mother turned to Alfred. "May I?"

Alfred looked embarrassed. "If you choose."

So she kissed him.

"Good night, mother," Marion said, as if dismissing her. Oh, that was fun!

She and Alfred continued seeing each other, and it was fun. If she had to live for the present, she might as well enjoy it. One day she went to the shore with him, and it was wonderful, but she was among so many strangers that it dampened her enthusiasm, especially at meal times. Another time they went swimming, and after a terrible inward struggle she managed to dive for the first time. She didn't feel at ease in the water, so they listened to some records, then went to the club and danced every dance.

Tuesday, September 15, 1925, he went to George School. But he wrote her regularly. He was concerned about his soccer: they had put him on the first team, but he wasn't playing as well as he had thought he would. "I hope you have confidence in me; maybe that will help."

"Why, they just couldn't have a team without you!" she responded encouragingly.

She wrote him five letters in the course of a week. Actually it was hard to fill that many pages, as she didn't want to get too personal, lest others read them. So she wrote of what she heard, saw, and did.

After two weeks at George School he came home to have his tonsils out, and to attend his father's wedding to Emma Taylor. He visited Marion as often as he could manage, and she visited him constantly while he was in the hospital. That was nice; she could see that he was very pleased with her company.

The month of October passed. Alfred corresponded with Mother also, and she wrote him sage advice. Marion wasn't sure how she felt about her mother's approval of Alfred. Meanwhile, to her he wrote "I think I would rather be an idealist than a man of the world." She wasn't sure about that either; idealists weren't known for success.

She remained wary of their separation. "It seems to me that just recently something has come between us," she wrote. "It's as if a barrier from nowhere has sprung up and it is rising higher and higher each day. You know we said we'd tell each other everything. I wonder if we've been doing that?" And "Will you tell me something which I might have done which would raise a barrier between us?"

Alfred replied "Frankly I know of none." Yet she was not completely reassured.

"Have we been right in all we have done?"

He assured her that they had. So why wasn't she satisfied?

At the end of the month he returned to West Chester and visited her. She wore a nice outfit with a short skirt, but something was lacking. Later she learned that he didn't like short skirts; he preferred long full sweeping skirts that gave way to every movement. So she had turned him off, when that was the very opposite of what she wanted to do. Damn!

After he left, she went up, undressed, and sat on her bed. She thought and thought, but she could not do anything, so she went to bed.

But next day it was much better. They heard Rachmaninoff's "Second Concerto" and Dvorak's "New World Symphony," absolutely lovely music. On the way home he asked her never to destroy his letters, and asked about last night. She replied "Something departed from us, and left us slightly estranged. More than anything, I want to get back that something which was lost." But this night they did regain it, and it was wonderful.

Then he returned to George School, and her concern resumed. Was the awful separation prying them apart despite everything? News filtered back from other sources, such as him looking at one Helen W, an attractive girl of that school. That bothered her a lot. Yet what could she do? She wasn't there.

She wrote "I think when I marry I want my husband to carry me off to some secluded place and keep me there for a long, long time. Just the two of us! And our life will surpass anything that has ever been felt by two mortals."

He asked her permission to acquaint himself with the girls there. "You are free," she responded with private regret. "Because I love you I want you to be free." But there were tears behind that letter.

News filtered back that Alfred had asked to fuss Helen W, but she had declined. To fuss was slang to call socially on a young woman. So he was taking her up on her release, and she couldn't express her hurt. But it did encourage her to respond in her fashion. She started dating Carroll again. Of course she told Alfred in a letter: "He begged me for another, so I guess I'll try it again."

Of course he took it as a breach of her faith. But what did he take his own pursuit of Helen W for? Could no man ever be trusted?

Then he fussed Karen S, and Maryanna W, and Hannah C. It seemed they liked him, but he hardly cared about them, so they weren't threats. Still, this was getting out of hand. Something had to be done. But what? She was not on the scene.

She thought about it, and realized that she would have to go to George School herself.

That decision made, she continued to date other boys, and let Alfred know. She went out with Bud, hoping, she told Alfred, that he wouldn't mind. No more than she minded his dating other girls!

Thursday, November 25, he was home, and called on her. "Oh, I'm so glad to see you!" she cried, running forward to hug him. Yet she remained aware of that wall between them. Indeed, soon he left her and went to talk with his friend Robert. Alfred liked to talk with those who he felt truly understood him. Two hours later he returned to her. She met him in her bathrobe, titillated by the notion of her seeming exposure, and he was very affectionate. He saw her as sweet and mystic, and she was glad to play that role. But why had he had to leave her for those two hours? Would he have done so if he had known that Robert saw him much as a woman saw him?

Next day he had John's car all day, but was in a perverse mood—she didn't like that moodiness—so things were indifferent. They went to the movies, and he evidently didn't like it as well as she did. Then they went to the Committee Dance at the Century Club, and she knew she had him under her spell. She felt his annoyance when Steve cut in, and Alfred had to dance with Ruth. Later he reported "When I dance with you, you seem to be a part of me. When I dance with Ruth I feel her bust but don't know where the rest of her is." Translation: Marion yielded to his motions, staying exactly with him; Ruth did not, so only her most prominent aspect touched him.

Then on their way home they met Carroll, and she asked him to visit her that evening. She could see that annoyed Alfred something awful. Well, what of him and Helen W? Did he get the message? Evidently not. Next day he phoned her, but she remained annoyed, and it showed.

Saturday they were together again, and she tried to be diffident, but he kissed her, and that destroyed her negative mood. She just couldn't resist a kiss! On Sunday he kissed her four times.

Then he had to return to George School. She hadn't told him of her decision to join him there, as the arrangements had not yet been made.

Their correspondence continued. Alfred wrote that he talked with Marianna W, but this was not really a date this time; she told him about Pantheism, the doctrine that the universe, taken as a whole, was God, and the laws and forces of the universe were all that God was. He found it an interesting concept, and so did Marion. Was every person merely a little part of God, and what each person did changed God a tiny bit?

The tender memories continued too. "Last Thursday evening," she wrote. "Do you remember when I was going to change my dress and you sat on the piano stool and I stood by? That silence was so full of everything, so beautiful." He had drawn her nearer, his head had rested against her body, and they had remained thus until dark fell. There was something about it that bespoke a friendship stronger than words.

Yet her present life seemed pathetically meaningless. "Do you see how your precious letters brighten this drab existence?" she wrote. She mentioned that she had reached a crisis in her life and had to choose between two paths, but the one she wanted would be difficult to follow. She didn't clarify that it would mean uprooting herself and going away to boarding school, so as to be closer to Alfred.

Carroll left school, never to return. That hardly helped.

"In a week you will be home, and I won't be blue," she wrote Alfred. Then she would tell him why she was blue, and hurt. "Something has happened inside of me, Alfred. I am tired of all this empty, senseless, noisy, glittering chatter. I want something substantial." The girls she knew were so artificial, with never a serious or beautiful thought, not really knowing the meaning of friendship.

She gathered from Alfred's letters that he had similar sentiments about the people he knew. The teachers at George School were superior and caring, with much excellent advice he would try to follow, but the other boys just weren't much.

And what about the girls? she wondered. He was still trying to get a date with that Helen W. She hated that.

He asked her to save his letters to her, so that later he might recover them and add them to his Journal, filling it out. She wasn't sure she liked that either, for more than one reason. First, they were *hers*, the part of him she possessed, to read and reread at leisure; she didn't want to lose them. Second, she wasn't sure that she wanted anything that personal going out of her control; who could guess who else might read them, at school or anywhere? But at least there was no conflict at present; she was saving them.

Meanwhile she wrote more to him. "I want to write poetry and I hope some day to write more. I want to do description. That is a story with a description in a poem. I want to write about beautiful lakes, a sunset, a sunrise, a mountain, a tree, or a bird." In fact she wished she could simply be in such a lovely scene, instead of here in dull reality.

Then at last it was Friday, and Alfred was back in West Chester. He couldn't find a car, so walked to her house to see her. Surprised, she had been asleep;

she had though he would wait until Saturday. She thought he might kiss her, but they just talked, and it was nice. But there were odd notes. Alfred had fussed Eleanor at George School, and at one point she had been swearing; he didn't like that.

"But it's common among girls," she told him.

"Well, I hope you will hold yourself above that."

Did he reside in the real world? "I have sworn as badly as any in the past," she confessed. "But in future I won't."

"Swearing is needless and useless for men too."

She tried. When the occasion came to say damn, she changed it to darn. But that didn't satisfy him.

"One is as bad as the other. It's the thought behind swearing that is wrong."

"Then I won't say anything," she said, piqued. Sometimes Alfred was better appreciated from correspondence distance.

But she did appreciate his appreciation of poetry. On Saturday he had her read Edgar Allen Poe's "Annabel Lee" to him twice. It was a nice poem, very sad and feeling. Oh, to be loved as Annabel Lee was, only not then to die. It seemed he wanted to take her in the Dodge to the top of some high hill overlooking a vast expanse of country, then have her read a poem of her choice. Instead they were confined to a room, and she wished there could be some kissing or petting, but evidently he wasn't in the mood. The wasted opportunity made her irritable. He had such awkward moods! Later he became playful; they even wrestled a bit. But that was as far as it went.

He confided that Monday in Camden he had bought a copy of the risqué VANITY FAIR magazine, and a package of Pall Mall cigarettes and a box of matches. Then in a waiting room he had puffed away on one while glancing through the other. She knew that such behavior would get him in serious trouble if his father ever found out, just as it would with her family if they caught her smoking. She did it anyway. But she gathered that Alfred thought she shouldn't, just as she shouldn't swear. What was all right for him wasn't all right for her. And why wasn't it?

Then something odd happened. It seemed that Alfred had a long intimate talk with his friend Robert, and learned that Robert cared for Alfred in much the way Alfred cared for Marion. Alfred was amazed, but took it as a statement of friendship. Marion did not comment, but she knew that some girls felt romantic about other girls instead of men, and some men felt that way about other men. So Robert *was* that kind! But she knew Alfred wasn't, so it really didn't matter. It was just an oddity.

Thursday, Christmas Eve, Alfred and his sister Elinor came to help them trim the Christmas tree. Elinor was a sprightly young woman, and knew what was what. Then on Christmas Day evening Alfred came to see her. She wore her velvet dress. He was feeling delightfully amorous; he could not keep his hands off her. They went to the dance at Kennet and just cut loose; it was wonderful.

But Saturday was the opposite. Marion was at her Aunt Marian's house, not totally pleased to be there, but Family could not be denied. She called Alfred, hoping he would find a way to get her out of it, but she couldn't come out and say that directly. He came over after a while. "Will you come in?" she asked.

"I guess I might as well if there's nothing better to do."

Some response! Keeping company with her was the last resort? She met it with cold silence.

"I guess I'll go in and see Aunt Marian," he said at last.

Instead of staying with Marion herself? "I'll go up to Frannie's."

"Shall I go up with you?"

"No. I'm perfectly able to go myself."

After she returned from Frannie's and he finished talking with Aunt Marian, they did get together, and Alfred realized that he had been insensitive. He apologized, and things were patched up, but some damage had been done. Maybe she had been rude too; she couldn't expect Alfred to read her mind.

Tuesday was mixed, again. They went with Ellis to Burdettes to dance, and Dot kept asking Alfred to dance, but he stayed with Marion. But when Marion got tired and curled up in a chair, Alfred did dance with Dot. What bothered her was that he seemed to hold her as close as he did Marion, when he thought she wasn't watching. "Take me home, Ellis," she said. "Return for Alfred when he has finished having his good time."

But Alfred intercepted them. "Remember how I told you that dancing is meaningless unless it is with you," he said, disturbed. "Did you think they were just words?" He looked so upset that she had to believe him, and they made up and embraced.

On Thursday, the last day of the year, they were part of a party of six, and again parts were wonderful and parts were bad. Somehow it seemed that when Alfred was in the mood for petting, she wasn't, and when she was, he wasn't.

On Saturday she did something daring. She had read in his Journal how he longed to put his hand on her abdomen. She took his hand and set it flat below her waist. He seemed to be quite transported.

But finally the Christmas vacation ended, and after one frenzied parting embrace and kiss Alfred went back to George School. Now there was no mixture of emotions; she simply felt lonely. It was letter time again, and they flowed back and forth, passionately.

Sometimes he relayed funny things. Once it seemed a student's father was trying to get in, the door being latched from inside. "Piss in the keyhole and swim through!" the student called. Another time a woman was similarly balked. "Grease your ass and slide under," a girl called. Oh, naughty! A girl had relayed the news in Chemistry class. Alfred professed to be shocked that girls could speak that freely to boys. He had that idealistic image of an utterly pure and innocent female gender.

They were together when he had time off from school. She was thankful that the separation had not broken up their relationship. Yet it was under a strain. She was doing her best to maintain it until next school year, when she could join him at George School.

"I hate to say this, but I believe it to be true," she wrote. "I hope you will forget for the present that I am a girl—think of me as Marion." Because girls were a dime a dozen, and there was more than a dime's worth at George School. "My one hope, desire, and aim is that I may prove true to you. I am sure that I love you and I want to show you that I can be constant. If I can only prove myself true and gain your faith and confidence, I shall be satisfied." She pondered, her emotion running high, then added: "But Alfred, I can't think of it without becoming so very breathless! I don't know why, but the very idea of it! It affects me strongly somehow—but it is only a dream. A fire—you—and I—each other!"

She wrote to him every day, and he wrote to her every day, though the letters did not necessarily arrive that regularly. She received one wherein he described his impression of himself, not wholly positive. She appreciated his honesty, and tried to be supportive: "It is only natural for you to have some faults (don't ask me to name them for I can't think of one, I can't see them, but maybe you have them.)"

Another day she wrote about Carroll, being honest about her contacts there. Alfred might not like it, but she didn't like his fussing other girls either.

He still had some interesting thoughts. "A great many people do not regret the right things," he wrote. "No man knows himself until he has suffered. The value of literature is in proportion to the thinking we do as a result of it."

In March came the spring break, and he visited her again. It was late, and she was in bed, but she donned her bathrobe and went down to meet him.

They hugged and kissed, and it was wonderful. She was aware that her robe was open at the top, but did not close it with her hand. There was a certain guilty pleasure in showing him "by accident" what she wasn't supposed to. But his friend Henry was with him, and soon they had to go.

They did manage to meet again before he had to return to school, and it was wonderful. He wrote her a very nice letter saying so. He also told how he had been with Henry to several places, but missed her. Sometimes he could be so sweet!

Another weekend she asked him to take her mother to Wilmington, and he did. When they got home, they wanted to make biscuits, but her mother objected. That made Marion angry, though she tried to conceal it. But sometimes Alfred made her angry too. When he asked her what he could do about himself, and she told him that he seemed to expect everybody to come and bow at his feet.

Yet when they discussed reasons for marriage, she said it was all right to marry for love alone, but not for money, while he argued that love should be primary, but money was necessary in practice. "The finest car is not much good unless there's a road to run on, and the better the road, the longer the car lasts." He did have a point.

Another time he was tired, and said he felt a "dog-like" devotion to her. That candor appealed to her; she approached him, put her arms around him, and pressed her body against his. They remained that way for half an hour; it was as though they were absorbing each other's love. Later they wrestled in a manner; he threw her around a fair amount, not roughly, and they had more body contact. He kissed her tenderly on forehead, cheeks, lips and hand. It was nice being the object of such attention.

He read her Robert's questions to him, and his answers: did he ever see her in a sexual light? No. But he thought that Robert would call it sexual attraction that made Alfred love her breasts. Marion didn't trust herself to comment. *Were* breasts sexual? If not, why did men look at them?

Then the spring break was over, and he was back at George School. He wrote telling her of the enjoyable vacation, of hidden happiness, and of his love for her. It was almost better having him away, because then he wasn't moody and was affectionate.

In April he landed in the school infirmary with a pink eye infection. She wrote him a letter on deep blue paper, with white ink. She also told him of her good dialogue with Walt, whom she really liked. But then she received a letter from Walt, and feared she had hurt him terribly. She had merely tried to clarify that she liked him as a friend, not as a boyfriend.

Alfred was home a weekend in the middle of May, and she was thrilled to see him. But he was in one of his moods, and this turned her off; why couldn't he save the moods for when he wasn't with her? She made herself cool and aloof, disappointed in him. She could have moods too.

The letters resumed, again seeming almost better than direct contact. Later in May he visited again, and they had a serious talk. He asked her of the future, and whether they would ever separate, and how. She said that she had often had the feeling that they had started to separate. He read her the comment made by Henry, concluding that she liked Alfred less than he liked her. She didn't like that judgment, or Henry.

"Last summer I was a dreamer and romanticist, as I want to be," he said. "My school life has changed me so that now I am less of a dreamer. The school does not contain or tolerate anything that is not material. I am becoming analytical, a hunter for facts, a lover of thought, a person who is deep in his own pursuits. This analytical quality is carried over into all branches of my life, and I am hunting out reasons and laws for all things."

"Even love?"

"It is not my policy to carry this over into affairs of the heart, yet I do, and I analyze them. You know I am undemonstrative of my affections, and I shall become less so as time passes. I will be a man who will seem to care more for his books and pursuits than for his wife. It will seem unnecessary for me to show affection for you as it would be for me to show it for my best male friend. Consequently if you would dislike such a man as I have described, you will dislike me in the future."

Marion was shocked. He was truly being brutally analytical about a thing that should be spared that cruel treatment. Was this what she wanted? She would have to think about it, long and hard.

He looked at her as if expecting an immediate answer, but she could not give it. This was just too big and awful to assimilate right now.

Later in May they went to a play. His cousin Ellis came to visit with them, and she realized that Ellis was paying her too much attention. He was smitten with her! She was flattered, and did not mind that Alfred was plainly jealous. That had a beneficial effect, for he was more attentive as they returned to her home. He kissed her, and didn't want to leave, but had to, for it was late. She was privately pleased.

Next morning he was back. She was in her green dress and tried to be alert, though she was logy from the lateness of last night. He told of his drive to Ellis's home after that. "I was sleepy, and although my eyes stayed open,

I found myself dreaming. I would see the road and all would be well. Then, unconsciously, I would be asleep and seeing the same road, and queer things would happen. There would be obstructive curves, and just before each one I would wake, and see no curves. I saw many spots which looked as if whitewash had spilled, like the ones on the tennis courts yesterday. I saw cars coming, but there were none. Once I saw a great hay wagon in my path, and I jammed on the brake, which action woke me to the realization that the road was clear. Three times the bump of going off the highway woke me and I righted myself."

"You should have stopped," she protested. "You could have had a bad accident."

"I suppose so," he agreed. "Louis and Henry and I want to go on a social walk. Should I ask some strange girl, or Eleanor?"

That chilled her. He was asking her whom else to date? Had he no sensitivity for her feelings? "I cared about Eleanor once." Then, getting even, she mentioned Carroll, who wanted to come back to her. "I see him, then deny him, then see him again. I can't make up my mind."

"He is beneath you," Alfred said, evidently nettled, as she had intended.

"I suppose Walt is more my social level."

He didn't seem much better pleased with that. Then she had mercy on him, and gave him the picture of her he had wanted so long, a good one. On the back was the inscription "Not for just an hour, not for just a day, not for just a year, but always, Marion." She had adapted it from a popular song.

Alfred's father didn't like the amount of time Alfred spent with Marion, and reprimanded him. So when Alfred was home in June, and she and her mother met him at the trolley and brought him home, he did not arrange to take her out somewhere in the evening. It was a rejection, and it hurt.

Saturday he called when she was eating. "Could you call later, Alfred? I haven't yet eaten dessert."

"I'll have time tomorrow to talk," he said gruffly. That annoyed her again. She wasn't refusing to talk with him, just trying to finish her meal so she could be clear for it. Why did he have to react that way?

Then there was the bad letter. She had written about what Ellis had said Emma had said to Walter, and Alfred reprimanded her for that. Surprised and dismayed, she had been unable to answer. She couldn't relay innocent gossip without being held culpable?

When he came to her house, they sat on the swing. He refused to be serious, further annoying her. "I don't like you any more," she said, almost meaning it—and he joked about that too. It was maddening.

When he did get serious, later in the day, it wasn't much better. "I read a story about the nothingness of life. I thought that when I have lived my youth and am married to the girl of my choice, the best of my life will be over. What does it matter whether we live or die?"

"It does matter," she protested. "It has to matter." But she lacked his ability to reason such things out.

He stood up and faced her. "Will you stand up?" he asked.

Uncertain what he was leading up to, she stood.

"What do you think of me?" he asked.

"I don't like what you said about the best of your life being over once you marry. I don't want to believe anything like that. The best should just be starting then."

"What about me, as you have seen me today?"

Did he really want candor? "I like other boys to be that way, but I don't like it in you. You're different."

He stood erect with his head up and face firm. "I am glad. I should be very sorry if I had to be like others."

"That's a relief."

"I don't care how cross or cold you become. I like you better for it. Nothing you could do in an instant could change my opinion of you."

"You've said that before," she said.

He nodded. "You can't expect me to be the boy I was. I have changed."

"Yes," she murmured.

"It is as if a treasure were buried on the beach, and the waves washed over it, and each wave covered it more. The treasure is still there, but harder to get to."

"Yes," she said again, though she found this confusing.

"You, too, have changed, and in the same direction. I wish it didn't have to be, but it is."

There was something overwhelming about this. She found herself crying, and turned away.

"Your watch," he said. He had borrowed it in the course of the day; she had forgotten to recover it.

She held out her hand. He started to put the watch on, but she was sobbing too much and drew her hand away. She hated making a scene like this! She went to the wall of the house, seeking some sort of cover.

"Good bye," he said.

What did he mean? She couldn't answer.

"Good bye, Marion."

She still couldn't answer. A silence stretched out between them. She had to get control of herself somehow.

Finally she went to the door and opened it. "Good bye," he said a third time.

And all she could do was sob.

She saw him step off the porch and walk toward his home, looking neither right nor left.

Next day he phoned, but she wasn't very animated. It was just so difficult at times to be with Alfred. Other boys wanted to hold her hand, to kiss her, even to touch her body where they shouldn't. Alfred was deep and unpredictable, evoking thoughts she couldn't properly handle. She didn't know the rules of his game, or even whether it was a game.

Three days later he visited again. They sat on the swing and he took her hand. "Have you regained your sense of feeling yet?" he asked.

"I'm not sure. You changed so much on Sunday that I didn't think I'd care, but today you are so much yourself that I love you all over again."

"Why did you cry?"

"Because I didn't like to think that what you said was true. I don't want to have to change."

He kissed her. She buried her face in his shoulder. It was all right. But not quite perfect.

Next Sunday they had another dialog. Things were still somehow imperfect. "One is reluctant to go when one has something on one's mind," he said. "And the more weighty it is, the more reluctant one is."

Oh, no—this was going to be another grim session.

"Shall I get it off my my my mind, or save it?"

"Go ahead. Things couldn't be much worse than they are."

"You advise me to relieve myself of it?"

As if it were a session on the toilet. "You may as well." She hoped it wouldn't overwhelm her again.

"Have I ever lied to you?"

"I don't think so."

"I'm not going to now. I love you."

What game was this? "That's funny."

"It's not funny."

Was he serious? "Then what is it?" She was on the swing, he standing, facing her, one foot on the ground, one foot on the porch, bending towards her. The whole scene seemed somehow unreal.

"Please—will you forgive me for being so childish and disagreeable?"

That much was easy. "You are always forgiven."

"But I've been nasty this afternoon." He paused. "Do you believe me, Marion?"

"I want to."

"I hope you will." He turned and walked quickly away.

Then he went to his Uncle Walter's farm to work for the summer, directed by his father. Also a religious conference. So Alfred had less time for her, and they both suspected that his father was trying to break them up by making their association inconvenient. At this point she was not entirely reluctant; it was emotionally wearing being with Alfred. Still, they did get together often enough. Unfortunately the conference filled him with notions of Christianity; he had bought books on it, and was eager to expound on it. She found it boring, and said so. She had accepted no religion; it wasn't romantic. Nothing was interesting any more; everything bored her.

Then his father eased up, and Alfred had the use of a car again, and they had some happy times together.

In July one time he got quite affectionate, kissing her repeatedly. She got sleepy, but not as sleepy as she pretended, curious what he would do. He stroked her hair, her neck, her side, and finally put his hand on her breast, stroking it through the material of her dress. Now this was not boring! She should "wake" and discourage him, but she was getting pleasure from his pleasure in touching her. Her body truly turned him on; it was her power. He kept kissing and embracing her, taking joy, and it was her joy too.

But at last he had to leave. "It's an agony to love like this," she said. "Nobody can take tonight away from us. Tell me that you love me, and that you'll always care."

He obliged, but she suspected he was doing so more from his head than his heart. Still, it was a phenomenal evening.

Alfred's work on the farm continued through July, leaving him little time for her. Her mother told her that she had heard that the J's loved themselves first, then any who come after. She relayed that to Alfred, and he agreed it was true.

Her doubts continued. She told Alfred that he should not see her any more, that he should forget her, because she had almost accepted another boy and might do so again. What had happened was that Carroll had told her he loved her and asked her to come back to him. She was sorely tempted, and was on the verge of doing so. Then he laughed and said "I don't want you. Go to Alfred; he may want you." That hurt more than anything else in her life. She didn't want to do that to Alfred, so it seemed better to break it off now.

But he didn't break with her, as she had rather known would be the case. At least she had made the overture.

Alfred continued to work on the farm, and was evidently too busy to write. But in mid August he came to see her. Now she told him her news: "I am going to George School next year." She thought he would be gratified, but he didn't seem to react. That was odd.

There was to be a fireworks exhibition, but she wasn't sure where it was. Alfred knew, but didn't tell her, and she drove from place to place searching. Finally he did tell her, and they saw the last few minutes. She concealed her annoyance; it was just Alfred's way.

The farm work continued, which meant she was mostly alone. But he did tell her of an interesting dream: they went swimming, and she robed and disrobed at his house. She lived the scene as he described it, as if it were her own dream. They swam and sported in the water, and touched each other naughtily under the surface. He liked to feel her breasts and she liked to let him, as long as no one saw.

Then they came inside, dripping. "I'll dress with you," she told him, feeling wicked.

"No you don't, Marion," her mother protested. She hadn't realized that her mother was there until that moment. "Come over here." She indicated a separate room.

"I'm going to hang my suit," Alfred said. "Shall I hang yours too?"

Marion agreed before her mother could protest. "Yes, of course." She turned to her mother. "Shall I give him my brassiere also?" Oh, the temptation!

Now they were beside the bay window outside Alfred's house, but the scene ended, so she didn't see her mother's reaction.

But the pleasantry of the dream was spoiled a few days later when she learned of Alfred's visit to the house of Lois W with his uncle. They played music and sang, Alfred on the sax, Lois on the piano. Alfred didn't say so, but he was evidently taken with her. Marion knew Lois, who was a wonderful and talented girl. That was the problem.

Then there was Jane A. Alfred was noticing too many girls. Was he going to fall violently in love with one of them? "But you are the most perfect combination, the only one who is complete," he assured her. "Others are likable, but you are lovable."

It wasn't enough. When he visited, she had it out with him. He wanted to know who else she might be seeing, but wasn't telling her who else *he* was seeing. "Why should I tell you everything that happens?" she demanded.

That seemed to surprise him. Apparently it hadn't occurred to him that she should have the same rights of association he did.

"Mother and Father and everybody says that both of us being at George School will kill everything that there ever was between us," she said heatedly. "So a few days won't make much difference."

"But all I think about is you! No other relationship has any meaning. I visit you whenever I can."

She knew better. "Don't you think you had better not come—ever?"

"Why don't you get a knife and stab me?" he demanded angrily.

"You talk about understanding and faith," she retorted. "You expect me to have it all. You need to hunt around for some." She was in tears, unable to control her sobbing.

"I have faith in you. I have not ceased to love you."

"Good bye."

He gave it up. "Good night." But he did not leave immediately. He placed his hands on her shoulders. She did not look up.

"Please don't think, tonight," he said. "What seems big tonight will seem smaller in the morning. Please forgive my outburst." Then at last he left.

But three days later it was almost like old times. He picked her up, and opened the car door for her, but she turned to him. "Kiss me hello."

"I'm not sure."

"I'm sure," she said. "Awfully sure."

"If you are, I'm sure I am." So they kissed.

It had surprising impact. For the moment, all doubts were banished.

"Why did you hesitate?" she asked.

"A kiss is a tiny marriage ceremony, and it should mean the same thing in a small way."

That was a really interesting concept. Only Alfred would have come up with it.

Then they were at George School. She spent a social hour with Alfred, and she confessed she was feeling homesick. He reassured her. But she had the feeling that he wasn't eager to be with her.

He was in her History class, but he paid her no attention there. It was as if he didn't want others to know he even knew her, let along think they were a couple. This wasn't at all what she had had in mind when she decided to come here. She seemed to be more separate from him than she had been when they were at different schools.

Still, there were the social hours, and he spent half of them with her, and the others with assorted other girls: Jane A, Eleanor M, Marianna W (twice),

Dorothea D, and Miss Micherell. Actually she asked him to fuss Marianna, who was a philosophical girl, and safe. But what really hurt was his suggestion that they each fuss others. He truly was losing interest, and there seemed to be nothing she could do about it. Of course his parents disapproved, not of her specifically, but of his being with any one girl too much, so that was another wedge. He was evidently compromising, trying neither to make his father angry nor to make Marion unhappy. But this was hardly ideal for her.

They traveled home together for the Christmas holiday. They missed the train and had to take the trolley, and her mother met them. Then they were separate for the holiday itself. The day after Christmas she wrote him an impassioned letter, regretting that they had been going their separate ways, but really did need each other. "You don't want to come back anymore? You want to end the most beautiful friendship that has ever been? We have worked together, played together, laughed together, wept together, but never again? If this is so, it is my fault . . . Alfred! The girl you left last summer, the girl you left the summer before, the girl who loves you more than anything in the world, is calling to you. She needs you—wants you! She will be waiting for you on Tuesday. You will hear her call, and you will stay by her side and help her—you will not go away?"

They did meet Tuesday. They kissed, and he played with her hair, and they embraced freely. At last, in ecstasy, she placed her hot body right against his and squeezed him as if she'd give it all to him if she could. It was a phenomenal evening.

Then she fussed Alfred's friend Bob C. Veary wrote her a letter, questioning that. She responded: "If you must know, Veary, it's this way. I've known Alfred since I knew anyone and ever since I can remember he has been *first, last,* and *always.* As far as I know now, he always will be. He is awfully nice to me too—makes me have a great time etc.—but up here he is so quiet and things haven't been very exciting until Bob C came along. I like him. I think he is heaps of fun, but I realize that he can't be compared to Alfred."

They were home in West Chester in early March, and had a great date, hugging and kissing repeatedly. It was just like old times. Two days later back at school they had Social Hour together, reminiscing.

She suggested to Alfred that he fuss her Swedish roommate, Linnea S. He did, and it turned out well. Almost too well; Marion got a bit nervous about that, though of course Linnea would not try to take Alfred away from her.

Meanwhile she fussed Bob again. He was attentive, personable, and clearly taken with her. But there was a certain diffidence that bothered her. "What's the matter?" she inquired. "Is there a louse crawling on my hair?"

Bob smiled, knowing the reference: a poem by the eighteenth century Scottish poet Robert Burns, "To a Louse," wherein a louse was crawling on a lady's bonnet at church, unbeknownst to her. She thought the rapt attention of others was because of her prettiness in her Sunday outfit. "O wad some Power the giftie gie us, To see oursels as ithers see us!" he said, quoting the key line.

But she had little patience with classic verse at the moment. "Then what?"

"Alfred is my friend."

Then it came clear. He didn't want to impinge on his friend's prerogatives. But now the image of banana salad came to her mind. Alfred knew they would separate when the school year ended, so he was easing off the relationship, getting used to it. She had to do the same. No more banana salad. "And mine. But he wants us both to be free to see others. He insisted we fuss others. He's fussing my roommate Linnea. But what good is it fussing if we don't fuss?"

"I don't think I understand." But he was flushing; he did understand.

"We may be committed to others. But tonight it is just the two of us. Let's act as if we mean it. Otherwise it's meaningless."

Finally, cautiously, he held her close. And later, when they were out of the view of others, they kissed.

She realized that she liked him more than she had thought. She had always been with Alfred, but Alfred could be moody and difficult, and he had hurt her innumerable times. Bob was not that type. He was less objective, more feeling.

It was a virtual explosion of realization. *She liked Bob better than Alfred.* And what was she going to do about it?

Alfred fussed her April 29, and asked her to go to the George School dance with him. Now was the time. "I'm sorry Alfred, but no."

He looked at her, not comprehending.

"I have decided to go with someone else, if he should ask me. Perhaps you can go with Linnea."

It was some time before he understood, and she had to gently suggest that there would be other occasions, providing him some hope, before he was satisfied to leave. He smiled as he went, but it was plain that he felt no smile. His expression papered over a void. She felt so guilty, so sad for him, yet she knew it had to be done. She had to make the break firmly, to free him as well as herself.

Then he was gone. She dissolved into tears. She was crying partly for herself, but mostly for him.

He was the one who had decided that he should not be dependent on her, and should not monopolize her attentions. The only way to do that was to separate. He had said he expected it to be hard on him, but he would emerge the stronger for it in time. He would always treasure the wonderful association they had had. He had hoped she understood. Now she had made it real. They were learning to live without banana salad.

Thereafter, until the school term ended, she went with Bob, and Alfred associated with her roommate Linnea, apparently not because he liked her, but because she was destined to return to Sweden and there could be no serious relationship.

Regardless, Marion had become part of Alfred's past.

# JOYCE

Joyce M was an athletic girl approaching twenty. She did not like to ride when she could walk, but here in the neighborhood of Woodbrooke College there were too many people. It wasn't necessarily safe for a girl to walk alone. Not even between the nearby town of Selly Oak and Woodbrooke. She had been warned, and she respected the judgment of those who warned. The world was not necessarily ideal.

But if she couldn't walk alone, as she preferred, with whom could she walk? That was the problem. She was not an outgoing person. Oh, she could handle classes readily enough, and recite material before a moderate group. She wasn't shy about that sort of thing. But when it came to personal relationships, it could be difficult. Her thoughts and feelings were her own; she might be willing to share them, as she did on occasion with her mother and sisters, but not with a stranger. Even with a person she knew, she tended to clam up. Not because she wanted to, but because she just somehow couldn't speak aloud what she felt.

She had tried keeping a diary, but that tended to be perfunctory; even there her most private thoughts would not come out. Instead she copied out poems she liked, about nature, beauty, and death. Especially death; the concept fascinated her, and she underlined the dread word wherever it appeared, giving it authority. But who else would even understand that? She knew better than to speak of it, even if she had the ability. Others had not lost their fathers when they were almost too young to fathom the void, and did not understand how the awareness of death could be a constant presence. So what would she have to say to anyone she might walk with? Because when people walked, they talked; that was the way of it. She just couldn't do that.

There was another student who liked to walk; she had observed him striding around and beyond the campus. Would he do for company? Walking with a man was even more of a challenge than with a woman. She had never dated, never really associated with boys in school, other than purely as classmates. Never as *boys*. It wasn't that she disliked them, just that the whole idea of a boy/girl relationship was beyond her ability. She would have no idea at all how to conduct it. So while she saw boys and girls getting together, playing tennis, seeing plays, dancing, even kissing, and felt some desire to engage in that sort of activity, the subtle emotional barrier was simply overwhelming.

It was October 6, 1928. They were hardly more than a week into the term, and already she was feeling confined. She wanted to get out and around, to explore the whole surrounding countryside, the paths and fields and forests. To commune with wonderful nature. And she couldn't do it alone.

The man turned as the class ended, briefly facing her, and for a moment their eyes connected. Joyce froze; he had caught her looking at him! What could she do? So she smiled, as much in embarrassment as welcome, and turned away.

That was all, but it was potent. Somehow it seemed that there was a link between them. She knew it was ridiculous to read too much into a chance meeting of gazes, yet she felt it. There was something.

The following days were mostly classes and getting to know the names of the other students. Occasionally she encountered the young man again, and each time their eyes met, there was, if not a spark, a connection, perhaps even a bond. Occasionally they spoke. She learned his name: Alfred. Alfred J. She suspected he had similarly learned hers. So they were becoming acquainted, if indirectly. Still, she lacked the ability to approach him about the matter of walking together.

Then on October 29 they chanced to sit next to each other at breakfast. She hadn't done it on purpose, and was sure he hadn't either; it just happened. Now was her opportunity to ask him about walking. But she said nothing. She just couldn't. He didn't say anything either, yet she had the impression he wanted to. Was he uninterested, and all this was purely in her head, or could he be as shy about this sort of thing as she was?

She observed that he did not socialize with girls, though he appeared to have no aversion to them. So it seemed likely that either he was committed to someone in America—for he was American, his accent gave him instantly away—or he had some private difficulty approaching others. She knew exactly how that was!

So it continued through November and December. Joyce was now interested in Alfred for more than mere walks, though they had now walked together, though not by themselves. She thought he could be a kindred soul. She had not encountered one of those before, and wasn't really sure what one would be like, but she was intrigued to a degree that surprised her. Every fleeting contact with him was special in some subtle way. And, darn it, she did think he felt the same way.

The term ended, and it was time for her to go home. It had been a good term, well worthwhile, and she had learned a lot. But she was unsatisfied, because she felt her intractable diffidence had balked what could have been a far greater experience. Yet maybe she was imagining it. She had never even talked with Alfred, outside of trifling incidentals.

It was a biting cold night as she bundled up warmly with wool leggings and everything for her drive home with Reginald Reynolds, a family friend. She was happy to be going home, as even the best school experience could become to a degree tiresome, and she had been long away from home. Alfred was there as she left; had he come to see her off? She tried to smile at him, but wasn't sure she succeeded.

Then they were on their way, and all that was Woodbrooke was past. Except that so much wasn't past, because it had never quite existed.

Next term she would definitely ask Alfred to walk with her. That should not only open up the countryside for her exploration, something she longed for, but enable her to get to know him better. But she knew that despite her resolution, she would probably lack the gumption to speak to him when she had the chance.

Her mother Ella greeted her warmly as she arrived at Caradon, her home in Winscombe. So did her younger sisters Ruth and Nancy. Oh, it was so good to be back!

After things settled down, she talked with her mother about it. "There is this young man—he's American—I think he is like me."

"And you never said a word," Ella finished.

Joyce had to smile. Her mother knew her. "Neither did he. His name is Alfred. Alfred J. He seems nice, but quiet. I see him walking alone around the campus and fields. I get so jealous of that! I wish—I wish I could have—" She shrugged, unfinished.

"Write him a letter," Ella said. "You do have his address?"

"Yes." That was the answer. She could write when she couldn't speak. So she wrote Alfred a nice card that really said nothing at all, except the implied need for contact.

Then she focused on being with her mother and sisters. The four of them had been together almost all her life, though Ruth was three years younger, and Nancy four younger. They were all December births, and there had been a miscarriage between Joyce and Ruth, accounting for the spacing. The truth was that Joyce hardly remembered her father; she had been only only three and a half years old when he died. She remembered Ella's grief, though, and that more than the death itself had colored her awareness of it. Her earliest clear image was of her mother's sorrow, and the loss of the warm male presence in their house. What was death, and why did it come so suddenly, bringing such devastation? She tried constantly to understand, without much success. But she had learned that others did not share or appreciate her concern, so she kept silent, on that and other things. It had become a difficult habit to break. She knew Ella hoped Woodbrooke would help open her up, as it were, but so far it hadn't.

Would Alfred understand? She thought he might. That was a phenomenal lure. To have someone she could talk to about what mattered, without being, if not condemned, at least looked askance upon. But she couldn't know without asking, and she dared not ask.

Ruth was her usual sensible self, and Nancy, now just sixteen, an exuberant teen. Nancy brightened the air around her. Whatever they did together was cheered by her enthusiasm and laughter. She had never known her father, so had no gloom of his loss. Joyce almost envied her that.

Near the turn of the year Alfred's reply arrived. She was so excited she almost dropped it on the floor. The letter resembled her own, in that it said nothing of substance, just his passing impressions of Wales, which were favorable. But it was verification of their contact, and wonderful. It was amazing how much meaning there could be in such a simple act as exchanging letters. It flavored her thoughts for the rest of the day, and beyond.

Ella nodded knowingly. "Men come in all kinds," she remarked. "Many are not worthwhile. But those that are, can be very special. Frank was. Do make contact if you can. We need to know, one way or another." Frank was her father's name. She fought off the renewed awareness of death it brought. After all, it was time for her haircut, making ready to return to school.

On Friday, January 11, 1929, Joyce was back at Woodbrook for the start of the Spring term. Alfred was there; he smiled gladly when he saw her, and she managed to smile back, briefly. Again that cursed reticence balked her.

Their occasional contacts resumed. She saw Alfred walking out with Todd T, and wished she could join them. Surely she could have, had she just managed to come out and ask. But she couldn't ask. Then two days later when she entered the common room he was sitting there, but soon he had to go. She knew he wanted to stay, and she wanted him to stay, but it was beyond either of them to be obvious.

Joyce also noted that Helen N was making a play for Alfred. She tried to suppress a surge of jealousy. After all, she had but to say one word, and she knew Alfred would be with her. But she couldn't, and so by default he went to the one who had no such handicap.

However, in a few days it became apparent that Helen's ploy had failed. The fly had slipped the web. Joyce tried not to gloat inwardly. After all, she was not the competitive type. There was also his friend Katia, from Bulgaria, whom he had helped come to Woodbrooke; she was interested in him, but he regarded her as just a friend. Odd how such things were evident to all except the participants.

January 25 they sat next to each other at the bookfair, not entirely coincidentally. Three days later they sat next to each other at dinner. It seemed that neither of them could be overt, but they could drift together.

In February they were in some kind of game, and she won, and Alfred congratulated her, clasping her hand briefly. At least he could be impulsive; she could not. Another day they skated together, with another couple, and that was nice, because she could skate well. She was competent on ice in a manner she was not in dialogue. They skated again; it was a convenient pretext.

Then she was ill for a few days, and out of circulation. It happened on occasion; she was a bit more prone to illnesses than she thought was appropriate for an outdoor girl.

Soon after her recovery Alfred told her of his dream of her. He was dreaming of her? She liked that. Later in the common room they gazed at a big map of Europe and talked about travel. They agreed that Paris was nice. It was easy to be with him when there was a suitable subject to talk about. She did like to travel.

Then the spring term was over, and she still had not walked alone with him. What was the matter with her?

She went home, while Alfred traveled Europe: France, Germany, Spain. She envied him that, and wished she could have traveled with him. But of course that wouldn't have been appropriate, even if possible.

"I have learned some things about Alfred," Ella said. "It turns out that his father is a wealthy man, well known in America."

"Joyce's boyfriend is rich?" Nancy asked, heedless of embarrassment. "Tell us all about it!"

"But I have no interest in money," Joyce protested, blushing. "And he's not my boyfriend."

"You said you sat beside him for a meal," Nancy said. "For you, that's a love affair."

They all laughed, but Joyce quailed inside. There was too much truth there.

And as it turned out, what Ella had to say was very interesting. Joyce had never dreamed that Alfred had such a background; he had never spoken of it, or acted like the son of a rich man. Also, his mother had died when he was fifteen. He had never mentioned that either.

Surely Alfred mourned his mother as Joyce mourned her father, long after others had gone on to other concerns. Did death color his soul, as it did hers?

Friday, April 26, 1929 was the start of the Summer term. This time, Joyce swore to herself, she would be more forthcoming with Alfred, not because of what she had learned, but because she simply wanted to be with him.

Alfred greeted her with a warm clasp of the hand when they met on the way to Lickeys. Their eyes met frequently on other occasions. It was definitely warming up, yet still she could not simply come out and say she liked his company. At least sometimes now they walked together on their way from one class to another, and it was becoming easier to talk, albeit it not of anything substantial. What would he think if she told him of her fascination with death? Of how she had a notebook of favorite poems she had copied out, with the word death marked? She wished she could tell him, and thought he would understand.

She received a letter from Ella: she and several friends would be having a picnic in Stratford, twenty five kilometers south of the school. Would Joyce care to join them? Oh, yes! But she needed clearance from the Warden, as they called the school headmaster. As it happened, Alfred was at the Warden's table with her May 11 when she asked.

The Warden frowned. "I understand your desire to attend with your mother," he said. "But you would be taking the last train back to Woodbrooke, after dark, and it is not appropriate for a young woman to travel alone."

She had not anticipated this. She spoke before she thought. "Suppose I go with another student? Such as Alfred?"

"That would be suitable," the Warden agreed.

Then she realized what she had done. She was half appalled. She turned to Alfred. "That is, if you—I mean—"

"I shall be glad to go with you, more than glad, if it is all right with your mother," he said graciously.

"I'm sure it will be!" she said. "Oh, thank you! I do so want to be there."

That was the breakthrough. The pressure of the moment had made her act with uncharacteristic boldness. As it turned out, Alfred was not only willing, he was thrilled to be invited. Thereafter he became much more talkative with her, which helped because she was not at all good at such dialogue. He carried the conversation and she was quite satisfied to listen and agree.

Three days later, rather than wait for a ride from Selly Oak back to Woodbrooke College, she preferred to get some exercise. "Anyone for a walk home?" she inquired brightly. She knew Alfred would volunteer.

"Yes!" They had done this walk before, but in a larger group. This was the first time she had had the nerve to ask him, however indirectly, and the first time with just the two of them. But if they were to travel together tomorrow, this was appropriate.

It was Tuesday, May 14, 1929, a pleasant day. "You're from America, aren't you?" she inquired as they walked. Of course she knew that; she had seen his home address on the listing of students. No need to mention her mother's research. She was just inviting him to talk. He surely had no idea what an effort it required for her to do this. Other girls could handle boys effortlessly, but she had to labor to be incidental.

"Yes, West Chester, Pennsylvania." He seemed shy. She understood exactly how that was.

She still had to get him started. Emboldened by her success so far, she tried again, feeling giddy. "What does your father do for a living?"

He smiled. "He grows mushrooms. He is called The Mushroom King." Then, before she could express interest: "What of your father?"

She frowned. "He died sixteen years ago. Mother raised my sisters and me. I hardly knew him." Yet how little that described the reality.

He was immediately contrite. "I'm sorry. I shouldn't have asked."

"No that's all right. It was a considerable event. There was publicity, though not exactly about him."

"I don't think I understand."

"You see, he was on the Titanic."

"The Titanic! The ship that sank on its maiden voyage in 1912?"

"The very one. He was one of those who did not make it to a lifeboat. That's really about all I know."

"Your mother—widowed with young children. It must have been terrible for her."

"I'm sure it was, but she coped very well." Better, perhaps, than Joyce herself had.

"I look forward to meeting her tomorrow, at Stratford." He looked so happy as to be on the verge of turning handsprings.

"I'm sure she'll find you interesting, being from America." She hesitated, then said it: "Actually, I knew about your father's business. Mother mentioned it."

He was surprised. "What would your mother know of me or my family?"

"My father was a businessman, and knew what was what. She picked up some from him, and then had to learn more when he died, settling his estate. Your father is known in business circles. I think Mother did a bit of research on you. That was all." She was being far more talkative than normal, feeling guilty for having deceived him about what she had learned. Had she said too much?

"I am the third of four sons," he agreed. "The philosophic one."

"I am the first of three daughters, the quiet one." Sociable Nancy would have found that understatement hilarious.

Then they came to the Woodbrooke campus, and separated after making arrangements for the trip to Stratford.

Joyce telephoned her mother that evening, to be sure it was all right to bring Alfred along. She knew she should have done it before, but it had somehow seemed uncertain until that actual walk with Alfred. "Of course it is all right, dear," Ella agreed immediately. "We have discussed Alfred before; I am getting curious about him."

"He's nice enough, Mum," Joyce agreed. "But I think he likes me." As if that were a problem.

Ella laughed. "Of course he likes you dear! How could he not? You're a wonderful girl."

"Perhaps too much, I mean." Though that was surely an exaggeration, considering her reticence. How could any man actually be interested in her? And what would happen to that interest, once he learned of her obsession with death? But mainly, she had needed to warn her mother that there was more here than coincidence. Joyce did not know exactly how she felt about Alfred, but the feeling was strong, and she needed Mum's more objective judgment.

"Oh. Well, we'll see tomorrow, won't we?"

Yes, they would. Her mother was a keen judge of character.

Next day they traveled to Stratford, catching the trolley and train. Alfred talked about poetry and his love of nature, and she was glad to agree with him. She wore her good brown suit with an open shirt and a skirt with colored links. She normally didn't dress up, but she would be meeting her mother's friends, and of course there was Alfred.

They arrived early—it was a matter of when the trains ran—so did some boating on the Avon. That was fun, both because she loved boating and because she loved doing it with attentive company. It was almost as if they were a couple. She had never done that sort of social thing before.

In the afternoon they reached Stratford and rendezvoused with her mother and her friends. One was named Nora, another was an actress named Joyce. So there were two Joyce's present. Mum took an immediate if discreet interest in Alfred, engaging him in conversation, drawing him out. Her friends, knowledgeable about such things, cooperated. Alfred never realized that he was being investigated.

They were even able to attend most of the evening show before train time. Everything was just so nice.

During their ride back to Woodbrooke, Joyce invited his reaction to the day. "I hope it wasn't too much of a burden, meeting all those older women."

"They were wonderful," he said enthusiastically. "Your mother is a remarkable woman. She reminds me of my own mother." Then he was silent.

And his mother was dead. What could she say? That had gone wrong. "Perhaps your father would remind me of mine."

"I hope not. Oh, my father is all right, but—" He shrugged.

That wasn't much better. So she shifted the subject. "You seem to like the outdoors."

"I love it," he agreed. "The city oppresses me. The open country, especially forest land—unspoiled nature—it's so wonderful to experience."

"Yes!" she agreed enthusiastically. "I get out in the country every chance I have."

"We must try it together some time," he said. "I often spend Sundays exploring neighboring hills."

She had noticed his absences, and wondered. "That seems delightful." Thus it was that they agreed to do it, and made a tentative date two weeks hence.

It was after midnight by the time they walked from Selly Oak to Woodbrooke. "It is tomorrow, technically," he said. "I shall consider this to be my birthday celebration."

"Your birthday? I didn't know. I didn't mean to spoil it for you."

"Oh, no, you haven't spoiled anything!" he assured her. "I could not have had a more delightful time."

Nor could she. "I'm glad."

"Do you know, since meeting you, I find I have come to appreciate the connection between nature and poetry. I never did before."

"Oh, yes, they relate," she agreed. It was so wonderful to be talking like this with someone who understood.

Then they were home. There was nothing to do but bid each other goodnight and separate. It had been a phenomenal day, but she was of course unable to express any part of that. It was late, but it took her time to settle into sleep.

The next time she talked with Mum she got the word. "Alfred is a fine young man, not at all spoiled by the wealth of his family. He is definitely smitten with you, Joyce."

"But Mum, I'm not smitten with him. Not in that manner. This is awkward." But even as she spoke, she knew it wasn't true; she did like Alfred, more than she quite knew how to cope with.

Ella was not fooled. "You could do worse, dear. You should give him a chance."

"We have a date to go hiking in the woods on Sunday, June second."

"Excellent, dear. That will give you a better chance to know him in a good context and sort out your impressions."

"I'll try," Joyce agreed bravely. But this business made her nervous. Her relations with men had been slight; she didn't really know how to relate to them. Mum said that was because she had lacked a father's influence, yet her sisters were not so diffident in that respect.

May 21 was a kind of field day. Joyce and Alfred sat beside each other at breakfast, but the spell of Stratford had faded, and they hardly communicated. If only she could be outgoing and friendly! But she couldn't, and neither could he. That was perhaps one reason she found him intriguing; he had the same sort of limitation she did.

But how did he feel about death? She would never dare ask!

Another afternoon she was reclining on the lawn when he returned from Yearly Meeting. He joined her and just bubbled over about everything. He had taken a walk in the country. She had never seen him so effusive. Her mother was right: *he truly liked being with her.* That was a dazzling revelation, though she knew it shouldn't have been. How could she ever have generated such enthusiasm? It was difficult to believe, yet wonderful.

But all she said was "I saved you a seat at the entertainment." With the help of Miss Fowler.

He told her of a small statue of Joy he had bought in London.

"I would like to see that," she said, intrigued.

As the day ended, she said "Good night, Alfred." It was the first time she had done that.

"Good night, Joyce."

That was all, yet it felt like a milestone. They were acting as if they were keeping company.

The day before their date she found a note from Alfred in her mail slot. He had worked it all out.

The library Birmingham June 1, 1929

Dear Joyce,

      The first tram on Sunday leaves Selly Oak at 9:10 which is too late to catch either of the morning trains. I think therefore that if we set out promptly at 6:45—or if it looks better, a quarter before seven—we shall be able to walk it comfortably, catch the 8:05 from Snow Hill and have combination breakfast and lunch in Bewdley when we arrive at 9:20. Then we plunge into the forest—I hope it's really a forest which deserves the name—and we shall follow whatever inclination strikes us until the return train leaves Bewdley toward 7:30.

      As for food, I have not thought of it beyond breakfast. If you think it should be thought of—that is if you think it wise to take anything along except some apples to munch in the early morning, I leave it to you. I am of the impression that neither of us cares a great deal about such details, or likes to carry bundles or boxes of food.

      If it rains, I'm not sure it would make much difference to me. I like forests in the rain just as I do in the sun; but you must feel quite free to change your mind if you think it best, with or without reason. I shall be ready by the side door shortly before 6:45, and if you do not come by then I shall know that you are not coming. I should deplore such an occurrence, though.

      If I do not get back in time to see you tonight, we shall set out in high spirits at 6:45 in the morning. Will it be the first, or the second time that I have seen you up before breakfast?

Alfred

Unfortunately she realized that she should not go at this time; it turned out to be the wrong time of her month. She did not want him to think she was ignoring their agreement, so she dragged herself up, dressed, and went to the side door at 6:45 AM.

"Joyce!" he exclaimed as she arrived. Impulsively he clasped her, delighted to see her. Of course he thought she was going.

"I'm sorry," she said, feeling awful. "I just came to tell you that I won't go with you today. I have a cold, and it's raining, and I don't think it wise to expose myself right now. I hate to let you down, but—"

"That's all right," he said quickly, though she could see his disappointment. "We can do it next weekend instead."

"Yes, of course," she agreed, relieved.

"I do appreciate your coming to tell me, instead of letting me wonder."

"It was the least I could do," she said, nevertheless feeling guilty.

She returned to her room, and he went on his journey of exploration alone. She had done what she deemed to be the right thing, for sometimes she did get ill when she pushed her limits, and did not care to gamble. But mainly, she could never have handled her situation out in the countryside with a man; it was bad enough with the bathroom close by. But of course that came near the top of the list of things she could not bring herself to mention.

She made sure not to disappoint him again. On Saturday, June 8, 1929 they met as he had planned before, setting out at seven in the morning for the Clee Hills. They weren't sure whether they were going to the Brown Clee hill or the higher one farther north, but their inclination was toward the latter. Joyce had to admit this was fun; she did like exploring the countryside, and did like Alfred. Just not as much as he evidently liked her. Perhaps that would change. Perhaps, as Ella and Nancy thought, it had already changed. She was not versed in love, and did not know what it felt like, or how to manage it.

At Cleobury Mortimer they took a very amusing jerky puffing little train up the valley. The trip took an hour and twenty minutes. She might have read a book if she had thought to bring one, but as it happened, Alfred had: he read aloud from Lowell, which was all right, but not completely to her taste. Yet what would Alfred think if he knew her real taste?

At the end of the line they got off and bought some food: tomatoes, oranges, chocolate, biscuits. They left the station, eating as they walked. This was her dream being realized at last: to explore countryside in compatible company. With someone who appreciated nature as she did.

They passed a little hotel and hesitated. "Do you think this is a proper establishment?" she asked.

"It's hard to imagine an improper establishment in such lovely country as this."

"I mean, could we use their facilities?"

"Oh." He pondered a moment, which was a mannerism of his. "They shouldn't object."

They went in and used the toilet. It would have been extremely awkward had the need come in the forest.

Then they went up the hill, cutting across the fields, climbing over fences, passing trees, and crossing brooks. There were sheep grazing who seemed content to live and let live. It was delightfully bucolic. She would never have dared do this alone. The forest, yes, but the rest of the trip, no.

"Isn't it amazing," Alfred said. "I marvel over the simple fact of being able to walk over an English meadow. I appreciate everything there is around us."

She smiled. "You don't have meadows in America?"

"Not like these. They are, well, more commercial. They don't tolerate intruders well. The ambiance differs."

"You're in love with England," she teased him. It was as close as she could come to speaking of that emotion.

"Yes, I think I am," he said seriously. Was he similarly limited? Was there more he had to say, if only he could?

They were in no hurry, pausing often to gaze at the gradually expanding vistas behind them, or to contemplate the ants that were scurrying to conceal the eggs that they had exposed by kicking an old stump. "Maybe I shouldn't have done that," he said. "I wasn't thinking."

She hadn't thought of it that way before. "I suppose you're right; we have no business molesting creatures who mean us no harm." Thereafter they left the stumps alone. She liked that awareness in him, his caring for natural things.

He looked at a large tree. "I wonder why the roots spread out instead of going down into the earth?" he asked.

"To prevent themselves from falling over in high winds," she said. She had pondered that question herself, and finally figured it out. "Even so, many trees are blown over in storms."

"There must have been a bad storm here," he said. Indeed, there were a number of fallen trees.

They followed a little streamlet up the hill. "This one's a baby," she remarked as it diminished.

"Isn't it odd how streams start alone, and find the company of others only as they age," he said. "They become more dependent as they grow, instead of less."

She hadn't thought of it that way. Alfred was forever coming up with odd thoughts, and she liked it. "Like people, maybe," she said, smiling. This was as close as she could get to flirting: the hint that the two of them were coming together like streams.

He nodded, smiling back. Then the mood faded; neither one of them knew how to take it further.

She squatted to scoop some clay from the edge of the stream, squeezing the lump to fathom its nature. "This must be as old as time, in some form."

"There is another fascinating concept," he said. She was pleased by the implied compliment to her observation. She doubted that anyone else would have cared.

They walked along a grassy trail. It was a succession of beautiful things.

The hills were like great rounded mounds. They climbed up over them, higher and higher. There was heather, gorse, and some little flowers. They circled a quarry and attained its highest pinnacle, where there was a pile of rocks. They sat on the rocks, letting their eyes sweep slowly around the horizon in a nearly complete circle, for only a little was shut off by another hill. They didn't speak, but only watched.

A stiff wind was blowing rain at them. Joyce was glad she hadn't come last weekend; this would have been bad. She could not have afforded to get wet down. As it was, it was refreshing, for she was better now. This was nature, through and through, air, earth, and water.

They took a few pictures. "I don't suppose I could take one of you?" he asked somewhat wistfully.

She laughed. "Windblown and wet like this? I'd rather not." He did not press the matter. But again she was flattered. He didn't care how she looked. That might have seemed insulting to an ordinary girl.

They went down into the quarry, finding some shelter from the wind, and ate more of their food. "I have found that I can't eat in the forest or on the pinnacle," he said. "There seems to be some antagonism between food and the appreciation of beauty. Food becomes a material thing, somewhat gross in its nature. I rebel against it while I am in surroundings of beauty."

"Now you have ruined my snacks while exploring," she chided him. Yet she liked the thought.

"I do have my own ways of viewing things," he agreed. "I thought of our trip to Stratford as a celebration of my birthday. Of course it was more than that; I was glad to be with you and to meet your mother."

"She was glad to meet you." And Joyce valued Ella's judgment. Had Ella not approved of Alfred, Joyce would not have undertaken this excursion.

"I have news that is going to make the rest of my term here so happy that this day seems like another celebration."

"Oh?" She didn't quite trust this.

"My sister Elinor is coming."

"You are close to her?" She was relieved; this was a safe subject. Joyce valued her own contacts with her sisters, though they were not all that much like her. They lacked her awareness of death, having no memory of their father.

"Well, not ordinarily. We quarrel as siblings do, but we get along also. She can be very good company when she wants to be. And she's from home; I didn't realize how I missed it until now."

"I love it at Woodbrooke," Joyce said. "But I miss home too."

They went down across the mounds and through marshes and long grass. They came to a lake, which they skirted. Then they struck out for the top of another peak that seemed higher than the one they had been on. They walked across a rolling expanse of heather with little bare patches of blue stone. The rain was blowing in their faces. She could see that Alfred enjoyed it as she did. This was truly nature!

They proceeded up another hill, but then spied a lane leading down through the forest to the left, and paused to look. On the left was a green forest with a floor of grass that was different from what they had seen. They went to look at it more closely, then saw on the right a dusky forest of black fir trees, green only at the top. The forest floor was dark and shadowy, a dull red, covered with needles and extending in all directions beneath the branches. It was a mysterious place, but enticing, and they went exploring.

Soon they were in the middle of it, standing and gazing about at the dim dark specters of trees with here and there a well of bright light in a small glade, but dominated by the mysterious dull red light. They wandered down into a glade where masses of stones were lying in disorder. On the left was the dark inscrutable city of ghostly trees, while on the right were young green trees in striking contrast. They stopped and looked, mystified. There was nowhere to go without leaving this odd place, so they sat and gazed.

However, there was something she did not mention. She was soaked through, and increasingly uncomfortable. There was really no way out, as they could not abruptly go home, so she simply had to endure it. She determined to do so with grace, not spoiling Alfred's so-evident joy of the occasion.

"I know," he said suddenly. "This is the place where I have to read poetry."

What? "Perhaps," she said guardedly, not at all sure he was serious.

"I like to go into some wild, natural place and read my favorite poems aloud," he explained. "Thus the thoughts merge with the setting, enhancing both. It's a wonderful experience."

"Oh," she said. "Of course." At least she could get off her feet for a while; she hadn't realized how tired she had become.

He brought out a small book of poems. There in the dim dark forest he read the American poet Edgar Allan Poe, "Ulalume" and "The Raven." "Are you familiar with these?" he asked.

"I'm not versed in the Americans. Those are unusual."

"Poe was unusual. His life was as strange as his poetry and fiction. He was the child of theatrical parents, but was orphaned early in life. He lived in England for a time, then returned to America as an adult. When he was twenty seven he married his thirteen year old cousin, but she suffered long illness and died in eleven years. He wrote the poem "Annabel Lee," addressing his love for her. He had many jobs editing magazines, and was very good, but never stayed with them long. He had a problem with alcohol and drugs. He disappeared, and turned up in an alley in another city, and died soon after, aged only forty."

"He was certainly remarkable," she agreed. "Of course we have had similar in England. Samuel Taylor Coleridge was addicted to opium."

"And was another very fine poet," Alfred agreed. "Here is 'Annabel Lee.'" He proceeded to read it. It was a very feeling story of a boy who loved a young girl, who died, leaving him desolate.

Joyce was touched. There was no love like lost love, poignant in its very hopelessness. More significantly, for her, was that this was a poem about death. Was it possible that Alfred related to death as she did? She would have to add this marvelous poem to her collection.

Alfred continued reading poems, lost in their magic, but she remained bemused by the wonder of the tragedy "Annabel Lee." How very sad it was! It was as though they were in the presence of Poe's sepulcher, there with the dim dark phantom trees in the dull red forest, lit with small penetrating rays of sunlight, with the music of the laggard drops of rain on the leaves. Now she could appreciate how Alfred saw it.

"One thing disturbs me," he said, breaking off from the reading. "It is that this life of mine, this capacity to love the forest, and indeed the forest itself and the meadows with sheep and the changing clouds—all these things were not given to me because I am worthy of them. The bounty of the world gives to me a million times more than I am worth."

"I love them too," she said. "But I never thought I had to be worthy of them."

"Perhaps there is a lesson to be learned from this. I don't know what it is, but some night when I am thinking, maybe I shall know what it means for me."

"Maybe you will," she agreed. He had such remarkable thoughts! She had anticipated a day of exploration, but never a session like this. She wasn't sure what she thought of it.

"I find that I don't care about the time," he said. "What is time to me? I care only to lose myself in the beauty of the forest and of the poetry, to enunciate the innermost sympathies of my heart through the poetry I read to the dim dark trees of the forest, and to you. I am transported, feeling the impact of the beauty around me impact against my being, not through my eyes nor through my brain, but direct. I am merged with the forest. Why should I care for time or train? I want only to read on and on until darkness closes down and I can read no more. And if the train goes, what should we care? I can see us walking down the little track in the valley in the darkness of the night. Or if not, there is that friendly little hotel we saw to welcome us."

He couldn't be serious! He had to be speaking more figuratively than literally. Taking it that way, she found she agreed. In fact, she found that she was bursting with an indefinable emotion. Could this be love?

He read Walt Whitman, clearly transported. So was she, but not in the same way. She was trying to comprehend the burgeoning feeling, so that she hardly heard the poetry. How was it possible that she could be here, in this lovely glade, soaking wet, almost shivering, yet feeling an internal radiance that warmed her from the core?

She would have to tell Alfred about death, because if that turned him off, it had to be done before she was lost. But she couldn't do it right now. Maybe the next time they were alone like this, she would find the courage. Then she would know whether it was safe to let herself love him.

He ceased reading, and she emerged from her reverie. Time had passed; it was late. Yet she had hardly begun to consider the ineffable hugeness of this feeling. She couldn't speak.

They got up and made their way back down through field and forest and to the station. Alfred was smiling, clearly well satisfied with the occasion. Joyce was of course relieved that they had made it back in time for the train, but that was a somehow distant concern. She remained mute, unable to compass the emotion that claimed her. She saw herself as a zombie, her body a mere shell around a spirit that wanted to suffuse the universe. She depended on Alfred for guidance, being uncertain she could navigate on her own.

As they came down the hill toward the station they saw two small foxes at the edge of the woods. "Oh!" she exclaimed, for the moment delighted. Foxes were seldom seen, because they were hunted. It was a spot tuning in of the physical realm. Then she faded back into the spiritual realm, still attempting vainly to gain some proper understanding of it.

The jerky little train took them down the hill with much greater speed, compared to the upward climb. At seven in the evening they had their supper, spread out before them on the seat. They had the whole carriage to themselves. Just as they seemed to have the whole world to themselves, relating to each other in a manner that was so far beyond words as to be a different dimension. Was love like this, saying ordinary things, doing ordinary things, while the emotional situation was extraordinary? How could she know?

When they changed to the regular train they found it crowded and had to stand in the aisle. Joyce could have done without that; she was tired after a pleasant but rather wearing day and wanted to get off her feet. Fortunately her body was only a little part of her being. The rest did not need to sit; it was already floating.

"Look," Alfred said. There outside the train was a phenomenally bright rainbow, a perfect arch, with a dim outer arch outside it. "Another gift," he said. "Plenty heaped on plenty."

She could only nod, agreeing.

In due course they transferred to the tram to Selly Oak. Then they walked back to Woodbrooke. As they walked past the chip shop, it turned the light on. That was an invitation, so they went into the warm room full of the odors of cooking food, and bought some fairly sizzling hot chips. They paused to eat them on the bridge over the canal, then merrily walked the rest of the way home. As they entered the Woodbrooke gate she gave a small sigh of relief. It was so good to be back!

As they neared the door, Alfred paused and turned to her. "I am glad that we have been together, and you must know my gladness without any words."

She knew she should say something, and she wanted to, but she couldn't settle on anything, so was mute. He had been such a gentleman throughout, and it had been a wonderful excursion—so why couldn't she say so? But she couldn't. The magnitude of what had to be said was impossible to fit into mere crude language.

There was a play in progress, so they had a whispered good night in the hallway. Then at last she was able to return to her room. It had been a bit too much of a day.

She slept well, to her surprise. She woke to the conclusion that if this was love, she needed to learn more of it. She would go with Alfred on another hike, and this time she would broach the matter of death. Then she would know.

In the next few days the camaraderie between them increased. They had dinner together at Huang's. He bought oranges for her. She invited him to play tennis. For the first time she was having a social life with a man!

When she went upstairs at night she gave him a look. She wasn't sure what it said, because she wasn't sure of her own feelings, but hoped that some of those chaotic volumes sifted through to him.

June 17 when she came out on the lawn, Alfred was there, and she was glad. They played doubles tennis against Doris and Jack. It wasn't great tennis and the score didn't matter, just the delight of participating together.

"When will you be in Paris?" he asked.

"In early August, I believe."

"That's when Spencer and I will be passing through."

"Surely we will meet there." It was another date.

She did not go on another country excursion with him, because she had company right at that time, unfortunately. She did walk with him and sit by him at plays, and talk with him between times. They did some punting on the pond.

June 24 they walked through fields in the morning, and she almost told him of death, but was unable. What they had together was so nice she couldn't risk losing it. That evening they saw *Pygmalion*; they were both great fans of George Bernard Shaw. They talked and talked, about everything and nothing, except that one dread subject.

Alfred glanced at Shaw's preface to *Androcles and the Lion*. "What do you think about immortality?"

She did not want to admit that she had not read the whole preface to that particular play; after all, it was a hundred pages long, while the play itself was only fifty. "I think it's ridiculous. Death can't be balked." Almost, then, she asked him, but again the moment passed without being exploited.

Another time, another play, Alfred asked whether he was imposing, going with her when she might prefer to go with someone else. "By no means," she assured him. "I prefer to go with you, because others make silly comments. You never do."

"There is no doubt we are good playgoing companions," he agreed. He seemed almost to be ready to say something more, and she was eager to hear it, but that moment, also, passed. When were they ever going to get really serious?

June 29 they had a long walk and talk. By then she was fed up with the school term, yet had little pleasure in the prospect of going home, except for the hills. She wished she could say more, but she couldn't. Instead she encouraged Alfred to talk.

One day he played "Rhapsody in Blue" for her. It was lovely. Another time he put his arm about her as they walked. She was delighted, yet could not say so. Damn her incapacity!

The evening of July 3 they walked out around the neighboring fields, talking. The evening was so still and the world seemed so good. They came back, but couldn't break off, so walked out again, around the field, until coming in again at 8:15. But they were still talking, and so they went out yet again, talking of many things, but principally of people who were different from day to day, showing different aspects of their natures, often not understood by others. They were of course talking about themselves, but couldn't say so. They really were kindred souls, and it did seem more like love. This companionship was immeasurably precious.

Finally at 9:45 they ended it, having missed the lecture because of their dialogue. They had never talked like this before! She felt thrilled and dizzy with it. She had been looking for this all her life, thinking it was just company for walking she wanted, but now the walking was for the sake of the company.

On the last full day of term they walked again, down Muddy Lane and across fields, munching fresh grain from the stalks. He asked her many questions, and she tried to answer, but there was always that infernal reticence, making her responses incomplete. She wanted to share everything with him, but simply could not; her internal censor governed. She hoped he would touch her, taking her hand or putting his arm about her, but he didn't, though she suspected he wanted to. He was being too damn polite, and she was too damn inhibited.

They didn't return until 6:20, so they took the 6:30 tram for the Shaw play. Somewhere along the way Alfred made an odd remark: "I'm glad you are wearing no stockings. I don't like to see you in stockings." But then she realized that he meant he preferred her natural rather than artificial. She liked that. They decided that they should have ice cream after the play, in huge quantities.

After the theater they looked for ice cream, but found none, so walked down from Selly Oak. Her brotherly friend Ralf was there, and he volunteered to get some cigarettes for her. So she was alone with Alfred longer, hoping he would take some advantage of the situation, but he was perfectly polite, and she couldn't take the initiative. So their time alone was wasted in that sense, but it was nice just being together.

Next day, July 12, 1929, Alfred and Ralf saw her off. They met in the hall at 3 in the afternoon and took the tram in to town. They had plenty of time, so they went and had the ice cream they hadn't had the night before, and then were just in time for the train. They put her things on it, then paced the platform until the train started moving. She jumped on, then reached out to accept Alfred's proffered hand. Only a brief clasp, but it felt like a loving touch. She knew he loved her though he couldn't say it; she regretted that she had never been able say it either. They were too much alike in this respect.

She gazed back as the train pulled out, seeing Ralf and Alfred standing together. Her friend and her dear friend. She was more than tired of the routine of school, but now she hated leaving it. But surely she would see them again. Alfred would be sure to look her up in Paris.

Back home after the term ended, she talked with her mother and sisters. "I feel so guilty," she said. "Alfred is such a nice man, and I know he likes me. But somehow I was never able to speak of that with him."

"What, is he stupid or pushy?" Ruth asked. She was seventeen, and had opinions about men.

"Not at all! He's very smart, and the opposite of pushy. He's rather shy, really, in some respects."

"Did you kiss him?" Nancy asked. She was still sixteen and romantic.

"Heavens no! We barely touched hands as I jumped on the train for home."

"Then how do you know he likes you?" Nancy had evidently forgotten their prior dialogue on this matter.

"He loves her," Ella said. "That's what makes it awkward."

"How could you let him go without a kiss?" Nancy asked. "If a smart, nice man loved me, I'd want to give him a real chance."

"Of course you would," Ruth said with a smirk. "That's why Mum keeps you at home."

"Still." She gazed challengingly at Joyce.

Joyce sighed. "It was the hike in the Clee Hills that made me realize," she said. "He had it all planned out, and it was very good, really, except that it rained."

"Let's be fair," Ruth said. "We can't blame him for that."

"I don't. I had already canceled once and didn't want to do it again."

"He didn't know how readily you can catch a chill," Ella said.

"He doesn't know," she agreed. "We thought it would be a clear day, but once we were fairly there, the rain came up. I was uncomfortable, but tried not to show it. So I just kept a stiff upper lip and bore with it. There was nothing else to do."

"And for that you refused to kiss him?" Nancy demanded.

She was incorrigible. "No. It was when we found a lovely dark pine forest with a glade. It was absolutely beautiful."

"What did he do?" Ruth asked.

"He said that was the place he had to read poetry."

Both girls laughed. "He had you alone in a deep dark forest and he wanted to read poetry?" Ruth asked.

"He *did* read poetry," Joyce said. "Edgar Allan Poe, Walt Whitman. For over an hour."

"American poets, of course," Ella said. "He's American."

"Actually some of the poems were impressive. There was this one about a girl named Annabel Lee, really a child, but he loved her. Then a wind came out of a cloud and chilled her and killed her. It gave *me* a chill."

"It would," Ella said. "Fortunately you did not catch a chill on that occasion."

"Far from it," Joyce said, thinking of her revelation of love.

"So instead of exploring the forest, he was sitting there and reading," Ruth said. "Wasting the time you had."

"No he wasn't," Nancy said with sudden insight. "He was reading love poems because he loves you. I'd have kissed him."

"I know you would have. That's the difference between us—and between me and Alfred. I can't say certain things."

"So what are you going to do?" Ruth asked.

Joyce spread her hands. "What *can* I do? I am the way I am." In love and unable to express it.

"Your tragedy," Nancy said.

"Don't tease her," Ella said sharply.

"So write him a nice letter saying you can't see him any more," Ruth said. "That will give him the summer to get over it."

"I can't do that!" They assumed that she did not like Alfred the way he liked her, and she wasn't ready to clarify that aspect.

"Give him more of a chance," Nancy said. "You might change your mind."

Joyce looked helplessly at her mother.

"He *is* a nice young man," Ella said, perhaps catching on. "And you're a nice young woman. I vote with Nancy. You don't have to make any commitment. Just be steady and see how it plays out. In time he will return to America, and that would be a natural ending, if that's the way that seems best."

"And if you find you really don't want him," Nancy said, "Send him my way."

They all laughed, knowing that it could never be that simple.

*

Somehow Joyce missed Alfred in Paris; their schedules did not after all connect. He had been traveling with his friend Spencer in Spain, and had written to her about it in July. It seemed they had arrived in Paris the day before she left. If only she had known! But Paris was a huge city, and there had been no time to get in touch.

She returned home to Caradon, then arranged for one last fling of the outdoors before the school term. She went boating at The Broads, that coastal section of Norfolk where the streams were so lazy and the meadows so low. One day she misjudged and got dunked, swallowing a gulp of water. She thought nothing of it, but that evening she suffered nausea, and diarrhea in the night. It passed, but ten days later she got sick again. This time it was more serious.

"But I thought you were done with that last week," Nancy protested. The past few days were hazy; Joyce did not remember leaving The Broads or arriving home, but here she was in bed, attended by her sisters.

Joyce shook her head ruefully. "So did I. I know I shouldn't have gulped that water but it did look clean. I thought the diarrhea washed it out of my system. But now it's back, worse. I have this awful headache, and I feel nauseous and hot. Feel my hand." She extended it.

Nancy touched it. "You're burning! Oh, Joyce, you must go to the hospital!"

"Mum's arranging it," Joyce agreed. "But before I go, I wanted to tell you of my dream. It was of Alfred."

"Alfred! I thought you didn't like him that well."

Joyce shook her head. "I do like him, just not in quite the way he might like. Maybe I like him better than I thought."

"If you aren't delirious," Nancy said, smiling.

"I may be." Then she described her dream, reliving its vivid images.

She had decided to visit Alfred's family, so as to get to know him better. They boarded a huge ship together and steamed for America. There was something familiar about the ship, but she couldn't quite place it. Alfred was very nice, telling her of all the special things about it, because he had traveled this way before. It was like a grand vacation.

Then the ship collided with an iceberg. It was mortally damaged, slowly sinking in the water, and no one was coming to help. "We must get on a lifeboat," Alfred said urgently.

They hurried to the lifeboat. It was almost full. There was room for only one more person. "Get on," Alfred said.

"No, your father would be desolate," Joyce protested. "You must get safely home. You get on."

He started to protest, and she knew she would not be able to change his mind. So she took the matter into her own hands. "I am done for anyway," she said. "I'm ill, like Annabel Lee. Fare well, Alfred." Impulsively she kissed him, hoping not to spread a germ. She had never done such a thing before, and would never do it again.

Then she jumped off the deck and plummeted down toward the water. She knew the shock and cold would kill her; she had no life jacket on.

"Then I woke," she concluded. "Just before I splashed."

"Joyce—that was the *Titanic!*" Nancy exclaimed. "Father perished there."

"I remember," she agreed with a wan smile. "I hope Alfred made it safely across."

"Because you saved him! You do love him."

"In that moment I did," Joyce agreed. "In my delirium. But it was not to be. I sacrificed myself."

"But it *can* be," Nancy insisted. "Soon Woodbrooke's Autumn term will start, and you can tell him."

"Perhaps." Joyce was feeling worse, and there was an awful finality about it. "But if I can't, I hope you will."

"No, you must!"

Then Mum entered the room, and she knew it was time to go to the hospital. "Please," she said as she faded out.

*

They did their best at the hospital, but it got worse. Now she was hallucinating as her fever raged out of bounds. Yet it wasn't all bad, because being out of her mind enabled her to look, as it were from a distance, at herself, and form conclusions she had not been able to before.

For one thing, she did love Alfred. It seemed strange only because she had never before experienced the emotion, and had no basis for comparison. For another, she understood why. It wasn't merely that he was a decent, handsome and intelligent man of her own age. It was that he was like her in certain key respects. He was shy about expressing intimate personal emotions, as she was. He could perform an impulsive embrace or touch a hand, sometimes, but never speak of love. He liked Shaw plays, and nature, and hiking, and ice cream. And death. They had never talked about it, but somehow she knew that if she had broached Death, he would have understood and agreed. She kept a personal diary with references to death, underlined. Others did not understand, thinking it unconscionably morbid, so she did not discuss it openly. He surely kept a similar journal, maybe not referring so much to death, but he would have understood and accepted her passion in this respect. His mother had died when he was young, much as her father had died; he knew how it was. He was a kindred soul.

As the fever took her body, her spirit shied away from the heat. Then it departed entirely, flying clear of the hospital, looking for Alfred. She had to tell him what she had come to understand. That they belonged together.

She flew across the countryside, seeing the hills and fields and houses. She came to the great lighted city of London. She found him in a room there, pausing in his travel from France to Woodbrooke. He was asleep, for it was night.

How was she to tell him, when she had no body and he had no consciousness? She knew she did not have much time; when her fever broke, her spirit would be drawn back into her body. She had to tell him now, while she could.

Ah, but he was dreaming. She could relate. She entered his dream and infused the body of the one he was dreaming of, a pretty young woman. It didn't matter who it was; she animated the image and faced him.

And found she still couldn't speak. So she simply gazed at him, pouring out the love and understanding she had discovered in herself. He saw her, and came to her, and clasped her, and kissed her in the utmost of love, all over her forehead and cheeks. How like herself: even in his dream he couldn't kiss her on the mouth. But it was enough. She had come to him and been with him, doing what they had never done physically.

Then her fever abated, and her body summoned her. She sank into oblivion.

Nancy was there when she woke, hours or days later. "Oh Joyce, I was afraid for you," she said. "You look so—so—"

"So deathly ill," Joyce said. "Nancy, there is something I must tell you."

"Don't strain yourself," her sister said quickly. "Just get better."

"I dreamed I visited Alfred in his dream, in London, and loved him. But I don't think he knew it was me. I took a different form. So if I can't tell him—"

"Oh, yes, I'll tell him! I will! But I hope I won't have to, because—" But Joyce did not hear the rest. She had exhausted her energy and fallen into a troubled well of sleep.

*

Nancy gazed at her mother with horror. "She didn't make it?" she asked, appalled. "I visited her just a few days ago, and talked with her. I thought she was over the worst of it."

"This was a bad one," Ella said. "Typhoid can be deadly. They did all they could for her at the hospital, but it wasn't to be."

"Oh, Mum!" Nancy burst into tears. Then, almost irrelevantly: "Does Alfred know?"

"Word is going to Woodbrooke now," Ella said. "He will know very soon."

"This wasn't the way it was supposed to end," Ruth said.

Then the three of them hugged each other close, crying together. Their beloved sister was gone, victim of the illness she had picked up, apparently, from bad water while boating. It was a crushingly sudden family tragedy.

And how *would* Alfred react?

For now Nancy was obliged to tell him of Joyce's dreams. Both of them. That was hardly the worst of it.

That night she slept badly, tormented by her sister's sudden death. Maybe it was romantic when the poet Poe's beloved Annabel Lee died, but Joyce was real. Nancy's own dreams were fragmented, but one stood out in her memory when she woke. It was a continuation of the first one Joyce had told her, about sailing to America.

She, Nancy, had joined Alfred on the ship, trying to prevent Joyce from jumping. Somehow in the dream it make sense that if she could do that, Joyce would survive the terrible illness and not die in the manner of Annabel Lee.

But to stop her she had to become her. Ghostlike, she infiltrated her sister's body. *Do not do this, Joyce!* she urged. But Joyce was determined, and

Nancy, in her effort to thwart her suicide, became her. Now she was Nancy in Joyce's body.

Alfred grabbed her arm. "For a moment I thought you meant to jump," he said. "Now sit there and be at peace."

"I'll try," she said as he lifted her to the seat.

The boat dropped, alarming her. Then she saw that it was being lowered on pulleys; all was in order. She was safely on the lifeboat.

And Alfred was on the ship. "Alfred!" she screamed. But it was too late. She had saved herself at the expense of him. She could do nothing. She burst into tears.

She didn't see the ship sink, but it was gone and they were on the turbulent sea. She felt horribly guilty for being alive.

In due course they were rescued by another ship. She made it safely to America. There was Alfred's father the Mushroom King, looking like an older version of Alfred. "I'm so sorry," she told him. "I tried to save him, but he wouldn't have it."

"We understand," the man said. "We will take you home."

They took her home. The house looked like a giant mushroom. Alfred's little brother Phil was there, so she married him instead.

Nancy woke, and realized it was all nonsense. Reality had not changed. She would still have to tell Alfred of Joyce's dreams.

*

Saturday, December 14th, 1929 Alfred came to visit them at Caradon. The Autumn term at Woodbrooke had ended, and he was about to travel to Frankfurt, Germany. It seemed his family encouraged him to travel, and it gave him practice in foreign languages.

"Welcome, Alfred!" Ella said, giving him a quickly motherly hug. "These are my daughters Ruth and Nancy."

Nancy was suddenly shy in the presence of the one who had so loved her sister. He was a surprisingly handsome young man, well dressed and polite: her picture of the ideal beau. It was up to Ruth to speak to him. The visit was brief, and by the time Nancy was ready to tell him of Joyce's dream, he was gone. Had she really tried?

Later in the month Ella received a nice letter from Alfred. She shared it with the girls. The address was Der Berg, Westerburg, Germany. He said:

My dear Mrs. M,

A burg signifies a sort of castle on top of a hill. But this castle, where I am now living with the Strobel family, is not only a great, hulking, shapeless, fathomless, thick-walled, dark-stairwayed, maze-passaged landmark, but is also surrounded by beautiful forested rolling patchwork country with a magnificent skyline which was covered by a light fall of soft flaky snow last night so that I can scarce leave my window, which looks out on a splendid sweep of landscape.

It is no wonder, then, that every glance from my window, every touch of the cold wind, every curve of the silhouetted skyline brings with it the thought of her whose heart was in these things. As I sat just now on a snowy mound on the side of a wooded hill, watching the clouds above the black trees across the valley, I thought and thought.

Nancy had to pause there. Joyce was dead; she might have resented a stranger intruding his feeling, as if it could match that of her bereaved family. Yet he said it so well. Joyce's heart *had* been in the things of nature; she had reveled in them. It was that passion that had killed her; it had not been in her nature to distrust outdoor water. And Alfred, though he had come on the scene only in the last year or so, surely had loved Joyce as her family did.

Perhaps it matters little what I thought. There must be times, too, when your mind seems full to overflowing, yet still contains an emptiness, a wondering. So was mine. I can say in words that the power which had the right to make her has the right to take her—but still I wonder. I can say that there are beauties other than material ones, and powers of perception which are not the senses, and that life is everlasting. I believe these things with all my heart. But there are still things I don't understand, which make me wonder. I can evolve explanations, but still there seems something vital that I don't and cannot know. And though I submit to what it *is*, though I don't understand it, still I wish that Joyce could wander these snowy hills with me, explore this ancient forest with me, and with me watch the evening fall, as now it falls over the white valley below. It isn't the "with me" that is important. I want her to know what is hers, because it is like her. I want her to miss nothing which would delight her heart. And though I recognize the possibility, I cannot quite be sure that she will experience the delight which waits for her here.

"I don't understand either," Nancy breathed. "She bore ill will to no one. She was a creature of nature. Why did God have to take her?"

"Why indeed," Ruth echoed.

"We have to believe that God has his design," Ella said. "That somehow this horror is justified in the larger picture."

"I can't see how," Nancy said tearfully.

"Neither can I," Ruth said. "First God took our father, then he took our beloved sister. It's not fair."

Ella resumed reading the letter.

> All the thoughts which were crowded out by my work in the autumn flood to me now. I can hardly help writing to you, because I have Joyce so much, so very much in my mind. She seems my constant companion, and I picture her wherever I am, and treasure the few memories I have of her; so few, perhaps, but each one perfect in its way. There are many who think of her, and I join their number with gladness; yet I believe that she had an individual companionship with each of us.

"Yes," Nancy agreed.

"He truly loved her," Ruth said. "Even if she—"

"Don't say it!" Nancy snapped. "She loved him at the end. She told me."

Ella glanced at her but did not challenge her statement. She resumed reading the letter.

> My words are a bit stiff, I'm afraid. You needn't mind them, for you will be able to read the thoughts from which they spring. My thoughts are more of thankfulness than of disquiet, for I am daily mindful of the magnitude of the blessing granted to us who knew her.

Nancy had to laugh. "God grant me stiffness like that!"

"He expresses himself beautifully," Ruth agreed. "Maybe he was worthy of her."

"Maybe he was," Nancy agreed.

"He truly does love her," Ella said. "As we do."

"And he resembles her," Ruth said. "Wandering the snowy hills—that's her."

"And not being able to express personal feeling face to face," Nancy said. "Only in a letter after she's gone. That's eerily like her."

The others nodded. "I think we need to see more of Alfred," Ella said.

Nancy realized with surprise that it was so. Alfred was like Joyce, not in gender, not in appearance, not in origin, but in essence. They could get a bit of Joyce back by associating with Alfred. It was weird, yet true.

In January Ruth went to Woodbrooke. It had been planned throughout, and Nancy's turn would come when she came of age, but she envied her sister's opportunity to share campus and classes with Alfred. She would get to know him better.

She did. She reported that Alfred's correspondent friend Katia from Bulgaria was also attending; it seemed he had arranged for payment of her tuition to make it possible. It was not a romantic connection; they were just friends. Alfred did not seem ready for any new romance; Joyce had spoiled him for that.

In March Alfred and Ruth visited the town of Lichfield, just north of Birmingham, and later they went to London together. Between times they shared classes and played tennis together. "I like him," Ruth said candidly. "But he sees me only as Joyce's sister. There's nothing building here."

"Perhaps that is just as well," Ella said. "He has to work all the way through Joyce, as do we all, before he can be sure of anything else."

Then the Spring term ended, and Ruth returned home. Three weeks later Alfred visited again. He was startlingly handsome; when he gazed directly at Nancy she felt almost like swooning. It was as though he were seeing right into her soul. She tried to be polite and friendly, but feared she was fluffing it. She had not anticipated such impact. After all, this was only the second time they had met; she had no real relationship with him. He surely saw her only as Joyce's kid sister, a person of no consequence. As was perhaps the case. But she saw him almost as a kind of reincarnation of Joyce. Joyce hovered eerily in his aspect and manner.

Ella of course handled it well, and Ruth showed him around the premises, as the two of them were now well acquainted. Did Nancy have the right to be jealous?

After he was gone, she remembered again that she had forgotten to tell him of Joyce's dreams. Somehow it had never entered her mind.

"For a moment, I feared you would faint," Ruth said. "Alfred impresses you?"

"Yes," she confessed. "There's something about him."

"There's something about you, too. I think it's that you look more like Joyce than I do. He looked at you, and I swear, suddenly Joyce was among us."

"But I'm only seventeen," Nancy protested, afraid to be flattered.

"And impressionable. Not that there's anything wrong with Alfred. But he's still locked into Joyce."

"And I could only ever be the echo of Joyce," Nancy agreed. "Even if my nature matched hers, which it doesn't."

"You're more outgoing," Ruth agreed. "More social. And you like him better."

"I don't!" she protested, knowing how Joyce had loved him. But she did like him a lot. Foolishly romantic it might be, but Alfred excited her. The idea of sitting in a forest with him and reading poetry delighted her.

A few days later he visited again. Ruth and Nancy waited for him at the bus stop and walked him to the house. Nancy found herself becoming bolder, chatting merrily with him, her outgoing personality taking charge. It was easy to do; he was responsive to her verbal sallies and laughed with her.

This time he stayed at their house, Caradon; Ella had concluded that it was by this time appropriate for him to do so, and it was certainly convenient. In the morning he went out with the two of them to walk the countryside, and for Nancy all the long-familiar haunts became new as she viewed them through his eyes. He did love the fields and forest, as Joyce had. Nancy knew he was thinking of Joyce as he gazed around, his expression becoming serious. She felt the same; this country *was* Joyce in its fashion.

In the evening after dinner Alfred played his bassoon for them. Nancy had not heard this instrument before and was fascinated. "It is said to be the joker of the orchestra," he explained. "Because it can make such funny sounds." He demonstrated, producing a weird squeak, and they all laughed.

But he could also play seriously, and the music was lovely. Nancy was absolutely charmed.

"I see music and poetry as two aspects of a common art," he said. "I try to bring them together whenever I can. It is my delight to go alone into some hidden glade of a forest and play there, hoping no one overhears me, for they would consider me eccentric."

Nancy clapped her hands, delighted. "Oh, that sounds so wonderful! You must play there for me—for us."

As it turned out, the others demurred, setting it up for Nancy, and next day she went with Alfred to a copse she knew, and he played for her. It was marvelous, and she was thrilled. Yet she knew it was Joyce he was thinking of, rather than her.

Then they talked. "I do not wish to cause you pain," he said, indicating there was something on his mind.

"Joyce," she said immediately. "You're thinking of her. It's all right; we think of her too."

"Surely so," he agreed. "You are so like her, flesh of her flesh, people of her environment. How can you be otherwise?"

"She was our sister," she agreed, pensive.

"As I look around your house I am aware of something which I can perceive yet cannot keep, touch yet not grasp. Each time I perceive it, whether it be in the position of a cushion or in the appearance of a flower, I undergo a moment of realization, a flush of pleasure, and a pang. There is the cushion. There is the work basket. There is the broken arm of the sofa. Here is the book you have been reading. They speak. They speak to me. For me they are endowed with the life of the hands which touched them. It is a certain kind of life. That's what eludes me. How can I truly know of what I sense so vaguely. As I look at you—" He broke off, embarrassed.

"You see a younger copy of Joyce," Nancy said. "I am told I look a bit like her."

"You are a different person, of course," he agreed. "I know that, intellectually. Yet it is true. You put me much in mind of her. I don't mean to imply any defect in you as an individual." He shrugged. "But there it is."

Now at last she was emboldened to relay the message. "Joyce dreamed of you. Twice."

"I have dreamed of her so often." Then he paused. "*She* dreamed of *me*?"

"She asked me to tell you. She was in the fever, and it did odd things to her imagination. She dreamed she was going to meet your folks in America. But the ship struck an iceberg."

"The *Titanic*!" he exclaimed, laughing ruefully. "Of course."

"Of course," she echoed. "I was, you might say, on the way when it happened. In the dream there was room for only one more on the lifeboat. You wanted to save her, but she refused, and jumped into the water."

"She sacrificed herself to save me?"

"Yes, in the dream."

"I would gladly have reversed it."

"I know." But Nancy decided not to speak of her own dream; it really wasn't relevant.

He considered for a moment. "Thank you, Nancy. Thank you for telling me."

"I promised to, but it was difficult."

"You said dreams. There was another?"

"Yes. When she ran the fever, in the hospital, she—her spirit flew out—I know this sounds silly, but—"

"Joyce could never be silly."

"She flew to you, in London, and entered your dream. In another body, because her own was stuck in the hospital. She couldn't speak, but she looked her love at you."

Alfred's jaw dropped. "I was in London. I dreamed of Genevieve, one of my sister's friends. That was Joyce?"

"Borrowing her image," Nancy agreed. "She wanted to tell you that she loved you."

"She did, in her special way. No words, just a look." He looked awed.

"I promised her to tell you, but hoped I wouldn't have to. Because I wanted her to live." She shrugged, near to tears.

He nodded. "Yet she is still with us, in spirit, far greater, far finer, far holier, around us and in us, finding us, feeding us, making us."

"Yes," she breathed, awed by his vision.

"We stand in love, in reverence, almost in fear. Our thoughts go beyond, and pain us."

"Yes!"

"Yet is there pain? Yes there is, now. I know that there is suffering in silence. How well I understand!"

"Yes."

"I feel myself sometimes on that unspeakable edge, that edge beyond which is a fury of uncontrollable sorrow, of defiance hurled against the crashing wheels of the universe, of spirit mangled in a chaos of distress—that edge is always near."

"Yes." He was voicing thoughts she had not been able to formulate for herself. There was poetry in his soul.

"Yet far wider and brighter is the horizon of hope, hope for which we yearn, and to which we turn, longing for certainty and finding a satisfaction which lacks only certainty. On the edge we stand, our stinging pain lightened by the fair resplendence of the horizon of hope; or joy tinged by the proximity of the near abyss. Here we stand. Here is our life."

Beautiful. Nancy turned to him, kissed him quickly on the cheek, and fled, appalled at her impulse. She knew he had been talking about his feeling for Joyce. But it was her feeling too.

He followed her back, seeming thoughtful. She stayed out of his way.

"Nancy!" Ella said, intercepting her as she entered the house. "What happened?"

"Nothing!" Nancy cried as she ran to her room.

Later she learned that Ella had next intercepted Alfred, and they had had a long talk. She didn't dare inquire.

Why had she done it? Why had she interrupted his feeling discourse by such an intemperate act? Was she crazy?

No, not exactly. She had a crush on her sister's boyfriend who had no such interest in her. She had no business with such feeling; it was foolish. Regardless, she should never have acted on it.

Later while they were washing dishes she turned suddenly and caught Alfred looking at her. What was in his mind? Was he wary of her, lest she do something ludicrous again?

Then Alfred and Ruth went back to Woodbrooke for the summer term. But he wrote her a brief note, expressing pleasure at having been with her. She was utterly thrilled.

Unfortunately Ella picked up on that, tolerantly, and in her next letter to Alfred wrote "She was really pleased to have your note—perhaps I must not say more!" How humiliating could it get?

Meanwhile life continued. Nancy tracked Alfred via his letters to her mother and occasionally to her sister. How she wished she could be part of that correspondence! But that was a thing she dared not speak.

Then Alfred visited again, October first. She tried to be restrained when she saw him, but her heart was thudding. He was as handsome as ever!

Two days later Ella called her aside. "We must talk."

"Have I been making a fool of myself, again?" she asked. "I'm trying to behave normally, but I have to confess he thrills me so."

"You have been fine. I have struggled with my conscience, and decided to violate a confidence. I ask you to maintain it, however."

"A confidence?"

"Alfred shared something with me, uncertain whether he should. It gave me pause for thought."

"I trust your judgment, of course."

"My judgment may be suspect. I'm going to read you a poem Alfred wrote."

"If you wish." There was of course only one person who inspired Alfred to poetry.

Ella read the poem:

> I cannot say she is the wind
> For she has substance, form and speech;
> I cannot say she is a flower;
> She is not fragile, small, or white.
> Nor can I say she is a dream
> For she is real, more real than I
> The poet has not met her yet
> The painter cannot capture her
> She is not music, dance, nor flame
> She's not like anything I know—
> She's only all that she should be.

Ella paused. "Does this mean anything to you?"

"It has to be about Joyce. But that's odd, because it suggests she's alive. Am I missing something?"

"Here is the last line," Ella said. "'She's Nancy.'"

Nancy felt faint. "But that can't be! I am nothing to Alfred."

"He has been careful, because he fears it is your resemblance to Joyce that moves him, and he does not want to cause any of us grief. But he has been conscious of you since your first meeting."

"But it is Ruth he writes to!"

"Because he feels he has no basis to write to you. He is taken with you, Nancy."

Nancy sat down. "But I'm just a schoolgirl, with a schoolgirl crush. He can't be taken with me."

"There is another poem."

"Another!"

Ella read it:

> I delight to hear the sound of her voice
> To see the flowers she has put on my dresser
> To sip the milk she has left in my room,
> To share in the water she has left for me
> To live from food prepared by her hands
> To think of her, to be with her, to speak to her
> If there is any good in me, she brings it to light.

"It can't be!" Nancy repeated. "He loves Joyce."

"He does love Joyce. But she is dead, and he is alive, and you are coming increasingly to resemble her. You are inheriting that emotion. He is not sure it is wise, and neither am I. Yet it may be in order. You need to consider carefully whether you would care for a future with Alfred."

"How can I consider, when I can't trust my emotion?" She paused, then confessed. "Did he tell you I kissed him?"

Ella's eyes narrowed. "No. Did you?"

"On the cheek, the day he played music for me in the glade. I couldn't help myself. I fled."

Ella nodded. "That might explain somewhat. Joyce never did that."

"Joyce was not impulsive the way I am, even if she was smitten with him."

"True. You might actually be a better match for him than she was."

"I never said that!"

"I believe the two of you are attracted to each other. Perhaps it is fate. I think you should get to know him better, and try to make a judgment. The truth of this matter must be found in your hearts."

Nancy found this hard to believe. "You are—are giving me leave to court Alfred?"

"By no means. Merely to get to know him well enough to form a judgment. Thereafter we can reconsider."

Nancy felt dizzy. All this time she had thought Alfred barely noticed her, and he had been seriously noticing her. Their attraction was mutual. But was it sensible? She resembled the dead woman he loved; that was no proper basis.

There more she considered, the less likely it seemed. Joyce had been quiet; Nancy was talkative, despite being shy in Alfred's presence. Joyce had loved the outdoors; Nancy liked it, but also liked the indoors and people. Joyce had been somewhat shy; Nancy was if anything too social. Joyce had been fascinated by death; Nancy preferred life. She was not at all like Joyce underneath, however she might resemble her superficially. So if Alfred truly loved Joyce, how could he love Nancy? It was bound to be illusion.

Next day she walked with Alfred, over hills and fields, grass and hedged roadways. They talked as they moved, of anything and nothing. She delighted in it; she could do this all day, with him. She was indeed coming to know him better, and what she was learning was good. Almost she could believe that she would be a better match for him than Joyce would have been, in large part because she related to his mergence of poetry and music with the countryside in the way Joyce had, and because she did warm to him in a way Joyce had. And because she could express herself in a way Joyce had not been able to.

But back home, alone in her room, her doubts resurfaced. Alfred was wonderful, granted—but what of her? She was a smitten girl who might not really be woman enough for him. She lacked his formidable intelligence and education. They had common ground in significant respects, but there was much ground that they did not necessarily share.

Three days later they walked again, and again doubts were banished. If this was not love, surely it was approaching it. They went out to Shute's Shelf, and when they got tired, they rested and Alfred talked about land and the Quaker position against disproportionate wealth.

"Of course I speak as the son of a wealthy Quaker businessman," he said ruefully. "So I can not be certain of my own objectivity."

"But isn't the idea to use that wealth to make things better for others," she asked. "To ameliorate the ills of the world?"

"Yes, of course. But I'm not sure how many Quakers actually do that, once they have wealth. I suspect it would be better never to have it; then there would be no conflict."

"I wish I could do something about those ills," she said. "But I don't know how. I'm just a girl."

"A marvelous, well-meaning girl," he said.

She tried to stifle her flush of pleasure, but it came out anyway.

But again, alone, she doubted. This time something else occurred to her: what of Ruth? Ruth was closer to Alfred's age, and more intellectual, and she knew him better. He saw her regularly too; how did she feel about him? Nancy needed to know that, and she didn't think she could ask.

Somehow she managed, phrasing it as passing curiosity. She wasn't sure that fooled anyone.

"I like him," Ruth said candidly. "He's an excellent convenient companion. But he's too intellectual for me. Too serious. And I don't look like Joyce. So we're just friends."

Her sister was giving her leave.

Then Alfred was off to Oxford. He was applying to the University there, and he was surely smart enough to be admitted.

It was another six weeks, in December, before he visited again. Nancy was so very glad to see him, but still that doubt loomed. Did he look at her and see the echo of Joyce? If Joyce were subtracted, would there be anything left?

They chatted, and it was nice. But slowly she was coming to the conclusion that he would have to relate to her as Nancy, not Joyce, if there was to be any realistic prospect of a future between them. Until she was sure, she couldn't afford to let herself truly love him.

Then he was back to Germany. "I wish he could let go of Joyce," Nancy said, distraught. "Or I could let go of him."

Ella nodded. "She was not destined to be with him. Perhaps it was just as well it ended this way."

Nancy was appalled. "That she died?"

"That gives it a finality it would otherwise lack. I would not have sacrificed her, or any of you, for anything, were it in my control. But since Alfred could not have Joyce, because she would never have been able to relate that way, this may have been God's only way of freeing him to have you."

Nancy had her doubts that Joyce could not have related, but there was no point in arguing that case now. "I would never take him that way!"

"Nor would I have chosen it," Ella said. "When your father died, I pondered long on what it could mean, and concluded that I would never understand God's purpose, but there surely *was* a purpose. Now I have a similar conclusion. It was not your choice, not your fault, but it may be destiny."

"I can't accept it!"

Ella shook her head. "You must accept what God decrees."

"But we don't know that he decreed this!"

"We don't. So we must keep our minds and spirits open, and see what offers. If Alfred chooses you, I will not oppose it. But I think the decision is his alone to make. If he still can't let Joyce go, then it is not to be."

Nancy had to agree. The decision was Alfred's because only he could let go of Joyce.

Alfred visited again on Thursday, January 15, 1931. Again, it was nice being with him, but it was apparent that Joyce still governed him. Nancy was merely marking time, waiting for him to decide.

He was at the University of Oxford, and doing well. He was a vegetarian now; she wasn't sure exactly when that had started, but thought it was after Joyce died. The shock of that might have had such an effect. Worse, it seemed he had developed personality problems such as shyness and seclusion. Ella had recommended that he see a good psychologist.

"You think he's crazy?" Nancy asked, alarmed.

Ella laughed. "Of course not. We all have our moments. I had considerable difficulty after your father died, and a psychologist really helped me."

"You!"

"I did not bruit it about, not wishing to alarm anyone, least of all my children, but yes I did. That's why I recommend it. He has been under the strain of an extremely rigorous academic schedule, and has been away from America a long time. I think in addition he does not see his future clearly. Many things surely have bearing."

"Maybe he needs a woman to give him emotional support."

Ella laughed. "He surely does! But we have covered that before."

They had, indeed. What they had not discussed was the way Ella had become like a mother to Alfred, and he like a son to her. Nancy had no jealousy of that, and knew that neither did Ruth; they would have been satisfied to have had a brother. Maybe that had been the one who miscarried: their older male sibling. Alfred fit the role nicely.

But this was not brotherly interest she was considering. It was romantic. That was quite a different matter. What was suitable for a brother was not suitable for a lover. Especially not if he really loved her sister.

All they could do was wait.

Alfred visited them again in December. "It *will* be fun if Alfred comes!" Nancy said enthusiastically when she learned of his plan.

He was with them three days in January 1932. It was delightful. They walked and talked and did things together, having a continual good time, and she saw him off on the train. Was Joyce fading at last?

Ella shared one of Alfred's letters with her: "Nancy was an angel. My days with her were incomparable. A precious creature. She makes me think life is good."

"I think I'll swoon," she said, delighted. Yet there had been no kissing, no hugging, not even hand holding. Definitely no expressions of romantic feeling. Alfred was simply too damned proper.

Or he remained enamored of a dead woman.

Alfred was back at Oxford, struggling with the studies, and seeing the psychologist. Obviously he had not yet settled on his course of life.

Still, the letters Ella shared with her were evocative. In March he wrote of research he had done on the almost unknown Moroccan city of Xauen, which he had visited for a day. "Until 1920 no European had ever entered Xauen. It was known to exist, but no one knew exactly where. The name means 'Two Horns,' for it extends up two valleys." He described the landscape and the people he saw as he walked around the area, which was of course exactly what Alfred would do. Nancy wished she could have walked it with him. She drifted to sleep that night picturing marvelous distant Xauen, the enchanted city.

Another letter was less sanguine. "My next book will have to be 'How it feels to be crazy.' I cannot be convinced that I am wholly sane. It would be painful to go into detail. Now I have a headache and no ambition. How loose and purposeless is my life! London alone always spells dissipation for me. I wish I could get away from my own company."

"Poor Alfred!" Nancy said. "He really does need someone to reassure him and provide him company." Of course she was thinking of herself.

"He is seeing Doctor Hadfield," Ella reminded her. "I'm sure the psychologist is helping."

But not the way a woman could, Nancy thought. She was nineteen now, old enough. As old as Joyce had been when she first met Alfred. But of course she could not say that to her mother.

Then he wrote her a letter directly. He did not do that often, and she thrilled to each one. His words were friendly but carefully neutral. Yet why would he write to her at all, if he wasn't interested?

She dreamed she was married to Alfred. There was nothing to it but that; no sex, no house, just walking beside him with the awareness that they were married.

"Such fancies are natural," Ella said, unalarmed.

Then later: "Alfred says he had a similar dream."

Nancy almost fainted. "You told him!"

"Perhaps I shouldn't have. I thought it harmless. I'm sorry."

"No, that's all right, if he didn't take it wrong."

"He loves you, Nancy. He just can't say it, lest he see himself unfaithful to Joyce. So it may come to nothing."

"Would it actually be the right thing? I don't think I would want to live in America."

"I don't think he wants to return to America. He prefers Europe. That's really not the question. He has other issues to work out."

"He doesn't seem crazy to me."

That was where they left it. Alfred continued with his studies and his doubts. Nancy wondered if he was letting go of Joyce at last, but finding nothing to replace her, so he felt empty. That might actually be a good sign. But still he had to make his decision himself.

Meanwhile her life continued well. She was surrounded by friends, and was living a free happy existence. If she missed someone, she did not say so; Alfred was not part of their world.

But he was part of *her* world. One day they hiked together to Crook's Peak and it was marvelous. Almost she thought Alfred was going to say something significant to her, but he didn't. She had been primed for the scene: "Nancy, my feelings for you have changed. I see you as more than a companion." "So do I, Alfred." "I would like to—" "Kiss me?" "I realize this may be sudden and forward, yet—" This time he was interrupted by her kiss on his mouth. But it never happened beyond her fancy.

He took the summer course at Woodbrooke, then visited them as August turned to September, 1932.

They went to the Bird Hotel in Winscombe where he was staying, picked him up and brought him to the house. It was fun, as usual. But Alfred was pensive, as usual. She tried to bring him out by being jolly, encouraging him to do things with them, but this was only partly effective.

"He is still struggling," Ella said privately. "He has to have time."

Nancy did not want to be unkind, but she had struggles of her own as she got into higher education and increasing social activity, and was becoming impatient. She needed to come to some sort of decision with Alfred, so she could get on with the rest of her life.

"Come with me to Bridgwater Bay to see the sailboats," she urged him. If she got him alone, she might even kiss him again, more seriously.

"I am tempted," he said. "But am not certain I should."

That probably meant he wanted to talk with Ella. So Nancy went with other friends, and had a great time, but not quite what she had had in mind. Perhaps it was just as well, as she wasn't certain how Alfred would react to her naughtiness, had she actually indulged in it.

Alfred needed the address of his friend Arthur Moore, and she agreed to look it up and send it to him. So Alfred sent her a stamp for that purpose. So she wrote to him directly, though Ella was writing him the same day: "Dear Alfred, How frightfully extravagant of you to send a 1½d stamp when a penny one would have done,—think of all the things you might have bought for the ½d. If it wasn't for the fact that we're going to send two letters instead of one big one I should probably have written a post card and bought the strip of licorice at the job-shoppe myself. However, next time you feel inclined to do the same thing you might attach an addressed envelope to the stamp." Then she gave him the address, and added news of her plan to move. "I'm hoping to get a room about 3 minutes from the hospital with the Roakes, whose son was at Sidcot. Hope you're doing lots of HARD WORK—like me. With love, Nancy."

She visited him at his residence in Oxford a month later. His room was small but neatly kept; Alfred was admirably orderly. They talked, then he offered tea, but turned out to be out of milk, which she preferred. "I will fetch some," he said immediately.

"There's no need." But he was already off, leaving her alone in the room.

She looked around. On his small desk she saw a thick canvas-covered volume. Curious, she went and opened it—and discovered inside the cover a small collection of pictures of Joyce. That flame still burned, obviously.

She turned the pages, and found that the volume was filled with dated entries, starting 22 X 31, which would be October 22, 1931. "As I was taking tea in the old North Gate, a new range of thought opened up, pursuant to my conversation with Louisa. Is it well to confine myself to Spanish? After Mr. Brown's lecture on psychology I talked with Mr. Kalkhorst, who recommended a duel language degree on two provisions: that I wanted general training and not specialized such as would prepare me for a lectureship; and that my German was far enough advanced to go on with."

It was a diary! These were his private thoughts of almost a year ago. There were surely prior volumes. But few entries were in plain English; some where in some kind of abbreviated notations, others in what appeared to be Spanish, and others in German. She could read only a fraction of it. Not that she ought to be getting into this at all; it was confidential material. Yet she couldn't help herself; she was seriously interested in Alfred and in his continuing attachment to her sister. She turned more pages, expecting to be interrupted at any moment by Alfred's return.

There was an entry date the 14th of January in Madrid, Spain; she remembered he had traveled there. Then suddenly her own name leaped out at her. "Nancy was an angel." That was what he had written to Ella. She was thrilled anew.

But she couldn't dally. Anything she wanted to see, had to be seen in a hurry. She turned pages rapidly, skipping all the foreign languages passages, and came to two pages in straight English, dated Thursday, September 15, 1932. That was just after his visit to Winscombe. She read them, fascinated.

> We were sitting on a stile watching the boats on the broads. It was the day before we separated, and I was pensive. I had so much enjoyed these two weeks, but more than everything else, enjoyed being near her. I knew that I had come to love her beyond all belief, yet I was never able to tell her so, or even hint that I cared. When we were alone together, life was so good that we just had to care more about it than anything else; and besides, there was something in her or about her which made it impossible to bring our attention down to ourselves. She was not interested in self. And she was not a dreamer of dreams of love. She was a doer, who loved outwardly and actively, and was scarcely conscious of

it. So I dared not truly to tell her how deeply, how sincerely truly I cared for her. The telling of it seemed so much less important than the *doing* of it.

But as we sat together on the stile, I was doubly conscious that she would soon go away, and I wanted somehow to hint to her what was constantly in my thoughts. Her hand was resting on the fence, but I dared not put mine over it. Anything of that sort was simply out of place with her.

I said: "I don't know what I shall do when you go away. It's been so good being with you all this time." She was looking across the marshes at two boats that were trying to pass each other. "It's been jolly good fun," she said, diverting her attention from the boats just for a moment.

Inwardly I was talking ceaselessly. Good fun? I should say it has been, and a thousand times more, for me. It's been two weeks of heaven, and the prospect of ever doing anything else than this is unbearable. I want never to go back, never to stop sitting on this stile with you, never to have to leave you at all. Fun? This has been *life* for me, and I think I have never lived before. Shall I ever live again. But no matter. This is *life* here and now, and here is Joyce herself, no hope, no dream, no memory, but *herself*. This is her hand, that I could touch right now—by mistake, of course! And here am I just radiating love for her, and—

"They're coming," she said, and slid off the fence, looking toward the boat that was approaching along the channel. That was our last chance to be alone together, and to her it was like any other—first or fourth or seventh. And "being alone together" seemed never to have occurred to her! I got off the fence, and we walked along the bank toward the approaching boat.

Nancy heard a noise in the hall. "They're coming!" she whispered with a guilty smile. She closed the book and left it exactly as she had found it on the desk, then scooted back to her chair just before Alfred opened the door. She was ashamed of herself for snooping, yet what she had read was immensely significant. Alfred had written this almost two years after Joyce's death. It had never happened, just as Nancy's own fancy of kissing him on the mouth had not, yet here it was in his mind, still paining him. He must have thought that he might have saved Joyce from the typhoid fever if only he had been there. How she wished that could have been possible!

The rest of her visit was pleasant; Alfred was good company, and she tried to be the same. But what she had read weighed on her. She had invited Alfred to join her watching the boats on Bridgwater Bay, and he had declined; had that image of Joyce been on his mind?

When she returned home she discussed it with Ella, confessing what she had done. "I am ashamed, yet I know I would do it again. He truly loved Joyce."

"I wonder. You say the entry was dated only three or four days after his visit here?"

"Yes. At first I thought it might relate, but it didn't."

"I am wary of coincidence. Could he have been thinking of you? That is, when you invited him to come see the sailboats. That might have triggered the vision."

"But he named Joyce!"

"Yes. You are so close to Joyce in appearance that it reminded him of her. That could readily have been about you."

Nancy was amazed. "That's why he wrote it so soon after seeing me. It *was* partly me." Because she was alive, not dead, and looked too much like Joyce.

Then they were busy with their separate projects for six months, though they kept in touch by mail. Until he visited again in early May, 1933.

Their personal interaction was routine, but a bit strained. When he left, Ella explained why: "We talked in the shed while I worked on the loom and he worked on the lamp. He said his trouble seems to lie in loneliness. I sighed; how well I understand that condition!" She glanced directly at Nancy. "It's not that you and Ruth aren't great company, but when I lost your father it was difficult, and now of course both of you are increasingly finding lives of your own. I wish you could stay with me forever, but I also wish you to make great new strides as independent women, which means I do have to be alone again."

"I'm sorry," Nancy said. "I wish I could rewrite the laws of the universe."

"I wish Alfred could marry, but that's a separate problem. He loves you, Nancy, but he's uncertain to what extent that love is real. That is, does he love you for yourself, or merely as the image of Joyce? If you represent Joyce, then it isn't real. He is understandably wary of that. So am I. I think he wanted to ask me whether he should marry, and if so, whom, but with the leading prospect being my daughter, he couldn't."

"Leading prospect! What am I, a deal to be consummated?"

"You're a dear, lovely young woman. But your resemblance to Joyce may be your curse. I couldn't have advised him, even if he had asked, and not just because I am your mother. I truly don't know how the aspects of his feeling would sort out."

Nancy suffered a flare of ire. "I'd like to sort him out and be done with it!"

Ella nodded. "Maybe that would be best, dear."

"I wasn't serious!"

"Perhaps you should be. Do you love him?"

Nancy had to pause before answering. "I don't know. Oh, I certainly had a crush on him, but I'm older now, and while I consider him to be a fascinating and worthy man, I do have other prospects, and am not certain. I mean, suppose I *am* the image of Joyce? Is that any basis for marriage?"

"I think not. But that can be resolved."

"How?"

"You must do something Joyce would never have done, establishing your independence, that also forces the question in his mind."

"I agree. But what?"

"You might propose marriage to him."

Nancy laughed. Then, realizing that this was no laughing matter, she abruptly sat down. "How would that sort it out?"

"He would know you weren't Joyce. And he would have to answer you with a yea or a nay."

"But suppose he answers wrong?"

"Is that possible? If he loves you, he must marry you. If he loves Joyce, he must not marry you. His decision has to be correct for him."

"But that leaves me no decision! Suppose I don't want to marry him?"

"Then don't propose."

Nancy smiled ruefully. "Oh, of course. I do have to decide first." It was the tyranny of duel uncertainties. She had to decide whether to make Alfred decide.

Alfred had invited her to visit him again at Oxford; that was obviously the occasion. She had to decide before then.

She visited him Saturday, May 20. She had to struggle with the two old dames who ruled the roost at Swindon to let her go out alone with a MAN, but succeeded because she had to. He picked her up on a motor byke, her first ride on such a machine. It was scary but fun; she would never forget!

Arrived safely at his room, he was courteous and attentive, as always—and slipped up on the same detail as before. He was out of milk for the tea.

"Please, don't run off again!" she pleaded, laughing. "I'm sure I can somehow survive."

But he was off again, determined to have this detail right. Once again she was alone in his room.

She looked to the desk. There was the book. "Get thee behind me, Satan," she murmured. But she couldn't resist. She opened the book and turned the pages, skimming rapidly past the foreign language material. She saw that Alfred had pasted in some of the letters he had received from Ella, and one from Nancy herself. There were also pictures of them at Caradon, including one of her sitting in a deck chair. She was touched. But what she was really curious about was what he had written after her prior visit here.

She found an entry in English dated November 2, two days before that visit. Fascinated, she read it.

> We sat by my fire, I on the sofa and she in the big chair, half facing me. She was reading and I, pretending to read, was looking at her and thinking. After a while she looked up at me, then looked down quickly at her book, and a trace of color crept over her face. That look—at once it was a barrier compelling silence, and a meeting of two souls closer than they suspect! I rose, went to her, and sat on the arm of her chair, leaning across her. She did not stir nor look up, nor did the new tint of color in her face creep away. Gently I kissed her forehead, with a feeling of deep love, deep peace, and quiet understanding. In a moment I returned to the sofa, sat back against the arm, put my feet up, took my book, and returned to my reading.

Nancy whistled. Alfred had never done that with Joyce, nor with Nancy herself. This was another exercise in fond imagination. She liked it. He was so much more emotionally expressive in private writing than verbally, as he had been when writing to Ella of Joyce that winter in Germany. In writing, his true beauty of soul came through.

She turned another page. This took her to three days after her visit. There was a separate note on small Union Society, Oxford stationery, pasted onto the page. "I think Nancy exercises, or can exercise, just as much influence over me as anyone else. I cannot go against her in anything, because she participates in everything."

She paused, amazed. She had had no idea!

She looked under the note, and there for November 8 was another plain English entry.

We were looking at the map spread on the table. "You must let
me know if I make you walk too much," I said, "but you won't, I
know. You *must* let me see, somehow. How can I tell whether you
are weary or fresh unless you do? I don't want to overdo it, but I *so*
enjoy doing all this with you, that I have no sense of moderation
left." My arm crept around her as we leaned together over the table
and pointed out our route. Then we stood up straight without
moving and looked at each other. A rush of emotion swept over
me like a sudden tornado and the whole world vanished except
her eyes. The next moment she was close in my arms and I felt her
heart beating only less furiously than mine. All I cared about in
all the course of time and experience was as if by magic within the
circle of my arms; yet moved as I was, I felt a peace more profound
than anything I had known. She stirred, and slowly freed herself
from my embrace. I did not resist—I loved her too much to resist,
and was half dazed with joy and love. I looked into her eyes and
they seemed moist, and beyond the moisture was a melancholy, a
sadness, a shame which startled me. "I'm sorry," she said faintly.
"I shouldn't have . . . let you do that." "But Nancy," I burst out,
seeing heaven within my grasp yet not knowing how to grasp it,
"I mean it, every bit of it. Oh, if you only knew . . . I didn't think
it would come so soon . . . I thought . . . perhaps after when you
and I . . . oh, what can I say? How can I tell you?" I lapsed into
silence and led her gently to the chair before the fire. I sat on the
cushion, never releasing her hand. I could scarcely look at her, lest
I lose control entirely. God knows how near I was to tears. "I live
only for one thing; my whole life belongs to it; there is nothing else
in my world; I have waited, and longed, and dreamed . . . Nancy,
I love you with my life [sitting on the arm of her chair and taking
her head in my hands, and looking into her eyes]. "*You* are my
life. I wasn't going to tell you. . . . I thought I should have to wait
and wait . . . But *now* you know." And I kissed her tenderly on
the forehead.

Nancy would have turned more pages, but heard Alfred returning. She
carefully closed the book and moved well away from it. There was no question
now: Alfred loved her. Yet he had not said so, either at her last visit or since
then. He wanted to say it, but could not quite bring himself to do so. It wasn't
shyness so much as incapacity; it seemed he didn't know how.

Well, *she* knew how. Ella's advice was good: she would ask him herself.

He returned with the milk, and there was a small flurry of incidental activity as they made the tea ready. They sipped it, and talked only of inconsequentials. She would finish her tea, then do it. She would say *Alfred, please marry me. I think we love each other.* Ten words to define their futures, one way or another. She wasn't even sure which answer she truly wanted from him, just that she wanted it settled.

Suddenly, it seemed, the tea was done and it was time. She stood and took a step toward him. He was sitting on the other chair, beside the wall. He glanced up at her, evidently having no idea what was on her mind.

Then Joyce appeared behind him, approaching in ghostly splendor. She was startlingly lovely, with chestnut hair just long enough to toss, tanned, lithe, graceful.

"Oh!" Nancy felt faint. What was she doing? How could she usurp her dear sister's love?

Alfred jumped up to steady her. "Are you all right?" he asked solicitously.

And she saw that now there were two of them in the image: the woman and Alfred. It was a mirror on the wall, reflecting their upper portions. She had seen herself, at age twenty amazingly like Joyce at the age she died.

"Yes, of course," she said. "I think I stood up too quickly and got faint."

But it seemed to be a signal. It might be sheer coincidence. Yet who was she to say that Joyce had not chosen this way to appear to her, to remind her that she was trespassing? Alfred might or might not finally have distinguished Nancy from Joyce; he might indeed be free of her. But Nancy herself would never be free of Joyce. She was flesh of Joyce's flesh, soul of Joyce's soul. Joyce was inextricably within her in much more than appearance.

She could not marry Alfred. That shadow would always be between them.

The decision had been made, not the way she had anticipated, but it was nevertheless final. She would let Alfred go. She knew there would be a lot of crying the next few days; she was really jilting herself. But she would survive it. As Ella said, she did have other prospects. Oh, she would remain friendly with Alfred, and enjoy his company. They would continue as friends. But that was as far as it would go.

Alfred would have to find someone else to marry.

# NORMA

"You really must meet my friend J," Molly said. "He's such a great dancer."
Molly was an excellent dancer herself; she was in a position to know. "I met
him in Sevilla, Spain, last year, when I was a governess and he was taking a
semester there."

Norma was uncertain whether that was a first or last name, but didn't care
to confess her confusion. She did like dancing, when she had a competent
partner. "Perhaps," she said noncommittally.

"There's a party tonight. He'll be there. Come with me and see."

Intrigued, she agreed. It was January 7, 1933, and her social life was nil.
Of course she was busy with her studies at Somerville College, Oxford, but
that was only part of it. She had had one serious relationship, which had
not ended well. The man had turned out to be not as represented, and she
had had to break it off, with more pain than she cared to experience again.
She was over that now, but the memory remained. She intended to be more
cautious about investing her emotion in future.

That evening she accompanied her friend to the party. There were a
number of young men and women there, some of whom she knew. Molly
brought her to a handsome man. "Alfred, this is my friend Norma S, the
smart one. Norma, this is Alfred J, from America."

They exchanged amenities, then moved on. Norma was glad to have the
minor mystery of the name cleared up at last. At least now she had officially
met Molly's friend, so Molly would not be urging her any more.

There was some dancing, but other things were going on, and she neither
danced herself nor observed J—rather, Alfred—dancing. On the whole it was
a minor evening.

Three weeks later Molly took her on a visit to Alfred's quarters at Exeter
College, Oxford, and they talked about Spain. Molly thought she might
go there for a term, and of course Alfred had been there. He spoke Spanish

fluently, for an American. That interested her; Alfred was clearly fascinated with Spain, and had had experience there.

Then on February 4 Norma had a problem with a new radio kit; she couldn't make head or tail of the assembly instructions. Alfred came over and assembled it for her; like most men, he was good in practical matters. They talked of MacMurray and other things; it was clear that he was an intellectual. She liked that.

Their dialogue continued via correspondence, and on February 21 they had supper together. She found Alfred not only handsome, but compatible. He was well mannered and intelligent, in contrast to some.

Their incidental contacts continued through March, and she did dance with him on occasion. He danced with Molly on Thursdays, and sometimes Norma was along. The two were very good together on the dance floor, and Molly confided that she was on the way to getting serious about Alfred. "He's deeper than he seems," she said. "He loved a girl named Joyce, but she died of typhoid fever three years ago, and he never got over it."

So Alfred had loved and lost, as it were. That, too, was interesting. It reminded Norma of her own love lost, though that was not through death but, she felt, an unfortunate misunderstanding. But Alfred was not at all like that, to his credit.

Then Molly was away, and Norma had several evenings with Alfred in late April. On the 28th they took a walk together and went to the playhouse. They talked—and suddenly she realized that she was getting more interested in Alfred than she had anticipated. This was dangerous; she didn't want a repetition of her prior crash.

She considered briefly, and decided to slow things, to be on the safe side. "After all, it is not good social policy for people of opposite genders to meet privately more than once a week," she said, as if it were a minor consideration.

May 4 she saw Alfred coming, and immediately rose and threw open the window to welcome him. There wasn't time to talk, so he left her a note, reacting to her suggestion that they limit their encounters. She read it carefully, appreciating the precision of its formulation. He was elegantly accusing her of syllogism: a deceptive argument.

> I will not be party to a syllogism. I will not be dominated in
> what is personal and immediate by vague and general laws. No
> truth of conduct is true until it is personal and concrete. Your last
> proposition rings in my ears and rings false, because it was a mere

deduction, not a desire; and was indirect rather than direct. I do
not accept in principle the proposition "No two people should meet
more than once in seven days; therefore you and I must not." What
an artificial way to determine conduct! The only valid statement
to the same end would be "neither you nor I really want to meet
during the rest of this week, so let's not." Next to it in validity
would be "I'd rather not see you till Monday."

For God's sake, something simple and direct and true! It is
not "two people" who have been together, but you, N.S, who
have been talking with me, A.J. before Monday, let that be stated,
faced, sanctioned, and acted upon. Away with your "grandes
rasgos." You think "In ten years time, if we dined together more
than once a week, it would amount to at least 3000 hours of
conversation; which is too much; therefore I can't see you before
Monday."

She assimilated that. He did have a point, however devious. It was a
foolish general rule that should be modified in specific cases; she had quoted
it without thinking. But more important, he was saying, obliquely, that he
did not want to be limited to meeting her once a week. For all his posturing,
Alfred did tend to avoid direct statements of personal interest, so this was his
way of getting around that.

She didn't want to be limited either. Alfred had become too important to
her for that. So she wrote him back, gracefully yielding the point. At least she
had made the effort to be cautious. Hereafter they wouldn't care how many
times a week they met. She quoted from "The Fountain": "When I was a boy,
God held my hand, but I escaped from him." She was thinking of her own
recent conversion from the Church of England to the Religious Society of
Friends, or Quakers, but she would have liked that quote regardless. He was
interested, so she wrote out the whole of it for him. The essence was that the
boy looked everywhere for God but couldn't find Him, having forgot what
it was he sought. But then in his hour of need, God's light appeared within
him. Just as she herself had found God within her, in the Quaker manner,
rather than outside her.

Alfred was a Quaker. She realized that that had been a powerful predisposing
force in the background. She now preferred a Quaker association.

They did meet more often. They couldn't help it. It was like being caught
up in a whirlwind. Their common interest in Spain, their mutual scholarship
at Oxford University, their intellectual compatibility, and above all, their

spark-striking matching intelligence: everything contributed to the developing power of the relationship.

She sent him a note inviting him to a Somerville College dance with her Saturday May 13, and he agreed to attend. Meanwhile on the 10th they were reading a play together, but fell to talking instead. He took her hand, and she was ashamed to realize it was trembling. "*Que gusto es quererla*," he said. "There is so much love in me clamoring for an object." She wasn't sure she dared react; what had become of her social caution?

On the 15th she introduced him to her parents. Her father was a doctor, somewhat aloof, but he understood the significance: Alfred was a man it was possible she was becoming serious about. Then they went to the botanical garden. They talked, and clarified, for both of them were highly expressive when they got serious. "I am afraid," she said with candor she found painful. "Afraid of failing you."

"How could you ever do that?" he asked.

She didn't care to say, even if she were able to. The fact was that she knew she had somehow failed in her prior serious interest, for she had abruptly broken it off. That specter haunted her.

On the 16th they talked a great deal, and shared their first kiss.

On the 17th they doubted. They exchanged notes of caution. She wrote: "Remember we both have a great deal to fight against in ourselves. Things are not going to be easy. I want for you to ask yourself very seriously whether you are able to forgive me for anything I might do, or fail to do, and if not, what then?" She was trying to be fair to him, because she knew herself to be a difficult woman by the standards of what men understood; she was intelligent, assertive, and she preferred to have her own way. Those qualities, perhaps, had been what destroyed her prior romance. She wished she could get that out of her mind! But she was afraid it was already too late for any easy disengagement.

He replied by note on the 18th:

> There was a time when I neither condemned nor forgave, for to understand a thing was to have forgiven it already. I think there may be things even in you which I could hardly forgive—not things you could do, but motives from which you could act. Things which are unforgivable in me would tend to be unforgivable in you. I might make a list. If you consciously, intentionally, deceived me where you knew I trusted you wholly—that would be blamable. But not a case for forgiveness, as much as a case for disillusion. If you were

that sort of person, no amount of forgiveness would make you other. But I will not exalt myself and preach to you from above. I know that this is hard, and calls in many ways for a wisdom and a bravery perhaps beyond our capacity. To carry it through would be mad but immeasurably great. To fail will hurt more each day we go on. But this is still not the answer. The answer is long and must be thought and talked carefully.

I fully believe that we are strong enough to deal with *anything*, if only we can see it clearly; and we can only see it clearly if we dedicate ourselves to your standard of honesty—the whole truth in so far as we can know it or suspect it. I have never felt the spirit of honesty so strong as I have this past week—perhaps because if it is an illusion, I want to break it soon, immediately; and if it is true, I want to live it free and unafraid. I can't bear half values. There is only one gear—top—, on the car I drive now. I have been afraid you might not stand the pace. Yet the pace is only that of unrestricted life.

Neither you nor I is alone now. What you do is my business; what I do is important to you. (I am not taking you for granted, and shall not till you give me leave.) Hence I cannot guide my conduct without reference to you, nor can you without reference to me. In order to live at all now, it must be in close fellowship, honestly and fearlessly, and in deep understanding.

That is much. Perhaps it is frightening, or mad, or impossible. Perhaps it is a dream or a vision. But we can only see what it is together. I at any rate do not see clearly without you; and above all things I want to see *you* clearly. I am a poet (in desire) and believe that visions can be as true as facts, frequently much truer. But precisely because I am a visionary I want to know you *as you are*, completely nude. It is much, very much to ask, but it is true and you must know. Hand in hand with that longing goes my complete openness to you. I am a book you have bought and may read in at will, even though you be the first to cut the pages.

Easy? None of it is easy. Are you willing to face its hardship with me? I know you have courage greater than my own. I know too that many parts of your character are outside the domination of your will. I knew it in me too.

I want to know you truly, not to praise or blame you. I believe I can forgive anything, provided I understand. All I cannot promise is . . . time. When I cease loving you, if that is to be, I shall accept it, or try, without resistance. But until then I shall love you boundlessly.

Anything anyone does may harm anyone else in any way. For me to fear that my actions can harm if they are based on my real feelings, will do more harm than the actions themselves. Moreover just as I am confident nothing you can do can hurt me seriously, so it is likely nothing I can do, loving you freely as I do, can hurt you seriously. But there is an extra protection. So long as we remain intimate and honest, you must depend on me to tell you what hurts me, and I must depend on you to tell me what hurts you. Moreover, I am willing to be hurt by you, so long as it is unintentional. Result: there is no need to fear harming you so long as I can trust you to tell me immediately and openly of the times when I do. And to remove every trace of danger of fear, you must know that I am strong enough, and my love for you is strong enough to bear many shocks. If it is not, the sooner it can be shocked to pieces, the better. So let us be mad enough to be real, to express our feelings fearlessly even if they are likely to hurt one or both of us; and say immediately and truly and tenderly when anything does hurt.

This will be hardest for you, I believe, yet I cannot hesitate to ask it of you, because it is essential to me both not to harm you in any way and to lose my fear of harming you in ways unpredictable by me. Only thus can I love you fully and perfectly freely, and to love you thus is my greatest hope.

I am sure that fear of any kind between us is unnecessary and undesirable, and that perfect honesty is essential to displace fear, even if it costs much. You need recall how much I struggled to be honest enough to tell you that I did not want to love you. It will be a greater struggle to tell you of anything *you* do that touches me in my pride, my hopes, or any of my complexes. Yet I am convinced I must be fearless to speak and you fearless to hear, before we can be generous with each other. For me, rather much suffering now than any deception however pleasant, or any artificiality, or any fear. I want to be brave enough to love you perfectly. I want to trust you to be brave.

A jeweller, when offered a genuine string of pearls, throws them on the floor and stamps on them. He knows that if they are genuine, they will stand that and much more. If they are not, it matters little if they are broken. So do I want you to stamp on me until you know me as I am; and I am confident you, like the true pearls, are genuine and can stand much battering if need be. If not, no pleasure and no make-believe will fill the gap.

Norma considered that carefully. It was a rather fuller statement than she had anticipated; Alfred had evidently pondered and delivered himself of a significant essay, perhaps greater than the need. He was like that, and she did not fault him for it. Saturday the 20th she responded in more restrained fashion:

This is just to say I have your note—it hadn't yet arrived when you came in this morning. Do you know, first I was sure you would, then horribly afraid you weren't going to. But that's by the way. What I want to say really is that you really are quite right, whatever at any time it may be necessary for me to say to you must be said and not written—not like my landlady who writes me little notes asking me not to walk over her Persian rug! You see there are two quite different things which push me toward breaking off now, before things get any more complicated—the fear of having to hurt you, and the pure instinctive fear in me of any repetition of what I went through before. But I can conquer that. All I can say is, have patience with me—and I won't say it again because I know you have patience, far more than I deserve. May it not be wasted. But I have courage this morning. I'll see you Monday.

Monday, May 22, she visited him at his lodgings in Headinton. They were so wrapped up in their discoveries of each other that she missed the last bus home. It was too late for him to drive her back, because he was an undergraduate and had to be in by midnight. What to do?

"You can borrow my bicycle," he suggested.

She considered only a moment. It seemed the best choice. So he brought it out, and mounted her on it. That was difficult, because she was wearing a tight skirt. He gave her a push at the top of Headington Hill, and she was on her way.

That turned out to be an adventure. She couldn't stop for any of the red lights because she knew that once she got off the bicycle she would never be able to get on again. So she cruised down through the darkness without pausing. Fortunately, because it was the middle of the night, there was very little traffic, so she was able to get away with it. She made it to her own door, and fell off the bike, hardly the worse for wear. Alfred never knew; he had probably assumed that she could ride the bicycle normally once she got started, never having tried it himself in a tight skirt.

They met again Tuesday, but did not have time for any extended dialogue. She regretted that, but accepted it; after all, they did have other things in their lives. It was hard to be relaxed when emotions were great and time was limited. Alfred, however, had another impression.

Wednesday she received his further thoughts on the two days. Alfred was always thinking; that was one of the things about him. Evidently while she had been swooping down the hill, he had been analyzing their relationship. So next day he had written about it, and about Tuesday's briefer contact. Certainly what they had together was worth understanding, to the extent they could. It was so important not to make a mistake that could seriously hurt them both.

> No, I *will* not go to bed. Not till I have eased my mind of this—and yours too if I have troubled you. How I hope to see you through these times to what underlies! I shall try hard to make them infrequent. It was just a time of disunity with you, due to my own isolation. I was more conscious of me, obviously, than of you; conscious of me-in-your presence. What is this consciousness, and what this presence?

> Just that yesterday (Monday) you and I explored some of the intricate caverns of the human soul together. More than that. I hate saying what it was—as I have always kept silent about what meant most to me. A rare experience must be kept pure—vivid in one's life, but unanalyzed and unrelated—I mean unspoken, simply because it is whole and ineffable. But I am not being clear.

> Today, when more than ever I wanted to be gentle and true, I found myself being vague, unintelligible, inconsiderate and false. It was self consciousness. I wonder if you will understand. No, it is too complicated to express, and in words it will look impossible. Yet there is some connection between my having revealed whatever is real in me to you, and this self consciousness. I was uncomfortable and unnatural simply because I had been intimate.

That explained that. She reassured him when she saw him Wednesday. But Thursday she received another note.

I can't help feeling that I have worried you. I know I have
worried me. I hate being unreal with you, as I was tonight. I hate
the sort of self I can sometimes act like. There was no reason to
fear you just because I had discovered you; no reason to appear
oblivious of a truth just because it is the most obvious thing. I was
trying, or the devil in me was trying to act as if the previous day
had never existed. Another time let me be brave enough to face and
accept fully and willingly the truth that something very deep binds
us together. I think I am afraid of what I most desire.

Friday they met again in the afternoon, and went to their mutual friend
Anthony's rooms. Anthony was musical; he could play anything and do it
well. Once they were driving, and someone gave him a tin whistle; he played
it while driving, but then came a turn and he wouldn't break off the final
note to make the turn; someone else had to grab the wheel to prevent them
from crashing. He could be quite a character in his fashion.

She reassured Alfred again. She was worried too, because of the disturbing
power of their relationship; it unbalanced both of them, like a stiff storm
wind. But they simply needed to handle it. Meanwhile they played records,
and Alfred played the accordion. He was very good with it. She liked the fact
that he was musical. They kissed when they parted.

They did not see each other over the weekend—life got in the way
again—but Monday, May 29 was another big day. They met in the early
afternoon and went punting at Abingdon, south of Oxford. It was always
fun poling the little square flat-bottomed boats around, inefficient as it might
seem. The point, after all, was not efficiency but togetherness.

"I talked with Ella M Friday, before I saw you," he said as he poled. "She
is a very dear friend."

Norma knew. Ella was the mother of the girl he had loved four years
ago, who had died of typhoid. Her daughter had been depressive, and Alfred
resembled her in that; it seemed it had been natural for Ella to counsel Alfred
in lieu of the child she had lost. Norma had met Ella briefly, and liked her;
she was a sensible woman. "Of course."

"Yet I find myself resentful, because she referred to you as a 'friend'
of mine."

"But I am," Norma said.

"To me you are no friend. You might have been, possibly, but instead you
became the repository of my love. You are my lover if anything, and there is
much difference between friends and lovers."

She laughed. "There certainly is! But we are not lovers in the sense generally understood. We are friends who love. Ella is quite right. You should not resent her standard use of the term."

He shrugged. "Each person sees a thing in his or her own manner. For me, separation from you is pain, the pain of love. If a single day hurts so, how can I bear more? I thought of going away to Spain, but how can I, having found you here? My whole life is here."

Norma found she could live with that sort of devotion. Alfred was coming to know her better and better, and was becoming ever more attached rather than turned off. This was what love was supposed to be.

They pulled up to the river bank and sat on the grass. Each ate an apple, lying side by side without quite touching. They talked. Then she brought out her little soprano recorder, assembled it, and played the slow movement of the Beethoven Trio in B flat. "Both music and landscape are so much more vivid to me now," she said. "I see much that was hidden before." It seemed that love was enhancing her awareness.

"It does seem to be that way," he agreed. "When I loved Joyce, poetry and nature became more important to me, and I saw connections between the two I had never thought of before. I lost her, but the awareness remained."

Joyce. That was the name of the girl, Ella M's daughter. That was not a subject she cared to dwell on. "I'm not sure that you understand why it was that I drove so fast on Saturday."

"It was LeMarquand's question 'Are you falling in love?'" he said. "And I answered 'yes.'"

"It was the first time you used the word," she said. "It unnerved me."

"The first time I said with anything approaching directness that I love you," he agreed. "I have difficulty uttering that, though I feel it."

"So do I." And there it was: they had spoken of love, and confirmed it. That was a giant step.

They continued to talk of other things, not remaining too close to the fire that was love. But inevitably it returned. "Thursday, when we spent the evening in Anthony's rooms, then parted by the Lamb and Flag. I was longing to embrace you."

"I was longing to be embraced. Why didn't we do it?"

"Why?" he repeated thoughtfully. "I think there were seven or eight contributing factors, such as my constant effort at originality, my fear of displeasing, of overdoing, of establishing a precedent, of appearing to enjoy physical contacts in themselves, my desire to appear tender and delicate, with great love straightly restrained; the consciousness that we both *knew*, and there was no need therefore to express; in all these ways I denied myself the longing that I had to hold you closely in my arms, and left my own life unquiet until today."

"Mine is unquiet too," she said. "I feel that lack of completion very keenly." He had not expressed it precisely as she would have, but the essence was similar. Desire warred with doubt and tended to paralyze her, making her seem cold when she was warm inside. "I wanted to run back after you at the Lamb and Flag to seek what I had missed. To steal a kiss, in some little burst of freedom from maidenly reserve."

"I treasure those little bursts."

They changed positions then. He laid his head on her breast and she put her arms around him, holding him close. Oh, it was good to be close, and to lose those fears and those false strivings!

"This is very unusual for me," she murmured. "I don't know whether you are used to embracing people in punts, and I can't say I care, but it is definitely new."

"There is so much I want to tell you," he said. "But even now the old constraints remain, and I find extreme difficulty in speaking."

"That much I do understand. There are things I also would like to share, but can't readily voice."

"It is hard to speak about one girl to another, and hard to use language which has been misused so much as to have various connotations."

She would have preferred "*that* has been misused," as it was a defining clause, but this was definitely not the occasion to quibble about technicalities. "Perhaps if we try hard enough, we shall in time succeed."

And in time, after a long struggle, he managed to say what he had in mind. It wasn't fully clear, but what was important was the fact that he was uttering it. "I don't want to give the impression that I have known many girls, yet something in me always tries to give that impression, which is simply not true."

"Not true for me either," she said. "Genders appropriately reversed."

He smiled. "Duly noted." Then he turned serious. "Long ago, when I knew Marion G at high school, it occurred to me that the second or third girl I treated as I did her would be the last one. That is, the one I would not leave. At the time I did not think I would ever be as close to another girl as I was to Marion, but my brothers and friends knew better; at that age few if any such relations are permanent. But then I came to England and met Joyce, and though we never kissed or spoke of love, I loved her. Her sister Nancy I still see on occasion, and she looks so much like Joyce that whatever relation I might have with her may be no more than the reflection of Joyce, so I think she doesn't count in that sense. She's a fine and pleasant person, quite worthy, but not—" He seemed at a loss for the word.

"Did you kiss her?"

"No, never, nor spoke of such feeling, and she never spoke of it to me. We could be taken for brother and sister."

There could be more to that than he was saying, but it hardly mattered. "She doesn't count," Norma agreed.

"So you are really the third."

"After Marion and Joyce," she agreed, realizing that she had been too superficial in using kissing as a definition. The imprint of Joyce remained on him, perhaps accounting for his depressive outlook.

"I have kissed only girls that I loved very much. I would have kissed Joyce, had I known—" He broke off again, and she understood why. He did not want to speak of the death of his beloved.

"You are not very forward about romance," she said. "I think I have had to meet you more than half way. Would you ever have done anything if I had not made advances?"

He pondered the matter. "It is true that I tend to hold back. It prevents me from playing the masculine role. I believe it is simply fear of being unwanted."

"Of being rejected."

"Yes, perhaps. It is an effort of security, protecting myself from that. To find I am unwanted, when I want to be wanted—that would be too great a disillusion."

They stirred, and returned to the punt, still talking intimately of their affairs, and it was a happy time. It seemed time for her to be as forthcoming as he had been about Marion and Joyce.

"Gordon J proposed marriage to me last term," she said.

Alfred was amazed. "I knew nothing of that!"

She smiled. "How could you? You and I had not yet met, though I believe my friend Molly had mentioned you."

"Molly," he repeated. "She introduced us."

"Yes, she is concerned with your welfare. She urged me to meet you."

"Molly is my dancing partner, and a very good one. I like her very much, and I appreciate her loyalty. But I cannot ever remember having wanted to love her."

That was an interesting way to put it. "I had understood that she considered the two of you to be close." In fact Molly had even hinted at the prospect of romance. That put Norma in an awkward position.

"I am sorry if I ever gave her the impression that our association was more than convenience or friendship. I certainly want to do her no wrong."

That seemed to cover it. Norma was not cutting in on her friend's prospect. "I am glad to have that clarified."

"Gordon J—I know him only slightly. What happened there?"

"He is not my type. We associated, we danced, we talked. Evidently he had a greater interest than I realized. I declined, of course. It would not have been fair to either of us. For one thing, I was not yet over my prior relationship."

"I do not wish to be selfish, but I am glad you saved yourself for me, as it were."

She had to laugh. "It was not intentional."

They discussed Spain. One of the things she liked about him was his fluency in Spanish. He had traveled Spain, and spoke the language almost like a native. "Will you be returning there?" she asked.

"I had thought so," he replied as he poled the craft along. "But that may have changed. In my present life, the only reality is you, and you are not in Spain. I would not want to lay the burden of my absence on a loved one; the demands of it would be too great. I could never bear to leave you again. It is significant that the idea has entered my head of not going to Spain. I am not content to go for reasons."

"But surely reasons are why we do anything."

"According to *The Fountain*, while we live, we must live our dreams. There is no other way of passing beyond them into reality."

It seemed that he had really gotten into that book, once she had introduced him to it. "I can say only that that concerns the future, and I can't think of it. But it may be in instance of the necessity for thinking of the future."

"Yet living truly in the present brings about the appropriate future, which comes to us though we cannot see it on the way."

They discussed that further, and she found herself increasingly tending to agree with him. But there was another matter that concerned her. "If our relationship proceeds as it seems to be, what about finance? The love of money may be the root of evil, but it is practically impossible to get along without it."

"I reject that completely. If two people are ready to suffer and to die together, they have nothing in the wide world to fear."

She wasn't sure of that, but couldn't fault it as a romantic notion. "You have met my parents. I can't say that they completely approve of you, but they hardly know you yet. What of yours? What might they say if you told them of me?"

That gave him pause for some thought, which was significant in itself. "I hope they trust me to make a sensible decision."

"My parents are bound to ask you about your prospects and intentions. My father is a doctor; he is very meticulous."

He smiled wryly. "I surely could answer, but they would think I was crazy."

She had to laugh at that, though it really wasn't funny. His parents and hers were quite likely to be dubious about their relationship.

They brought the punt to land at six in the evening, then drove back to Oxford. On the way they ran out of petrol, and had to push the car half a mile to get some. So it wasn't a perfect date, but she was so exhilarated by their dialogue that she hardly minded.

Alfred had a tutorial to attend at 7, so she had supper by herself. When they rejoined he took her in his arms and held her closely. "It was just something I had to do," he said, almost apologetically.

"I had wanted you to put your arm around me for an hour in the punt, but I did nothing about it," she said. "I'm glad you finally had more initiative than I."

At 8 PM they came to Alfred's room. Norma lay on the couch and he sat facing her. "I want to tell you things, but I don't know where to start," he said.

"Tell me of your life from the beginning, and continue it day by day," she suggested. But immediately she reconsidered. "The high points."

"The high point was Joyce, and I feel incapable of it. She was— everything."

She didn't push it. She couldn't fault him for his loyalty to the girl he had loved, but neither was she eager to hear every detail of his experience with another woman. "I understand. I must confess that the novelty of our new relationship is such that I can't see it or interpret it. It is so new to me to give myself to you that I can't tell whether it is primarily a physical or a genuinely emotional experience. Nor whether any other man found at the same time in my life would have filled the gap likewise. I believe in the idea that there is one girl for one man, one man for one girl. But how can I be sure we are those ones?"

He looked surprised and nervous. "That echoes my thought. Suppose we are not that couple? If I awaken love in you for the first time, but am not capable of carrying it through to completion, I could leave you adrift, in possession of a great new power, and nothing to do with it. I don't want to harm you, even by loving you too well."

"Yet if we are that couple, it would be a shame to hold back."

He nodded. "It is such a relief for me to lose my fear and my worship of the physical expressions, that I want to keep on losing it at full force."

"If it is a gamble, let's gamble on winning," she said, overflowing with the joyous wonder of it.

So they passed the evening in gentle and loving intimacy, sharing the secrets of the lover and the beloved. He kissed her for every favor, and rested his head on her, and they looked deeply into each other's eyes, until they could no longer see them in the darkness. They were enveloped in warmth and goodness.

"Are there any signs of the recovery of your soul?" he asked her.

"I can't tell."

"Is your fear now quite gone?"

"It is, almost. But I am still dealing with something largely unknown, and I'm never on absolutely certain ground."

"I can't tell either. Are we destined not to know?"

They talked further—they never seemed to get enough of that!—and then Alfred took her back to her room. It had been more than enough for a day.

They continued to meet when they could, and exchanged letters between times. They agreed to try out the feel of marriage before actually deciding whether to do it, just in case that clarified some vital aspect. They knew this could seem odd to someone else, but they were not someone else, they were themselves. However reticent Alfred might be in person, he was expressive on paper, somewhat the opposite of her. They didn't necessarily mail their notes; sometimes they passed them to each other when they met, like students exchanging confidences while a lecture was in progress. The mails took too long for such urgency. June 3 he wrote:

> My darling, why must I delay in saying openly to you what
> never leaves my consciousness? Why must I hint and not speak?
> The moments which separate me from being your husband are
> unbearable. I want never to have to leave you. I meant what I
> said tonight. I want to *live* all the time, and you are my life.
> Can't we let the world know *soon* that you are my wife and that
> we are one person forever? I can think nothing else but that it
> must be so, that this thing is right. Why then delay? I cannot
> stand having something important in my mind which I have
> not communicated to yours. Yet I have. You know that you are
> my wife. It only remains to make absolutely clear that we both
> know and accept it.

She considered that. She was his wife. She tried it on for feeling. She liked it. She replied by note, as usual with greater brevity but no less feeling.

> Funny sort of love-letter. How bewildering and unorthodox this correspondence would seem to a biographer—not a bit like the Brownings! But I do love you for all that.

Then as an afterthought after it was out of the typewriter, she added:

> I asked Miss B what would happen if I married. She said nothing would. She hoped I would stay on.

Miss B was the house mother for the Somerville College female students. She had no real control over the senior students, but she did care about them.

The fifth of June was a bad day for Alfred. He had had some kind of accident the day before, and had received letters of criticism from both his aunt Louisa and Ella M, and had overslept. "Worse, I did not see you this morning," he concluded.

"But you are seeing me now," she pointed out. They were having lunch together.

"That makes it worthwhile," he agreed.

They had to separate again to accomplish their other businesses, but had supper together. Then they drove down a road in darkness and stopped by a haystack. They kissed and talked.

"About this matter we have discussed," she said. "I do know it. I see no reason to leave it as conjectural."

He gazed at her, his face invisible in the darkness. "You wish to—?"

"Yes, I will marry you."

Gratified, he took her in his arms and kissed her. They had made their engagement official.

But they did not yet announce it to the world. The prospect of telling their parents remained daunting.

Thursday night, June 8, they supped with the family in charge of the house where Alfred stayed. Mrs. Tagg made one or two knowing remarks, though she was obviously guessing; maybe she was remembering her own courtship. Then they went to Alfred's room, as he was too tired to go out.

"I had a long talk with Dr. H," he said. That was the psychologist he was seeing for his depression. "I mentioned every doubtful element, and he gave me the impression throughout that in this case there was no visible danger, even in marrying immediately. That surprised me, because he has said before that he doesn't like his patients to have significant changes in their lifestyle while they are in treatment."

"Good thing," she said. "We do not need him to decide our future for us."

They walked across the new road in the area, and back. He read her "The Guardian Angel," and they rested a while in quiet. Then he took her home.

She was somewhat disappointed. She somehow expected each of their evenings to surpass the previous one, but he seemed content to let them be even. "It is so good, after so much loneliness," he said as they paused in the hall.

"I want nothing in the world more than to be a good wife to you," she said.

"Contemplating my husbandship I see a vision of new values, new responsibility, new ability, new manhood," he said. "Yet I have fears and doubts, and you need to deal with me by telling me simple things, with nothing in them I can oppose."

"Then you must eat more," she said. "You are becoming gaunt."

"Yet applying general principles doesn't necessarily work. Others have tried that."

His queer mood wore her down, and she ended the dialogue. But she thought about it when by herself.

Next time they got together, she tackled it forthrightly. "You are giving me certain rights over you, and you must accept that. I don't expect this to be easy, but do expect that the goods will surpass the bads of it. There must be surrender and sacrifice, and we must accept them." He acknowledged that meekly enough.

"So you must eat more," she concluded.

In the afternoon they walked the parks, and she told him of her long morning's conversation with Miss B. "I clarified my own position in the process of explaining it to her."

"I tend to doubt the wisdom of talking much to any one, especially unrelated people, at this juncture," he said. "We both want to cry from the housetops that we are husband and wife, yet we must remember that from other people's point of view, nothing has happened. We are not even engaged."

"Yes we are."

"I mean, there has been no formal announcement. Without that, others see us as merely associating, whatever understanding we may have between us."

"Then we shall have to see to that announcement."

"But first we have to tell our parents."

She sighed. "True." She dreaded that, but it had to be done. "Meanwhile we need to decide on the wedding. I prefer as little commotion as possible."

"I agree. I should like to avoid every avoidable interference in our present life, especially every inner tension."

"No disturbance," she agreed, relieved.

"Well, there will have to be some disturbance, if we are to live together," he said. "One or the other or both will have to move."

"Which is complicated at the moment," she said. "So the only possible thing is to stop thinking altogether about this marriage until much later in the summer."

"I agree. At least until after term and after your time in Malvern. It is obvious that we are not going to marry this week, and probably not next week. So let us be in peace."

They left it at that. It really was a relief not to have their lives immediately disrupted. They both had so many other things to keep up with.

Saturday the tenth she brought him to her home in London. It rained, and they did nothing special until evening. Then they moved all the furniture and danced. Alfred was a good dancer, and so was she, but somehow it didn't work well.

They put the furniture back and retired, she to her room, he to the guest room. But after a time he come to her room and sat on her bed. She could not see him at all in the darkness. This made her nervous. What did he have in mind? "What is it?" she inquired. She was trembling uncontrollably.

"You said that if I found myself not sleeping, I might come and talk to you."

Oh. "Yes, of course." But suppose her parents heard them? They would not understand.

They talked briefly, quietly, her nervousness fading. Then he returned to his room and slept. She was relieved.

In the morning she was up before him. She brought him tea while he remained in bed.

"There is no more welcome sight than the face of the person one most loves," he said as he sipped.

She stayed with him a while, sharing the warmth of the bed, then took the tea things away.

They had music most of the morning, and snatches of individual reading. After lunch they went out in the car, stopped at Bledlow Hill, and read a chapter of *The Fountain* that reassured them about their doubts of love. Then he dozed with his head on her lap until it rained and they had to return to the car. They drove around.

"The reason we have not married is that you don't love me enough," she said.

He looked stunned, yet did not refute it. "I am dependent on you, and it is impossible to be your husband until I can be a well of love for you. I am holding back my feelings, and my life-habits put a check on those feelings. I must release them."

"Your release will be mine too."

"I find strength in you when I had none. You restore my peace of mind. I know my life is inextricably bound up in yours."

They drove back home. That evening they had more music and talked. But she was aware of tension in him, and she pressed him to tell her what was bothering him. Reluctantly he unburdened himself. "I am concerned that you are daring me to be a man. To claim you, when I can not. I fear there is some deficiency in me, and this may be what restrains me. I am depressed. It is unbearable to be away from you, yet I feel conflicted when I am with you. This wears me out."

She realized that she shouldn't have charged him with not loving her enough. It had sent him into a maelstrom of uncertainty. Yet it was not in her to admit error in such a thing. So she simply laid her hand on his arm, and gradually his tension passed.

After he retired she came and sat on his bed, and he relaxed and fell asleep. She did have power over him; she could make him relax.

She woke him with tea again in the morning, and they returned to Oxford by nine.

In the afternoon she went to Alfred's dancing practice and gave him several good suggestions. His technique improved immediately. Then they had tea in the Union, and supper at Goodcooks.

She met him again after his concert, and they drove around the country, feeling happy and playful. She felt mischievous, and he seemed to love it. They paused on the bypass by Woodstock Road, and he held her close. "I have been longing to do this since the concert," he said.

"I know."

He kissed her good night in her doorway, and got tense again. "What is it?" she asked gently.

"I can't understand how it is that I can love you as I do, and still not have applied for the marriage license. It seems almost as if the very fact that nothing stands between us is sufficient to make us suspect some imaginary difficulty."

That was an interesting thought, and it just might be true. "Sleep now, and if tomorrow you still feel this way, we shall think again." Then they parted.

Contacts were brief the next few days, but perhaps that was just as well, as they both had things to figure out for themselves. She had her studies as the term drew to a close, and the endless details of ordinary existence, and Alfred had his. Sunday the 18th Alfred and Anthony went to London to hear Duke Ellington. Then Alfred had his consultation, and it wasn't until Monday afternoon that they got together for tea.

"Spencer urged me not to postpone my marriage," he said. "Since it was an obvious certainty. I saw that I had been postponing it for reasons, and not through any real desire or necessity."

"So you feel that it should after all be soon?"

"Yes, if you agree."

"I do. I had thought we should put it out of our minds for the summer, but it hasn't left my mind, so it seems better to be done with it."

"Then let's do it immediately," he said.

She smiled. "Well, we do have to get the license. We can't avoid the forms."

"What about the marriage itself? What day?"

"This is Monday," she said, musing. "We can probably manage it by Friday."

"Friday it is," he agreed.

Anthony joined them for supper and the early part of the evening, and there was good feeling all around. Later they cuddled on the sofa. It was a happy night.

Wednesday morning Alfred went with Spencer to get the marriage license. They set the ceremony for 2:30 Friday afternoon.

Then Alfred and Norma went house hunting, and found a good place on Abingdon Road.

But that afternoon Alfred went to London to see Dr. H, who recommended postponing the ceremony until they were surer which directions Alfred's complexes were moving in. He suggested that Alfred might have some sort of sister complex. Meanwhile Norma talked with her mother, and came to the conclusion that it was unwise to be married on Friday.

They met in the early evening and exchanged impressions. "I am much disappointed," Alfred said. "But I see the rightness of it."

"Yes. We shall have to postpone it a few days."

Norma's mother was leaving on the train, and Alfred raced down to see her off. She looked at him closely the whole time he talked with her. Then the train pulled out. "I'm not sure she approves," he said as Norma caught up.

"Does any parent ever fully approve?" she asked rhetorically. "She knows I know my own mind."

Then they went to the Exeter College dance, neither of them in very good condition. Things had been so rushed and confusing! But it was a good dance and they enjoyed it.

At midnight they wandered out into the fellow Garden, up by the wall, overlooking the Radcliffe Camera. As the clock struck he formally proposed marriage to her, and she accepted. They already had a complete understanding, of course, but it was nice to do it officially.

At 2:30 in the morning they had supper. She had two glasses of tea, while he insisted on drinking several glasses of champagne. That annoyed her; he knew she did not like him to drink, and he drank more than a token. How could he do that, on this uniquely special occasion?

So she acted. She got up and departed.

It took him some time to find her, though she was waiting in the entrance. They danced, then talked.

"I was so disappointed that you chose this time to run counter to what you know are my wishes," she said severely.

"I am sorry. I was not thinking."

"I learned a lot this night, not all of it good."

"But you must know every truth about the man you are to marry. I can not choose times to show you what I am. If I am capable of disobeying your wishes, you must know it and take it into account."

"There are nevertheless limits."

"I hope I haven't disappointed you to the point of throwing me over. But even that is preferable to deceiving you in any way." He looked truly mortified.

He had surely learned his lesson. She had mercy. She went and sat on his chair. "It is all over. I will stand by you in spite of that or anything else."

He was clearly overwhelmed by a flood of emotions. He covered his face with his hands until he could collect himself. He cried silently, uncontrollably.

"That's all right," she said, trying ho reassure him. But her kind words set him off again, and again. Every tender thing she said or did seemed to increase his misery.

They went out into the garden, and he cried it off in his own good time. She tried to mask her embarrassment; it was not an easy thing to see a man shed tears abundantly, especially knowing that she was the cause.

At last it ended, and they returned to the dance. After that they went out into the country and lay in a field till 8:30. She was tired, and he wanted her to rest; he spent the whole time caressing her.

They returned to her room. "Give me the name of your father; we shall have to include him in the notice."

He gave it, and she phoned her mother. "Put the notice in the Times." Her mother might not completely approve, but she would do it.

Alfred went to his room to sleep. She got some sleep herself, but not enough. This whole business made her tense; it was so complicated. Perhaps she had overreacted to his drinking of too much champagne; it was a traditional thing for special occasions. Still, Quakers did not approve of alcohol in any form, and she did not like to see him being indulgent in that manner.

She roused herself in the early afternoon, logy from insufficient sleep, and went to rouse Alfred. But she was too tired, and wound up sleeping on the sofa in his arms.

After tea she went home and slept again, all night, hoping to recuperate from all the term's unrest and excitement.

The London Times ran their engagement announcement on Friday, June 23: Mr. A. B. J and Miss N. S. It was official.

Thereafter it was a haze of meetings, talking, arrangements as the considerable process of getting married proceeded. In July Dr. H decided he wanted to see Norma. She knew he disapproved of a patient of his suffering a significant life change before therapy was completed. But how long would that require? She had no intention of allowing a third party to interfere with her marriage.

So she went to see the doctor, and actually they talked compatibly about this and that. It was all perfectly pleasant. Thereafter Dr. H withdrew his objection.

"How did you persuade him?" Alfred asked, bemused.

"I didn't. The subject never came up."

Later Alfred asked Dr. H. It turned out that the doctor had taken one look at Norma and realized that there was no point in arguing the case, so had yielded gracefully. That indicated that the man did have some common sense.

More difficult, in its fashion, was her private dialogue with her mother, who took it upon herself now to do what she had not done before: she described the beastly mechanics of the sexual act. Norma listened calmly, masking her horror. She had had no idea. It seemed that this act was expected of married couples, and that men were insistent about it. It was supposed to occur often, especially at the outset, and simply had to be endured. Yet the advice seemed good: to close her eyes and think of England. It was normally finished quickly, fortunately. She would surely survive it, as her mother had. As all women did. It was a necessary liability of marriage.

They were married Saturday, July 22, 1933. James W and Molly were witnesses, and her parents were there, and Mrs. H. It was all quite routine. Afterward six of them dined very well at the Clarendon, quite happily. In due course the two of them retired to The George hotel. They took a room with one bed, but didn't sleep until late, because of the heat and the state of their beings. It was simply such a wonder actually being married!

She was relieved that though they shared the bed, Alfred did not attempt to initiate the mechanical act. He was content to embrace her, kiss her, and to talk with her. This she could tolerate.

Actually they had to separate in order to get effective sleep. It was just as well. Alfred was still to some extent afraid of her, and she encouraged him to tell her the causes. He found it hard to realize that he had taken the whole of his later life in hand, by marrying her. She certainly understood that; she was doing the same.

But in the course of the following months things soured. She found him to be essentially inconsiderate, inattentive, undemonstrative, and selfish, and told him so. His response was to become worse. "You never come near me unless you want something," she said. After that he did not come near her at all. What was the matter with him?

She concluded it was two things. One was that he did not love her enough to cater properly to her nature. The other was that their continence might be the root of it. They had not been sexually intimate, and for all the beastliness of the act, it was expected in marriage, so its absence was probably making mischief. So, reluctantly, she said so.

They decided to get books on the subject that Dr. H had recommended. But the library kept them under lock and key, to be issued only on the presentation of a letter from some responsible person. Alfred did not care to ask any of his friends for such a letter, and she could appreciate why; it was embarrassing. So she went to ask for it, and after a long delay, at the end of which she was asked the date of her enrollment in the library, and another delay, she was finally given the books. Each one contained a slip printed in red ink asking the reader not to leave the book on the desk when finished, but to return it to an attendant. This was ludicrous, as the books were freely on sale in London bookstores. Alfred was so annoyed that he wrote a letter to the editor of the LONDON TIMES.

The books did help, but it became apparent that Alfred was hardly more eager to get into physical sexuality than she was. They tried, but it just wasn't very effective. For one thing, there was discomfort verging on pain when he tried to penetrate, and he immediately left off.

Then Alfred mentioned to Dr. H that their marriage had not been technically consummated in the first three months. The doctor was appalled, and issued an order: consummate it forthwith. So they tried again, and finally managed it, though without any real pleasure on either side. How could it be that God had chosen to implement such a divine emotion as love in such an awkward way?

They looked for a residence to buy. One was called Ford Cottage, and it looked good. According to Alfred, his father had promised them any cottage in England they wanted. Alfred felt that they should search out the ideal cottage for their desires and needs, then see how Ford Cottage compared. She could not accept that; why go to the trouble of a search through England, when Ford Cottage was already here and good enough? Alfred had no permanently assured income, so could hardly afford any cottage, apart from his rich father. That bothered her.

There was also the matter of psychoanalytic treatment that had been suggested for her. She wouldn't consider it unless Alfred had it too, but he said he couldn't because he already had Dr. H.

They found another prospect, about fifteen miles south of Oxford. This was Slade Cottage in Charlbury. They moved there in October, when their residency at Oxford concluded.

Unfortunately things did not go well. Norma found that having her own residence palled rather quickly; there was too much upkeep. She had thought she would like to have her own kitchen, but that too became tiresome in a week. There was friction with Alfred about it, and he wound up doing much of the cooking and housekeeping. Meanwhile things at work were no better, with Miss B frequently unreasonable. Norma would not stay in that office another minute, if they didn't need the money. As it was they were living on five pounds a week, and though they had enough, technically, she objected on principle to being trapped at that level.

But mainly she was disappointed in Alfred. One Thursday before they moved to the cottage he was about to depart, and she desperately wanted company. She begged him in tears to stay with her.

"You can't wrap me around your finger," he retorted, and went off with Spencer to work on the cottage. What firmer indication could there be that he didn't truly love her?

Things came to a head Tuesday night, October 24. Alfred had been silent and moody all day. He gave her a long and severe lecture about her supposed self-righteousness in the evening about going to the Gilletts. What right had *he* to talk to *her* about self-righteousness? But she bore with it, knowing that reason would never show him the error of his ways.

Then when they went to bed he kept to his own side, ignoring her. She couldn't stand that. Discontented, she thought about it, and the more she thought, the more annoyed she became, until she was fuming. Finally she spoke. "If you want me, you must make some effort to keep me. You can't just stick to me intellectually."

He opened his eyes and looked at her. "Some effort?"

"If anything should separate us, I would date it from Thursday, when I called for you and needed you, and you failed me. I have had to build up my wall of protection again because you are not protecting me. You are losing your wife, and that thought frightens me. I am coming to despise you because you are not a man."

He just gazed at her with a certain seeming wariness, and she realized that she might be overstating her case. "I am no longer in danger of leaving you, but I can offer no proof that I will remain faithful. I'm sure we can go on living together quite happily anyway. I still belong to you and want you, and am waiting for you to claim me."

He did not reply directly. Instead he went to sleep. Well, so much for trying to explain something to him, or for making any positive overture.

Yet in the morning just before they got up he did hold her in his arms for a moment, and as she went to work he embraced her and kissed her goodbye. He was perhaps trying, in his fashion.

Still, there was no getting around the fact that their marriage was in trouble. She had dreamed last week that her wedding ring came off, and she was worrying and attaching importance to it. After all, it was the symbol of their marriage, which was coming apart.

Nevertheless, she had come not to heed or attend anything Alfred said. He had lost all credibility with her, and now his opinions made no difference.

Things weren't universally bad. The first week of November they got along reasonably well, and managed to have sex more than once. It was uncomfortable and she didn't like it, but at least she could be satisfied that she had done her wifely duty.

Then she missed a period, and realized she was pregnant. She wasn't sure whether to be pleased or saddened. What kind of a situation were they bringing the baby into? At least it gave her a pretext to quit her burdensome job; how could she work now? Many mornings she felt too ill to get up, let alone handle the rigors of a job.

Alfred was not completely supportive. That, combined with the dullness of the cottage, encouraged her to visit her family in London, where her mother was always supportive. But that was not entirely satisfactory either, because there was always the unspoken suspicion that something was wrong with her marriage, and she did not like to admit that. So after a time she would return to Slade Cottage, until its objectionable smells and Alfred's intransigence drove her away again.

Because they were often apart, they sent letters back and forth, and sometimes exchanged notes even when together. "You never have asked me what you could do to help," Alfred wrote. "Though often you have told me what I ought to get you to do. You don't realize the difficulties of getting you to do anything."

Well! As if she hadn't tried to be the best wife. He simply did not appreciate the efforts she made. So what was the point in trying?

For example, there was a time when he came to see her in London. They slept apart, but then he came and knelt by her bed in the darkness. She woke and invited him in, though she would have preferred to get the sleep. He joined her and was very passionate. She was not; sex never turned her on. But she was willing to submit. Then he broke off and returned to his own bed. She had done her part, but he had evidently been unsatisfied. What more could she do?

Later they had a bitter battle of words. He was simply impossible to please.

Her troubled pregnancy continued. Alfred was always after her to eat the right things, by his definition. Brown bread, not white, fresh greens, not cooked. How could she eat such things when he had brought them up while she was feeling bad? That gave them a bad association that always returned to sicken her again. It didn't help when the doctor her mother got in London said some of the same things.

Her pregnancy proceeded inexorably. Actually the knowledge that it would soon be over cheered her, and her spirits and health improved. Then came the first day of her confinement, Saturday the fourth of August, 1934. Anthony took them in. The hospital took care of her, but had all those rules and tests and violations of privacy. Labor was awful, a seven hour torment culminating finally on Monday the sixth with the birth of a healthy boy.

After that it was better. She rested in bed, nursing the child frequently, and Alfred bicycled in to see her every evening. He was completing his studies at Exeter, but made the time, without making any demands on her. So it was a happy time. Her only frustrations were her inability to go to Somerset with her family, and a sty on her eye.

After three weeks she was released, and returned to Slade Cottage with the baby. Soon enough the gloom came back. This simply was not the kind of life she craved.

She caught up on a lot of reading. One book she read was the second in the Jalna series by the Canadian author Mazo de la Roche, *Whiteoaks of Jalna*. The author was a Canadian woman, and the story was about the Whiteoak family of Jalna, an estate in southern Ontario. One of the characters was named Piers, and Norma found the name intriguing.

Then Ella M offered them the use of her house for part of the coming month of October. That promised to be delightful. Alfred visited there alone, traveling by bicycle, confirming the offer.

Meanwhile she was up against a deadline: she had six weeks to officially register the boy's birth, and for that she needed to name him. She had been unable to make up her mind. Anthony, their loyal musical family friend, seemed like a good prospect, and of course there should be a Family name represented, maybe Alfred's mother's maiden name, D. Some boys were named after their fathers, but "Alfred" might be confusing. Alfred had suggested his brother's name, John. Then there was that intriguing name in the Jalna series. How could she choose?

On the day the six weeks were up, Monday September 17, she hurried into the office, still uncertain, and compromised by listing most of them: Piers Anthony D J. Maybe he would grow up to be a writer and use some of them as a literary pseudonym. At any rate, it was done.

When Alfred returned she gave him a nice pie she had made. He was more affectionate than he had been for a long while. But she was wary, because his moodiness was always in the background.

Her caution was justified. She mentioned that her family the S's were coming to stay the night. He went ugly silent and set about arrangements to be absent for two days so as not to have to see them. He made no secret of his aversion to her parents. Yet of course she was the stuff of her parents; they had made her, in substance and nature.

As he was about to depart, they discussed that briefly. "You know I am close to my mother," Norma said as she nursed the six week old baby. "I suppose in a way I *am* her property."

Alfred leaped up and beat her about the head several times with his fists. "No you're not!" he shouted. "You're either mine or nobody's!"

Shocked by his violence, she nevertheless maintained her composure. After all, there was the baby. "Please go away."

He paused as Piers started to cry. Then he went.

She finished nursing the baby, then put him down and saw to her repairs. She had some bruises, but her hair mostly covered them; she could surely conceal them from her parents. The irony was that Alfred, as reprehensibly as he had acted, had nevertheless showed himself to be a man. So she could not entirely fault him.

They did go to Caradon, the M house in Winscombe. Ella was away and her two daughters were now living on their own, which was why it was free. It was very nice. But things remained strained, if muted, between them. There were scars that only their best moments briefly concealed. This marriage was essentially make-believe, and not in a happy sense.

Mrs. M returned, and it was time for them to go home. She was a very nice woman. She seemed depressed, but it was not expedient to inquire what was bothering her. The woman had had tragedies enough in her life, losing first her husband, then her eldest daughter. But she did seem to enjoy Piers. She had never had a son, only daughters. That seemed to be why she liked Alfred, whom she clearly saw as a son-figure. Her influence was beneficial; maybe if she had really been his mother, he would have grown up less moody.

They came back to Slade Cottage and put it in order. Wednesday the 24th they went to Oxford to celebrate Norma's 24th birthday by trying to buy out Woolworth's; it was fun to splurge on rare occasion. Next day Alfred went to London to see Anthony and his flat. Friday Norma did the house while Alfred worked on the Dog Grate, and they had a fire in the evening. Saturday she did the house again while he picked one of the apple trees and put another light in the kitchen. Baby Piers was well but habitually constipated; was her milk somehow wrong for him?

It was a reasonably satisfactory time. But Alfred's antipathy to her mother was a problem. When she visited and Alfred saw her holding Piers, he made himself scarce until she was gone. Later he wrote her a nasty letter suggesting that she could facilitate harmony by leaving them alone. That was of course outrageous, and Ella M cautioned him about it. "If Norma decides to take Piers to his Grannie for a few days, let her do so." Exactly. That did some good, as he respected Ella's opinion.

Things muddled on past the turn of the year. Then in February Norma missed her period again, and thought she might be pregnant a second time. They really hadn't had sex, at least no penetration, but Alfred had an one point been on top of her and had a reaction, and it was possible that had led to something.

Alfred reacted badly when she told him. They were in bed, and he leaped on her, beat her head, and tried to strangle her. "You bitch!"

She had been through this sort of thing before. She knew his fury would quickly abate. It was part of the beastliness of men her mother had warned her about. It simply had to be tolerated and concealed.

She spoke to him sanely. "It does take two, you know. These things happen." But then she lost control. The idea that he would so object to a baby! She sobbed. "I don't mind what you do to me. It is—" But she was unable to finish her thought. And of course there was no certainty that she was pregnant; it was merely a possibility.

They continued to have sex, such as it was, and she put in the diaphragm she had gotten. At least now there wasn't physical pain; the birthing of the baby must have stretched her.

On April 20 Anthony came to pick up Alfred's bassoon. Alfred wasn't using it, and it had a remarkably sweet sound; Anthony wanted to try it in the London orchestra. This led in due course to Anthony's decision to buy it, because it turned out to be perfect for him. Alfred didn't want to sell it; it was one of his most precious possessions. But in the end he agreed, but wouldn't spend the money; he put it in a fund earmarked for Piers' eventual education. She couldn't fault that, though they certainly could have used the money to live on.

The suspicion of pregnancy gradually became certainty. This did not smooth things with Alfred, who it seemed had barely wanted a first child, and never a second. She finally went to stay with the Sherlocks, taking Piers along, to get away from the tension.

They exchanged letters, bitterly. "Dear Madam," he wrote May 23, 1935, "Does it ever occur to you that there are some things which are best left to the vestiges of the affection you are trying to kill?" It continued for three pages.

She replied: "Dear Sir, My thought on reading your first sentence was 'there can obviously be no answer to this letter'; still I am writing an answer, not because I think it will do any good but because I have always tried not to ignore *any* gesture on your part that might be interpreted as an effort to make things better." She also wrote ". . . after two years of uncertainty, disillusionment and almost incessant discouragement I feel that the old defences have grown up again stronger than ever. And perhaps it is a good thing, for one can't go on indefinitely crying oneself to sleep at nights."

Yet they persevered, as did her pregnancy. Suddenly on October 22 she felt the contractions coming on so strongly that there was no chance to go to the hospital. Fortunately the nurse had arrived. Alfred carried her (Norma) upstairs and such was her distraction that she bit him on the arm.

The baby was delivered in just twenty minutes. This was a girl, Teresa Caroline J.

Surprisingly, things were better for a while thereafter. The nurse stayed for two weeks, which really helped. There were visitors. Piers said "Da-da" to Alfred, pleasing him. On occasion Ella M took care of Piers, enabling Norma to travel with Teresa. Thus they tided through into 1936.

Alfred told the Friends Service that they would be willing to serve at the Friends Centre in Madrid if one should be established. Norma told him that she would be unwilling to go to Spain with him; for one thing, where would the money come from? But as they explored the situation in Spain, which desperately needed help, she relented.

Thereafter it was all Spain and children: Alfred organized for the one, she took care of the other. It was a burden; she had not realized prior to having them how demanding children were. Could she have been that way as a child? She appreciated her mother's tolerance in retrospect, especially when she returned home and saw her mother with the children.

Alfred went to Spain for a month, March and April 1936, visiting eight cities and getting a clearer notion of the lay of the land, as it were. There was a good deal of attendant publicity. His report convinced the Friends Service Council of London that they should start a Quaker center in Spain. The people of Spain were coming to distrust the Catholic church there. Many of the priests were scamps, and the religion was a hoax. A real religion would be far more satisfactory. A mission could be set up in Madrid, the capital, and expand from there.

However, the Meeting for Sufferings, a body of the London Yearly Meeting, told them in July that they were much too young and inexperienced for such an assignment. But the Meeting didn't have much choice, because as far as they knew, Alfred and Norma were the only Spanish-speaking Quakers in the British Isles. So, reluctantly, they approved it.

They were busy packing, getting ready to leave with the children for Madrid, when the Spanish Civil War broke out on July 18. That changed everything. Yet it did seem that there might be work for Quakers to do in Spain, even if it wasn't exactly that they had planned on. So Alfred went to Spain again in September, this time accompanied by a much older and weightier Friend, John H. They drove into Spain with the spare tire stuffed with foreign money. No money was allowed to cross the border, but it was impossible to accomplish anything without it.

It quickly became apparent that they would not be able to go on to Madrid; the war prevented. But maybe they could start something were they were. They checked with the YMCA, and there Alfred met one Domingo R and his wife Margarita, who were extremely helpful. They focused on Barcelona, on the east coast: that was where they would start the operation. This was actually the beginning of a lifelong friendship, though they didn't know it at the time.

The first relief action that Domingo and Alfred got started was on Christmas Day, 1936, giving hot drinks of Cadbury's cocoa to refugee children from Madrid. The children would arrive typically in the middle of the night, from a long journey, cold, hungry, and scared. The hot cocoa was surely a great comfort. The main railroad station was constantly bombed but never actually hit.

Norma took the children to her parents in London in early spring, 1937, then went to Spain. She was gathering material for a fund-raising campaign. She crossed the British Channel to France and took the train to Toulouse, where she took an airplane, her first flight. The snow-capped Pyrenees were beautiful at dawn. They landed without event, a relief, and drove into Barcelona from the airport.

The air raid alarms sounded. This was another new experience; nothing like that had happened in England in Norma's memory, and it was alarming. The bus stopped, and everybody went down into a subway station, not very far below the ground. There was a group of school children with their teachers in the same shelter. Suppose a bomb came through the roof? She thought about that for a minute or two, then returned to ground level. She intended never to take refuge underground again.

The relief operation had already been expanded enormously. Alfred was very busy, and seemed happier than she had seen him. He was doing something challenging and genuinely useful, and clearly loved it.

And challenges there were. While she was there, the anarchists took over the city. This was disaster. The anarchists seriously believed that any manifestation of government was sinful, even a traffic light. They did however make an exception for the police; apparently unfettered crime on the streets was beyond their philosophy. Alfred and Domingo carried on despite them; hungry children could not be denied.

Soon Norma started her return trip to London. She was arrested at the frontier station and brought back to Barcelona under armed guard. Fortunately she managed to get word to Alfred, and he and Domingo came to police headquarters. They all sat up in comfortable armchairs and waited to see what would happen. Norma felt protected by her British passport, but later concluded that she should have been downright scared. In times of serious social disturbance the rule was often to shoot first and inquire afterward.

She had to stay the night at the police station. There was a succession of young men coming in and being issued revolvers from a huge open safe. In the morning the chief of police called her in and said it was a case of mistaken identity, and she could go. They even paid her train fare to the border.

The next time she went to Spain was in the summer, and she brought the children with her. They joined Alfred, and all went to Puigcerdá, a town in a beautiful green valley high up in the Pyrenees. It was on the French border, near the tiny country of Andorra. The international boundary ran through the valley, and they lived in a house right beside it. The garden ran down to a stream, on the other side of which was the small French town of Bourg Madame. Spanish and French soldiers had posts on the bridge, but local residents went back and forth quite freely.

One day she stood on a small stone bridge over a narrow stream in that valley and saw the water running white with milk. It was from a condensed milk factory that shut down because they couldn't buy sugar in wartime. The grass kept growing, the cows kept producing, and there was nothing to do with the milk except throw it away. There was no way to ship it out in liquid form because there were no tank cars. It was a light mountain line intended mainly for skiers. Children in Barcelona were dying for lack of milk, and here it was being thrown away.

Well, now. Soon the Quakers sent several tons of sugar so that the factory was able to resume partial production, and children were sent from the city to live in the large vacant houses of wealthy people who had fled the war. So the local Quaker unit distributed food to the children in ten ton Bedford trucks sent out from England.

Puigcerdá was at that time under anarchist control, and this made a problem similar to the ones Barcelona had had. The anarchists were extremely puritanical and heartily disapproved of women wearing pants. But the women with the trucks had to wear them. So the Quakers never quite knew when the anarchists might decide to shoot them in order to encourage the others. They also disapproved of women sitting down for cool drinks at one of the open-air cafés in the main square. Domingo once had to come from Barcelona to defuse the situation when an Australian woman with a different group took a drink in public.

There was often shooting at night, when the anarchists settled disputes among themselves. Once the racket was appalling. They got the children out of bed and lay on the floor, hoping no stray bullets would strike. In the morning they discovered that it was the French Bastille Day, July 14, and the folk of Bourg Madame were letting off fireworks.

Then scarlet fever showed up among refugee children, and they decided that it would be safer for their own children to take them back to England. This revived a familiar problem: French money was needed in France, lest Norma be arrested for vagrancy, but it was not allowed in Spain and could not be taken across the border. Money would have to be smuggled across. Norma made several casual shopping trips over the bridge to Bourg Madame and managed to accumulate a nest-egg in large, new crisp French bills. She knew she would be searched before being allowed to leave, so she pinned the money to the front of little Teresa's diaper. The child was walking, at age not-quite-two, but not yet talking. As the policewoman at the railroad station was searching Norma, Teresa clutched at her stomach and began to cry; the sharp corners of the new money were pricking her.

The policewoman looked at the child. "Poor little thing! She has a stomachache."

Norma picked Teresa up and hurried to the train, bringing three year old Piers along. They had made it!

But the train didn't move. What was the matter? Finally it started up and went the few hundred yards into France. And it had missed the connection; the Paris express had left. It was a set-up to force travelers to pay for a night at the station hotel.

Angry, Norma put their suitcases in the left-luggage office, got a cab, and drove with the children back to Bourg Madame. She walked to the middle of the bridge with the children and explained to the guards what had happened. They agreed that the children should spend the night in their own beds in the house by the bridge. So Norma shouted, and Alfred came out. He was surprised; he had thought they were already halfway to Paris. She handed the children over and turned back to find a bed for the night for herself. After all this, she wasn't going to go through it all again.

But as ill luck would have it, this was the day before the Tour de France, the great bicycle race. Cyclists had all the rooms, and it was impossible to find a bed in Bourg Madame that night. What to do? At last she gave up and walked back to the bridge. "If you don't let me go back to my own bed in that house there," she told the guards, "I'll just have to sleep under the bridge." They couldn't think of anything else to do, so they passed her through.

Next morning she crossed the bridge again, with the children, with no passport, no police search, and took another cab back to the railroad station. This time they got safely to Paris, and then back to London.

Several months later, without the children, Norma returned to Spain. Now they lived in a huge mansion, which accommodated their entire unit of twelve foreigners. A native staff twice that size came in by day. In the garden they could pick oranges, tangerines, lemons, olives, and figs. The oranges were bitter, grown for marmalade, which they couldn't make because there was no sugar. One evening a large open truck loaded with sweet oranges arrived from Valencia. They backed it up to the second story windows and rolled out ten tons of oranges by hand onto the office floor.

Another time they somehow got hold of a copy of the American magazine ESQUIRE. It contained a quiz by which one was supposed to be able to assess one's own personality. The questions were almost incomprehensible to everyone except Alfred, the only native American there. He explained them to the English, the English translated them for the Spanish-speaking staff, and they translated them again for the Catalan-speaking staff. The results were hilarious.

Alfred and Norma were invited to the Christmas dinner of a wealthy British couple who had lived well in Barcelona for many years. The table was set with linens, silver, and crystal. On a silver platter in the middle was one opened can of sardines: the main course. There were a few bits of bread and some broccoli. Food was short. They themselves lived on the absolute minimum that enabled them to function. At that time they were feeding just about every child under age ten in Catalonia. One hundred-pound sack of oatmeal turned out to be full of mouse droppings. They patiently picked the droppings out by hand.

The most distressing part of the job was turning away hungry people. They had a huge cellar full of food, but it was restricted to young children and older people with ulcers. The job of sending them away was rotated among the staff people, English, Spanish, and Catalan. No one lasted more than two weeks. They would come into the office and say "I simply cannot do this anymore." Sometimes people fainted from hunger in their waiting room.

One day a truck came from Marseilles bringing all sorts of extravagant goodies sent by their families in England, for their Christmas dinner. Norma had just had to turn down a request for help from the blind beggar's union of Barcelona, and here was this pile of ridiculous luxury food in the middle of their floor. They put aside a pound of coffee for the day when a bomb fell on their street. They would run up to the roof when the alarm was given and try to spot the parts of the city being bombed. The Italian airmen liked to bomb on Sunday mornings, taking off from Majorca. Norma was a Quaker pacifist, but she found herself hoping that one of Barcelona's few antiaircraft guns would hit something. And the bomb never did hit their street.

It got unusually cold for a Mediterranean city. The roses in their garden looked ridiculous with tiny pointed caps of snow. The mansion had no central heating, but that hardly mattered; when there was an air raid—and there were several a day—the main power switch was pulled and every light in the city went out. Norma was ever after to be nervous when the power flickered, and always knew where the matches and candles were.

They worked seven days a week, for as many hours as they could keep awake. Then London sent out a young doctor. He laid down a new law: on Sunday the office would be entirely closed and everybody would go out to the beach. They obeyed, and thereafter had one wonderful day each week, racing up and down the beach, screaming and throwing each other into the ocean, to the stupefaction of the dignified Catalans watching them.

They had a vague impression that the war was going badly for the Republicans, but it was impossible to get accurate information. Then in January 1939 they left for a brief vacation in France. The first French newspaper they saw showed that Barcelona was about to fall to General Franco's army. Alfred hurried back, while Norma, on orders from London, stayed in Perpignan on the southeast coast of France.

It was obvious that an enormous movement of refugees over the frontier was about to happen. Norma went from one French government office to another, trying to find someone who would start preparations to take care of all those people. Nobody seemed to be interested. She became aware that she was about to collapse herself; she didn't want to do it in the middle of such a large-scale human tragedy.

She returned to London and let her parents nurse her back to something resembling health. She was terribly underweight, exhausted, and suffering from the aftereffects of the crushing defeat of something in which she had profoundly believed. The forces of evil, as it were, were prevailing in Spain, despite all that good people could do. Nothing in the world seemed quite the same since.

She saw it happening from a distance. The thousands who had fled the Nationalist advance were hustled by the French into camps. These were bare spaces of sand surrounded by barbed wire for the men, and improvised lodgings for the women and children. Miserable accommodation, but probably not much worse than in Spain, except that in France they were surrounded by a hostile population.

Alfred was in Barcelona in January 1939 when it fell to General Franco's forces. What vehicles remained there were confiscated by the military. The general in charge threatened to hang Alfred in the main square of the city as a punishment for feeding "red" children. Actually they had been feeding children in need regardless of politics.

After some months, Norma returned to France, sent by the Friends to visit those camps. When she drove into a camp with the Quaker star on the panels, people came running "The Quakers are here, the Quakers are here!" They made lists of things needed, like sandals.

In June, 1939, they returned to Barcelona, this time taking the children along. Everybody in London thought they were crazy, but it seemed clear to them that war was about to begin in the whole of Europe. They had already seen enough of what war did to children to feel that their own must be spared that. At least the war was over in Spain.

This time they had a much smaller house on a street nearer the center of Barcelona. Domingo and Margarita Ricart shared the house with them, and they had a housekeeper. The new Franco government had taken over the large-scale operation literally overnight. The Quakers now fed mostly people who were out of favor with the new authorities, who were denied ration cards.

They had to drive out into the country in search of extra food, mostly eggs and fresh vegetables. Bringing food into the city was strictly against the law, so they had to smuggle it in. There was a cavity behind the back seat where a big sack of potatoes hid. Because of the Quaker star on the panels they were never searched. What would happen to the international reputation of the Society of Friends if a search ever took place?

There were shortages of everything, including cooking pots. When Alfred and Norma set out on an inspection tour, the car they used had the peculiarity of getting stuck in reverse gear, signaled by a difficulty engaging second gear. When it happened, only a mechanic could fix it. During this trip, Alfred felt the problem with second gear, and they resolved not to use reverse before they got home. Then they saw a shop that appeared to be selling cooking pots. Alfred couldn't reverse, so he drove around the block, pulled up outside the shop on a small hill—and automatically put the gear into reverse to assist the brakes. There was nothing to do but keep driving until they found a garage. They drove two miles up Spain's major highway in reverse. The peasant women working in their fields straightened up to gape. Fortunately in the next small town they found a garage. The man in charge forged a new piece while they waited.

Their year under the Franco government was uncomfortable. The new patriotism was everywhere. One day a man approached Norma wanting to sell her some kind of lapel button celebrating the new regime. She refused. That sent a chill through their group, and she realized that such independence was now dangerous. During movies a picture of Franco would be flashed on the screen, and everybody was expected to stand and give a fascist salute. They were also expected to salute the flag when encountering it on the street. Seeing how the flag could be used as in instrument of tyranny, Norma disliked such observances ever after.

They took over management of a small hotel in Tossa, a coastal town about fifty miles northeast of Barcelona. The English proprietors had gone to France with a group of children and could not get permission to return. Alfred and Norma discovered that they weren't particularly good as hotel keepers, but it was a nice place to spend a weekend. Nightingales sang interminably in the eucalyptus trees.

Their job assignment now represented the American as well as British Friends. Many people were still dependent on them for the food that kept them alive. Norma did not like life in this new, repressive Spain, but how could they desert this mission?

It was no better with Alfred. When not at work, he was distant if not actually hostile. He was endlessly critical of the way she managed the children, calling them "infants." There was no sex. He was obviously not a family man.

In November 1939 he made an inspection trip around the country, passing through Madrid and Valencia, and things were peaceful at home. But he remained chronically depressed on his return. He was inattentive to her and short tempered with the children; it seemed that nothing could meet his strict standards, whatever they were. Sometimes he did active work in the garden at Tossa, and that seemed to help. But in May 1940 he objected when she had to make a special trip to get Teresa's medicine, delaying his return to Barcelona.

In June, on a another trip to Valencia, he wrote her a letter: "If you decide to join me I'll always be glad to see you. Though I think you would find this sort of travel not conducive to clear discussion." Another letter a few days later was a bit more specific, saying in part "The best thing would be to get the children to the parents, because where they are they will neither be well fed nor educated. I hardly realized there could be villages so off the map."

There it was: he resented the presence of the children. But he had a point: Spain was hardly the ideal place for them. Yet was England really any better? It was obvious that war was looming and bombs would be falling. At least here in Spain that was over. Then again, what about America? His family was there, and it was far from the war scene. That would be better all around.

She tried to make overtures of friendship, as there really was no point in quarreling. But then he failed to get permits for them to go to America before Italy entered the war, and she was angry. It wasn't as if there hadn't been warning; Germany had invaded Poland in September 1939, and Britain and France had declared war. In April 1940 Germany invaded Denmark and Norway, and France in May. It was scary the way the Germans raced down through France toward Spain in June. Fortunately they did stop at the border, expecting Spain to join them at any moment. Of course then Italy officially joined the Axis. Now there were no neutral neighbor countries. How were they ever going to get out?

Suddenly things changed. Alfred was on another inspection trip at the end of June, which included a stop near the French border to meet a train from France. Hitler's forces were advancing rapidly, taking over the rest of France, setting up the pseudo French Vichy government. There were frantic arrangements to ship four hundred British people who lived in southern France to Lisbon, Portugal, for repatriation. The Quakers had been asked to help, so Alfred was there with a list of the people to assist, and a large sum of money provided by the British authorities. The plan was that these people would cross Spain in a sealed train. This would take several days, and food had to be provided. Naturally the fascist Spanish government would not provide it. Norma had spent several days in Barcelona going to government offices to get permission to buy huge quantities of staples—bread, eggs (to be hard-boiled), milk for the babies, and large crocks to be filled with drinking water. Alfred's trip to the border was to meet that train, if they could figure where it was coming in, and buy fresh food there and otherwise offer what help was possible. But the train never arrived.

And Alfred disappeared. He did not report to the next stop on his route, and they could not reach him by phone at any of the hotels where he was supposed to be staying. What had happened? Norma was extremely anxious. She asked at the government office: had he been arrested? She remembered her own arrest at the border in 1937; these things could happen. But they assured her that they had no idea where he might be.

Then one day the mailman delivered a very grubby picture postcard, mailed in Zaragoza, a hundred and sixty miles west of Barcelona. He had been arrested there, and had no way of letting them know until a prisoner who was being released managed to smuggle out the postcard. This was confirmation: the government *had* done it.

Norma swung into action. She sent the children to Tossa with an American woman who was a friend of theirs, and took the train to Zaragoza. But at the prison she learned that he had been transferred to Madrid. She had to take another train, this time at night, riding in a very cold carriage because other passengers insisted on keeping all the windows open.

In Madrid she stayed with an American Quaker; an American passport was a marvelous protection from official molestation. They went to the British embassy to ask for help, and an embassy person accompanied them to the head of the prison service in Madrid. "We have no such man in any of our prisons," the official assured them.

But by great good fortune they received help from a very weighty American Quaker, Howard K, who was able to threaten withholding huge amounts of money and food. Spain needed that very badly in this postwar period of reconstruction. Finally, grudgingly, the official revealed that a prisoner named Alfred J was indeed being held in the prison underneath the Puerta del Sol.

They were able to gain his release, on condition that he and his family leave the country as fast as possible. That would eliminate any evidence of a mistake on their part. Meanwhile he would have to remain in Madrid and report to the police twice a day, like any criminal. They never stated the reason for his arrest, but surely having so much money so near the border had made him a person of suspicion. Of course the fascists did not understand how a man or group could be seriously trying to help hard-pressed victims to cope. They had to believe the worst.

They learned something of the prison where he had been held. It was a former stable with just one high window looking out on the sidewalk where they could see the feet and legs of passersby. Alfred had at first stood under this window so as to have light to read the book he happened to have with him. "You're new here," a long-term prisoner said to him. "Soon you won't bother with that." There were just two rooms for men and women. All but one regular prisoner was male; the lone female was a Hungarian woman who had been in a Spanish port waiting for a ship to Italy on the day that Italy entered the war. The ship didn't sail, her transit visa expired, so she was put in prison. The men by common consent let her occupy the short bench that was the single piece of furniture, so she wouldn't have to sleep on the cold damp floor as they did. Alfred was luckier than some because he had a raincoat to lie on. The other women were streetwalkers who were rounded up every night and released in the morning. The sanitary facilities consisted of a drain in the men's room; periodically the women were herded there to perform as the men stood around to see what they could see.

They went shopping after Alfred's release, returning to the prison with armloads of blankets, food, and other simple comforts for the remaining prisoners. The awful place reminded Norma of nothing so much as a nineteenth century painting of Dante's Inferno.

She returned to Barcelona to close their office as fast as possible—and became ill with what looked exactly like the mumps. She was in the hospital with her face grotesquely swollen when the doctor from the US embassy came to give her a certificate of health. He sat beside the bed and solemnly signed it. Without the certificate, they could not have gotten their American visas. As it happened, little Teresa had gotten tuberculosis, at that stage undiagnosed; that, too, would have prevented their exodus.

There was another problem: they could not get tickets for the ship in Lisbon without a Portuguese transit visa, but the Portuguese would not give the visa until they had their tickets. They did have the money for them, courtesy of Alfred's American parents, but how could they get around this impasse? They had another stroke of luck: a young Spaniard they had once been able to help was employed in Madrid. He cut a corner and supplied the tickets. Norma got out of the hospital and went to the US consulate for necessary travel documents. A picture taken of her there for her her visa showed her looking the way she felt: about to keel over at any moment.

She collected the children and took the train to Madrid. They picked Alfred up and took another train to Lisbon, Portugal. At the border crossing point there was a very long platform, one in each country, and at the Portuguese end they served white bread and real coffee. What delight, after a year! In the Lisbon store windows were familiar breakfast foods. But the hotel they stayed in was infested by cockroaches.

The children enjoyed stopping to pick a piece of cork off a cork tree, and watching the toy trains of an amusement arcade, and riding in the pedal-boats. They of course had no notion of the horrendous happenings that had brought the family here.

After four days they went to the harbor and boarded the *Excalibur*. This turned out to be the last ship with refugees crossing the Atlantic. It was designed for two hundred passengers, and was carrying four hundred, but the staff did its best. Piers had his sixth birthday on that voyage; they lacked ingredients for a cake, so made a mock one of sawdust. Among the other passengers were the Duke and Duchess of Windsor, on their way to take up the governorship of the Bahamas, after the Nazis had failed to recruit them.

Alfred's father, the former Mushroom King, and stepmother were there at the New York harbor. Caroline N J was Edward J's third wife, the prior two having died, and understood about marrying into the family. She welcomed Norma, and their friendship was to last fifty years. Alfred had been somewhat alienated from his father, and was overseas when Caroline joined the family, but the J's were certainly supportive, both emotionally and financially. They provided a cottage where Piers stayed when he was ill, and helped them settle in. Alfred had been absent from America for twelve years. For Norma it was a new country, but also a phenomenal relief to be back in civilized territory without the threat of bombs falling.

Piers went to school, but Teresa's tuberculosis kept her in bed for six months. Norma taught her to read during that time, and it was effective; when she entered school, she already possessed a fifth or sixth grade reading level. That was in sharp contrast to Piers, who was unable to learn to read, and fell behind from the outset, taking three years to get through first grade.

However, the marriage itself did not improve. Alfred and Norma had no confidence in each other, no fellowship, no common activity, no give and take. Yet they did have the Quaker community of interest, which counted for a lot.

In 1941 they got interested in forming a planned community, considering the advantages, such as providing a better environment for the children, and demonstrating a pacifist alternative to war. They had to decide whether to rely on cash, or their own inventiveness and adaptability. They discussed food, and realized that a good garden would be in order. They could keep goats, and calculated how many quarts of milk that would provide.

They arranged to buy a large forest property in the Green Mountains of Vermont, with a century old house held together by wooden pegs. This was Hilltop Farm, where strawberries and blueberries grew wild, and there were many sugar maple trees. The nearest town was Jamaica. They moved there by the fall of 1941. Unfortunately one of the participating families, Leslie and Valerie J, left for a visit to Canada—and were not allowed to re-enter

America, not being citizens. Norma was depressed; this was a body-blow to their plans. She had thought they had escaped that sort of thing when they left Europe.

The Vermont winter proved to be savagely cold. The four mile trail to the farm was snowed in, impassable by ordinary vehicles. They had to take up temporary occupancy at Hope House in Jamaica, and the children went to the local school.

Then Alfred got a job teaching Spanish at Dartmouth, the college he had attended before coming to England. So at the end of January, 1942, they were in Hanover, New Hampshire, with the children attending another school. They had their goats along, too. The job gave them financial stability, but their marriage remained difficult. Things would set them off, and sharp words would be exchanged.

At the beginning of May they moved back to Hilltop Farm. Others came there to participate in the planned community, but there were differences of opinion. People were too individualistic, and there was increasing verbal discontent. An artist painted a picture of the farm on the kitchen wall, a lovely mural, with the words "Let not the seeds of war be found on these our premises." Later those words were painted over, as they seemed hypocritical. The seeds of war *were* there, even among idealistic pacifists.

Yet plans continued over the summer. They worked out the plan, with lessons for pacifists: 1. Non-violent, 2. Cooperative, 3. Complete. 4. Collectivists can express human individuality. Financing was a problem. They discussed white flour versus home-ground flour. Agreement was not easy. Alfred objected to wastefulness, such as lighting a fire instead of dressing more warmly, making buns that then didn't get eaten, spraying to get rid of all flies, then propping the door open. Norma had problems with the religious and cooperative aspects.

Finally it got to be simply too much. In November, as another winter set in, Norma announced her intention to leave. She did depart for a month, leaving the cooking, bed making, and child care to Alfred. Then she realized that this was too difficult for the children, and arranged to send them to a good boarding school in New York State.

In February 1943 there was a fire in the study. The kerosene lamps that were necessary in the absence of electricity were dangerous in this respect. Alfred ran down to the cistern to fetch water, broke the ice—and fell in. He managed to get out and bring water, and they did douse the fire. But many papers were scorched. It was an object lesson in the perils of isolated existence.

In the early summer of 1943 Norman and Winnie W came, liked what they saw, and stayed to participate. But overall the farm simply wasn't working out. People were at cross purposes, and few seemed to see the obvious solutions to problems. Finally, reacting to yet another pointless challenge by Alfred, Norma typed out her position:

1. A way of living which satisfied her need for constructive service wider than the comfort and security of herself, family, and friends. 2. A group of people who are seeking to eliminate the seeds of war, with friendliness and consideration the rule of life at all times. 3. An economy avoiding exploitation, sufficient to keep participants healthy and happy so that it seems worthwhile. 4. An economy of abundance based on the principle that the productivity of nature is the greatest single asset. 5. An attempt to establish better relations with townspeople. 6. A plan, and willingness to follow it.

Early in August Norm W suggested that if Winnie could arrange to teach at the Pikes Falls school, which was closer than Jamaica and not being used because of the lack of a teacher, the two of them might be able to stay at Hilltop over the winter. Alfred welcomed the idea, and Norma approved. The Williamses were young, he about 19, she 21, but very sensible and hard working people.

Winnie did teach. They found a trail through the forest that she and the children could walk, making the distance two and a half to three miles each way. It was a long walk, but they handled it. Unfortunately Piers was still wetting the bed, and constantly shaking his hands and head in a neurotic tic, and Teresa was chronically irritable. This life wasn't good for them. To make things worse, Alfred was getting more serious about the fantasy of astrology. He really thought he could fathom the nuances of people and the world by making horoscopes. How was it possible to proceed sensibly when pseudo-science governed?

Norma did her best. She prepared foods that she didn't personally like, for the benefit of the others. She took more interest in the children and gave them more positive instructions. She reflected on Norm Williams' good qualities and tried to get to know him better. She organized her work to fit everything into the day's plan. She adopted an attitude of encouragement and interest for all. She shared the substance of her reading with others. She made only necessary journeys. She used a yeast sponge to carry over from one baking to the next. She sang with gusto in their community choruses. She kept up to date with the mending, and made shirts and underwear for the men. She spun the angora wool. She did everything she could to help make the community a success.

Yet for her it was too much. She had tried, but simply couldn't tolerate this primitive life any more. Alfred had not come through on promises to finish building the sanitary privy. Things didn't have to be *his* way or *her* way; discussion might bring them together. She felt she had done what she could, but he had to show some initiative. "Yes, I think separate lives are best. I had a great hope this spring that it could be different, but if now we both agree it is best, let's go ahead and be as friendly as possible about it."

She went to Philadelphia and got a job with the United Peace Corps, leaving the children with Alfred and the W's. It wasn't an easy decision, but was a necessary one.

She returned in the summer of 1945, but it was clear that the planned community was a failure. Alfred was finally coming to agree, and they made plans to move to Wallingford or Rose Valley, Pennsylvania.

And so the trip to Philadelphia was made in late September, 1945, barely in time for the children to start school in Pennsylvania.

Piers went to the excellent School in Rose Valley, while Teresa attended the local middle school. The family stayed at Pendle Hill again. Both Alfred and Norma undertook psychological treatment, she for a father difficulty, he for a mother difficulty. Her father had been a doctor, rather cold and aloof; his mother had died when he was fifteen, and it clearly had left a mark on him. Whether that related to his vegetarianism she wasn't sure; what was the point, anyway? What was also clear was that they simply did not get along well together; their marriage was a shell covering a profound lack of togetherness.

The way he saw it, if his emotional life was cut off, he had to live intellectually. Yet she had been trying to relate to him emotionally. He just wasn't receptive. Meanwhile she had a number of complaints about his behavior. He had not placed Piers under clinical treatment; he was uncharitable to the children, and sarcastic; he used money in ways she had not approved; he interfered with food, the children, and medicine; he was on occasion irresponsible and unreliable; and he was impersonal, as he had been the last year in Spain.

But she noticed another change in him, as if he had a romantic interest, but not in her. That, oddly, made him easier to get along with. He was seeing a lot of Wilma B, one of his astrology associates; could there be something there? Certainly he had killed Norma's effort to be a good housewife.

In June 1946 they returned to Hilltop, and Wilma and her children joined them. To her surprise, Norma found she could relate to the woman, because she had husband trouble. It seemed that Wilma's husband had no regard for her needs, and demanded sex every day.

In August Norma sailed for England for a nice visit with her family, returning in October. This separation helped clarify her mind, and on her return she spoke to Alfred about a formal separation. They now had a house in Wallingford that his family had helped them buy. The children were with her, continuing in their schools.

Then one Saturday in November they argued about money, and he beat her about the head with his fists. She collapsed on the floor, and he left. She wasn't really hurt, physically, but it certainly underscored the point: it was not possible to live with him.

Thereafter he was away from the house most of the time, and she did not encourage him to be otherwise.

Then there was the matter of the pet. Piers said he would like to have one, and Alfred talked him into a goat. Next thing, they had bought Marcella, a full grown doe, from Alfred's sister Elinor. Later there was a second goat, Ann, and in due course they had kids. Piers tried to take care of them, selling the milk to the household for ten cents a quart, but when he was away at school they could break free and trespass on the neighbors' yards, generating mischief. Norma finally had to give them away, a year later, alienating Piers. The whole thing should have been avoided.

In the fall of 1948 Piers went off to the Westtown Friends School, and the following year Teresa went there also. It was an excellent boarding school, so they no longer lived at home for most of the year. Alfred's father paid the tuition and board. This simplified things.

By the summer of 1949 Norma was discussing the prospect of divorce with her friends. In due course she discussed it with Alfred, and he agreed that perhaps that was best. Divorce was frowned on in Quaker circles, but in reality they had no marriage. In Pennsylvania it was not easy; Alfred had to live elsewhere so that the official grounds could be listed as desertion. In May 1952 she sued for divorce, and in September it was granted. She was free at last.

Alfred would surely carry on well enough without her.

# GENEVIEVE

Genevieve F first met Alfred July 14, 1929. She was taking a steamer cruise and overland tour around Europe with her friends Marion and Elinor, seeing the sights, taking classes, shopping and having a good time. Sometimes there were even fireworks and other entertainments, and of course many evening concerts.

They met Elinor's little brother Alfred when they were in Dresden, Germany. She recorded it in her Trip Diary: *"Elinor's brother called, and will arrive tonight. Planned to go to Schillers—oh yes, had tea in the garden today, everyone stayed around and talked, played a little Victrola and danced a bit. It was quite lovely. Had dinner very late. Waited on the street corner for Elinor's brother and carried on 'in satch a crizy wey' as Fraulein Von Hoelzen would say. He surprised us and walked up. We watched a very happy meeting from afar."* They had expected him to arrive by car. *"—To Schillers and guzzled gobs. To bed 'krank' as usual."* Neither she nor Alfred had any notion at the time of the significance of the meeting.

Two days later she took a long walk with Alfred, and they talked of many things. He was a very companionable young man, three years her junior. Elinor seemed to have good taste in brothers.

They were back for dinner, foot sore and weary. He certainly could walk! Then the three of them and Alfred went to Schiller's until closing time. *"Gabbed and gabbed,"* she wrote in her trip diary.

Their usual routine of classes, sightseeing, shopping, and having a good time continued, as they absorbed the atmosphere of Germany. It was a largely carefree time.

On Thursday she and Marion were at Schiller's again when Elinor and Alfred walked in, so it was another nice gettogether.

Their constant activity continued, keeping them worn out. Dresden was wonderful. *"I could just weep at the thought of leaving Dresden—the soft moonlight, the violins across the water from Anton's—the sparkling lights of the bridges, the Old cobbled path—"* she wrote on Saturday.

On Sunday Alfred and Elinor went to the Albert theater. He was taking a lot of Elinor's time, but of course soon enough they would part ways.

On Monday July 22 they went after dinner to Linkes Bad and danced. Alfred wanted to get drunk, but it was rather difficult to do on champagne. It was amusing.

Friday they took the train for Frankfurt, while Alfred stayed in Liepsig. He was waiting for his friend Spencer T to join him, so they could set off on a summer tour of Spain.

Their tour continued, through Germany, northern Italy, Switzerland, and France, before returning to America. They arrived in Paris August 28, 1929.

Then came what turned out to be an astonishing interlude. It began innocently enough, as Elinor's brother Alfred came to join them in Paris on the last day of August. He was with his friend and Woodbrooke classmate Spencer, with whom he had toured Spain while the girls were touring the rest of Europe. This was really the conclusion for both parties. The two still had their hiking clothes on, but looked good. They took a metro to their locality and after some delay got their baggage. Genevieve and Elinor waited in the hotel while Alfred and Spencer went to their room to clean up.

Monday the boys came over, and they went as a group to the famous (or infamous) Folies Bergere. Genevieve was pleasantly surprised. Everything was so different from what she expected. The nude figures didn't bother her one bit; they were very lovely.

Next day the boys moved over to join their locale, making communication much easier. They went over to the community hall to dance, and had fun, but found all the French students walking out on them. The French girls were particularly peeved. It seemed that Marion was a magnet for boys, but she refused to dance. One nice French boy sang to them, and did dance with Genevieve, however. Then she got Spencer up and tried to make him jazz it up a bit. It was fun.

But she must have overdone it, because she felt bad and remained in her room most of the next day. She finally went down for supper, and planned to take a walk with Spencer before breakfast the following morning.

Thursday she overslept a bit but finally got downstairs. Spencer was there, and they went for a walk in the park across the street. They talked of Woodbrooke in England, where Alfred and Spencer were students. "I want you to join us there," he said.

"But I couldn't seriously think of going there," she protested. "Though I would like to; I understand it's a fine school. I have my steamship tickets already bought, for my return to America."

"But you can arrange for a later return," he said.

She tried to explain that this simply wasn't feasible. She couldn't desert her friends Elinor and Marion, and she had things to do when she got home. She was bemused by his interest. Spencer was a sweet thing, and she felt toward him as she might toward a child or an old lady—a rather queer mixture. She didn't want to be unkind, but what he asked was extremely impractical. She talked so long that she got back just in time to miss breakfast.

Later she and Marion went with Spencer to town on routine business. After supper they skipped her French lesson and took a bus to the Louvre and walked through the gardens. Then they toured other wonders of Paris. Finally, back "home," she sat on a bench with Spencer—and got the shock of a lifetime.

"Do you know why I'm so anxious for you to come to Woodbrooke?" he asked her.

"I assume that you are really proud of your school, and want to show it off."

He smiled. "That, too, perhaps. But it is far more than that. Genevieve, I love you."

She forced a laugh, thinking she had misheard. "I don't think I understand."

"I love you," he repeated seriously. "Absolutely and completely, ever since we met last week."

"You can't mean that! We hardly know each other."

"I have tested myself in every way and am positive of it. I am in agony about it. I would have preferred more time to tell you, but when I found there was so small a chance of your coming to Woodbrooke, I had to broach this matter now."

She was overwhelmed. "But this—this—"

"Genevieve, I am asking you to marry me. No, don't answer now; think about it, so that you can know your true heart. You can answer me in a few days."

"Maybe that's best," she agreed faintly. She felt as if she had nearly died from shock. She went to bed that night in a terrible whirl.

She was in a turmoil the following days, doing things and attending functions without really absorbing them. She talked with Marion and Elinor, trying to find her way. She did not want to hurt Spencer, but marriage was way too big a step for her to consider at this point. She wasn't able to figure out the situation so that things would be kindly and satisfactory all around. It was a terrible problem.

Friday passed, and Saturday, and Sunday. She still hadn't arrived at any conclusion, and remained "squee hawed" inside. They saw the Eiffel Tower, and much of its grandeur was wasted on her distraction. She had to get this straight!

Monday she talked it over with Elinor. Genevieve simply collapsed and went to pieces. The whole mental and nervous and emotional strain of her relations with Spencer had been too much. "Spencer is so terribly serious every minute," she said. "There just isn't a chance to let go and relax in his company. When I'm not with him, he's still constantly on my mind. I have to do something decisive."

"And that is?"

"I have to end it," Genevieve said. "Maybe in time there could came a day when I would be ready to marry him, but I can't make that decision now. So if it must be yes or no now, it has to be no."

"That does seem best."

She wrote Spencer a note, explaining how terribly hard this was for her, and that it would be impossible for them to continue seeing each other with things as they were. She knew they would not be happy together for one minute in the next two weeks. So it was best to make a clean break, dreadfully hard as that was.

Elinor took the note, and before long returned with his reply. He would take a plane home tomorrow, and would rather not see her to say goodbye. And that was exactly what he did. He was extremely decent about it, which made her feel even worse. She felt awful about everything, but also relieved to have at last arrived at a fair and straightforward understanding. His note said he would write to her from England. In due course he did, a perfect gentleman.

The girls were very supportive, knowing that she had done what she had to do. So was Alfred, on Tuesday. "Alfred was awfully sweet to me," she wrote in her diary. "I think he knows and knows."

Wednesday she cleared up, then went over for Alfred, arranging to meet him for lunch. Then she went down to take a table for them. This became a small adventure: some squirrelly French girls had rolled tubes and were shooting at her with bread spit balls. Lord what pills! She didn't even turn her head, trying to ignore the barrage so as not to give them the satisfaction of seeing her anger.

Then Alfred came, and it stopped. There was something about the presence of a handsome man that stifled such behavior among girls. Alfred was a comfort in several ways, not least among them his nonjudgmental attitude about the way she had separated from his friend Spencer.

On Thursday Alfred met some people, and plans for Friday had to be changed again. What affected Alfred affected Elinor, and what affected Elinor affected Marion and Genevieve. But there were plenty of incidental things to do.

Friday the thirteenth they went to the International Students league with Alfred. She was gradually recovering from the trauma of Spencer and life was returning to normal.

Saturday she and Elinor gabbed at breakfast. She looked out just at one and found Alfred, so decided to go with him the the catacombs. That was an experience! She came out all weak in the knees. Then they went shopping for wine. Alfred bought cherry brandy and she bough Bordeaux. After supper the group of them just strolled around. Paris was like that; it was always interesting.

Sunday September 15 they went to the Pavilion and danced. Alfred danced very well. He said he felt rusty, but he wasn't. Between times they held hands. But that made her uneasy. So she gently broached her concern. "I thought it was just friends with Spencer, but it turned out that he saw it another way."

Alfred smiled tolerantly. "Spencer is my friend and a fine man, but of course a relationship has to be mutual. It is surprising how fond I am of you, yet feel only a gentle love which demands nothing more. It is the love which is content with loving."

"Nothing more," she agreed, relieved. She preferred companionship without any deeper commitment. They were here in Paris to have fun, not to seek life partners.

Next day they went to the vegetarian restaurant, and to Notre Dame. "I am distressed by the open commercialization of the cathedral," Alfred said.

"It is for the tourists," she agreed.

They climbed the tower and dallied there as they gazed out at the landscape. Alfred told her how he was smitten with Joyce M at Woodbrooke, but somehow could never express his sentiment directly to her. "But we did have a marvelous tour of the Clee Hills. I will always remember and treasure that."

Genevieve was happy to agree. Her problem with Spencer had been because he had become too expressive of his feeling. The fact that Alfred was emotionally committed elsewhere made it easier to be with him. They could indeed be "just friends."

The next evening they danced until ten in the evening, then went to his room, where she found herself talking about her father.

"The sweetness of your humor worries me," Alfred said.

"Worries you?" she asked, surprised.

"I don't see how a person can be so equable, so responsive, so thoroughly gentle as you are. What a marvel you are!"

She had to laugh, with a tinge of embarrassment. "I'm just a regular girl."

"With a beautiful nature," he said. "I can see how Spencer fell for you. If I had not met Joyce, I would surely do the same. I am so glad to be with you."

She laughed again. What else could she do?

Thursday she dressed especially nicely, wanting to impress Alfred. He took her hand as they entered the gate, but said nothing. She was disappointed; evidently she had not made the effect she hoped for.

But the next day he told her that she had looked absolutely stunning, perfectly marvelous.

"That's a relief," she said. "I thought you didn't like my outfit, because you didn't comment."

"I'm sorry. Sometimes I don't know what to say, or how to say it. That's my problem with Joyce, and now with you."

That, oddly, provided the necessary perspective.

Then he playfully mussed up her hair. "What are you doing?" she asked.

"I'm making it look as if we have been necking."

She laughed again. "Would it matter if we had been?"

"Probably not. It's a game."

On Saturday they went to see *Marouf* and were much impressed. Whenever they went she and Alfred were linked by arms or hands. Others surely saw them as a couple, and really they were, for these few days. Then he sent her off to bed. "It is not wise to linger on a night so beautiful with a moon so bright," he explained. "You are such a sympathetic person and so responsive."

On Sunday he was working on tarot lessons, and told her about it. "On the first page is the question 'What do you want more than anything else?' I think perhaps harmony with the universe. Or to live a life of beauty." That impressed her; most people would have answered money or power or the love of the perfect companion.

On the twenty second they went to the Mosque for a long dinner. She appreciated everything. That night after reading some of *Sadhana* they sat on a bench with Elinor and Marion. His fingers found her hair and put it in an awful tangle. She would have been annoyed, had she not realized that this was his way of showing affection. He did have trouble doing that, even in a non-serious relationship. Hair could be put back in order; emotions were more devious.

Next day she told him all about their travels before getting together with him. She showed him some dance exercises; then they joined the gang, danced, walked up the avenue and he played with her hair again and finally left her at her doorway.

Finally on Wednesday the 25th it was time for them to leave. Alfred saw them to the station and to the right car. They had to travel to the ship, and return to America, their long delightful excursion drawing to a close. The last few days had been so busy she had neglected making entries in her trip diary, and now it was packed away where she couldn't get at it. That did not diminish the experience.

A few days later Elinor received a letter from Alfred, praising Genevieve. "Genevieve moves in an aura of light. I worship her. I dreamed of her, and in my dream I kissed her. And in my waking thoughts when I look back on our times together I think of her as the most lovable and lively girl that I have ever known, and one who rouses no conflict in me nor makes me uncomfortable in any way. It is a rare girl who is so attuned to my nature and yet so beautiful in her own nature. I thank all the forces of nature that brought us together."

"I'm glad he's in love with someone else," Genevieve said giddily. "Otherwise he might have been more expressive." And more like Spencer, perhaps.

*

Seventeen years later they met again. It was January 1947 in Philadelphia. Genevieve remained friends with Elinor, and Alfred was in the vicinity, so they got together one Wednesday for lunch. Alfred was older, of course, and so was she, but suddenly it was like Paris. They had so much to catch up on! Each of them was married now, and not happily. Genevieve had been engaged for nine years, from 1934 to 1943, then finally found herself in a marriage that was never consummated. In fact she hardly ever saw him. Alfred had two children, but his marriage had become a shell. They had each, with the best intentions, managed to make messes of their lives.

After that they lunched together fairly regularly, getting to know each other again. They were two different people now, having lost the carefree innocence of youth. Experience could be brutal! But the interest that had been sparked in Paris was regenerating. They had things in common. They corresponded, staying in touch.

Then in August they both attended the Sabian conference in Chaplin, Connecticut. That ignited their relationship. The order and detail of the events disappeared in the chaos of emotion. Alfred was carrying water in jugs, and when she made a kind remark, he hugged her, water cans and all. She welcomed it. That was perhaps the point at which their fate was sealed.

One night they swam in the lake, without suits. They danced together. They walked together, hand in hand. "I could not wish for a more wifely relation than you are providing."

That sent a surge of feeling through her. "You . . . my husband," she said, savoring it. In Paris it had been too soon, but now it was perhaps not too late.

They were constantly together, verifying their understanding. By the close of the conference they realized that their existing bonds must be broken, if they could be without unpleasantness. Her relation with her husband Bill seemed shameful and degrading; she was a kept woman, nevertheless unused. His relation with his wife Norma was unfeeling, passive, and worn out. Alfred's children need not suffer if the marriage was broken off gradually. Perhaps they would go to England with Norma, and stay there.

In September he made a qualified proposal of marriage, approximately: "Genevieve, I love you, and you would make me the happiest man in the world if you would be my wife, as soon as it can be arranged, and let me cherish you as long as we both shall live."

She hesitated, yet there was no denying her desire. "Yes."

Thereafter they were together whenever it was possible, but the complexities of their lives and the need for secrecy about their relationship prevented much.

In November they spent the night at Elinor's house, Saturday the 8th in different rooms. She was peacefully sleeping, but woke to find him watching her; he had run up to wake her. Then he climbed into bed with her and held her in his arms. It was sheer bliss. Her unconsummated marriage had denied her sex and children; Alfred clearly desired her physically as well as emotionally. They talked normally; the door was open.

They were together again November 15, but it was harder to be alone together, as others were noticing. Monday she wrote to her husband Bill, stating her lack of hope for the future, and showed it to Alfred. His hope seemed no better; his children both had whooping cough, and his wife was not hospitable.

In December Alfred followed a program that required him to write three words of self criticism each day, at least for the first week. He followed it dutifully, but she wasn't sure that this effort was worthwhile. Of course she did not say that to him.

Their sporadic meetings continued. She learned bits about his home life, especially his objections to the way Norma ran things, his daughter's argumentative attitude, and his son's dirty fingernails. Obviously he was not comfortable there, his annoyances merely the superficial manifestation of the deeper problems.

Sometimes there were slight problems between the two of them. Once Alfred reached around her to light a candle, but she shrank away, fearing the the flame would make her hair catch fire. He suggested that they travel together to a program in New York, but she felt that would be too obvious. She was concerned that he took her reactions to such things as rejections of him, which wasn't intended. Once they got free of their marriages and were able to be together openly, would similar differences develop between them?

In June there was an ugly scene. Alfred was blending bananas in the juicer, and she cautioned him to run it slow at first, so there wouldn't be a splatter. He pointed out that the switch went in progressive order from slow to fast, so it was like asking him to go through Harrisburg before Pittsburgh. That sarcasm hurt her feelings, and she cried. After a while he became aware of it and was sorry, and they made up. But there was a hidden emotional scar. Yet overall the wonder of their love continued to grow. They truly had picked up where they had left off in Paris.

In January the thermostat was too high, and it got up to 85° in the house. She nearly fainted in the bathroom. Alfred turned it down to 70° and things gradually improved. That was scary. Meanwhile Alfred always seemed to be fatigued; his situation was weighing on him.

In May Alfred happened to see a letter to Norma from a friend, saying that she was sorry that Norma felt it necessary to get a divorce. This bowled him over. There was nothing he wanted more than a divorce, and here Norma was thinking similarly. Genevieve agreed that this was actually a positive note, considering the larger picture.

Meanwhile her own divorce was proceeding, and in the course of 1949 she saw the whole of it through. Progress indeed!

Tuesday, May 16, 1950 she threw a birthday party for him, inviting their Sabian friends Stan and Indra C down. Alfred was 41. They did not know it then, but their friends' marriage was in trouble, and would be over within two years.

May 25 the University of Pennsylvania newspaper THE DAILY PENNSYLVANIAN ran a column by one of Alfred's students, Jack Kevorkian. It said in part: "The limitations imposed by my artistic ability make impossible a worthy tribute to an obscure, 20th century Thoreau on the faculty, the most honest and courageous person on campus, Alfred J." One of the things Jack had learned was that there was no absolute truth. Alfred did not make a lot of it, but of course he was pleased.

In June 1950 she asked him to get beer, but he had a problem with that. Not that it was alcoholic, but that beer presented manufacturers a way to make big profits, exploiting the public, in a way that wine did not. She found this difficult to understand. Beer was beer, wine was wine; why did it matter what profit the companies made, so long as the price was satisfactory to the consumer?

Then from June 15 to July 15 they went on a month long excursion sponsored by the Sabian assembly. They traveled separately, but saw each other often. They visited the Grand Canyon, Los Angeles, Reno, Salt Lake City, and Chicago. It was a grand tour. On Sunday July second in Los Angeles they had a small private ceremony in the Brentwood School Garden, reading their respective Blue Slip passages, and Alfred slipped the ring on her finger. After nearly three years of waiting, they wore each other's rings.

Then he was off to Hilltop Farm in Vermont for the summer with his children. They corresponded, of course. Alfred relayed social news that astonished them: their neighbor Natalie F revealed that she had had an affair last winter with Norman W. Her husband Harold knew about it and was distressed.

Then at last summer was over, the children went back to boarding school, and Alfred returned to Philadelphia. September 27 Genevieve bought a little organ whose air was pumped by foot pedals. Now she could accompany him when he played his big accordion. They made music together, literally.

On October 1 Alfred laid new floor tiles for her 44th birthday. She made a big chicken dinner for Thanksgiving, and Alfred enjoyed it without mentioning vegetarianism.

In May 1951 Alfred's Uncle Joseph died, and Alfred was a pallbearer. A week later his nephew Teddy J died of cancer, technically metastatic neuroblastoma.

Then it was summer again, this time just Alfred and his son Piers at Hilltop, and it was quite compatible. He was back in Philadelphia in September.

In May 1952 Norma filed suit for divorce from Alfred. In June they told the children.

Alfred and Piers were at Hilltop in the summer again. Alfred mentioned that he received four letters from Genevieve in one day. They were planning their wedding. Marc Jones agreed to marry them, and Priscilla would give the reception.

It also seemed that the affair between Natalie F and Norman W continued. Both were married—yet what could Alfred and Genevieve say? They had been through it themselves.

And back to Philadelphia in September, after delivering Piers to Goddard College. How glad she would be when these forced separations ended!

The divorce was final Monday September 29. Alfred and Genevieve applied for their marriage license.

The wedding was October 18, with 21 friends attending. It cost a total of $265.25, including banquet, rings, church, and flowers. There were favorable reports on it. It was a wonderful weekend.

How would it have been had they not separated after Paris for those seventeen years? Yet perhaps they had needed those other, largely negative, experiences, in order to fully appreciate the present.

November 23 her new address stamp arrived: *Genevieve D. J.*

There was another separation for a month, as Alfred went to Hilltop, and Piers hatch-hiked down from college to join him. Then Genevieve got there. Piers rode with Stan C to Philadelphia to see Norma, and hitch-hiked back to Hilltop a few days later. He took over the meals.

But Alfred was annoyed that Piers did not do other things, like cleaning, gardening, repairing, wood chopping, or roadwork. Alfred had not asked him to do these things. Genevieve in turn kept silence about both chores and annoyance.

The summer of 1954 was at Hilltop again. This time two college friends, Malcolm S and Robert P, joined Piers, and they logged. They bought a little tractor and power saw.

Alfred somehow got his head caught between two logs, got a bad nose gash, and gushed blood. Lois S patched him up.

Then Genevieve joined them at the end of July. The boys had their routine, working in the forest all day, with Piers returning early to make the meals and wash the dishes. Alfred fussed privately about what they neglected to do. He was even more critical of the other two than of Piers. Genevieve did her best to be noncritical and supportive.

It was not all work and irritation. They went as a group to two movies in Brattleboro that summer, *Gone With the Wind* and *Valley of the Kings*.

She returned to Philadelphia the end of August, and the others wrapped things up in mid September. Alfred delivered the boys to Goddard College, caught up on sleep, then drove down to Philadelphia alone. Another summer and its trials was done.

For her it was the time of menopause, which required some adjustment, but she handled it. Their friends Stan and Indra C broke up, and Stan's new girl was Rusty.

In February Alfred's father died at age 83. He had been "The Mushroom King," making his fortune growing and marketing edible mushrooms. Piers was in the city, working at Norma's office during his winter work term; he came over, and they two went together to the interment ceremony at Birmingham. She knew that Alfred had not been close to his father, but this was a sobering event for him. There were financial repercussions, with additional income now coming to Alfred, and some to his children directly.

In March they had a curious submerged difference. They were stuffing envelopes, and Alfred did it his way, which wasn't quite proper. She did not comment, as he could be excruciatingly sensitive to even implied criticism. She merely did them over correctly, and mailed them. But he must have noticed, and there was a coldness in him for several days thereafter. She regretted that, but wasn't sure how she could have handled it better. Alfred was, in a special sense, a difficult man; he meant well, but there were hard edges in him.

Finally, at the end of the month, he expressed himself about it. She apologized for causing him distress; what else could she do?

Saturday April 2, 1955, Stan and Rusty were married. Alfred and Genevieve were home that day, doing routine work and dozing.

In May Piers wrote that he hoped Alfred could take the truck up to Goddard at term's end. "That's curious," Alfred said. "He hitchhiked from there to Hilltop before. Why the change?"

"He's got a girl," she reminded him.

So Alfred drove to Hilltop by way of Goddard College. Sure enough, Piers introduced him to his girlfriend Carol Ann M, nicknamed for her initials CAM, and she rode with them to Brattleboro where she had a relative. She was a tall dark haired girl, almost as tall as Piers. They stopped at a traveling circus and sideshow in Montpelier, enjoying it. They spent the night on the road, dropped her off in the morning, and drove on to Hilltop. Now Alfred learned that Carol was Piers' fiancée, and they had made sure of physical compatibility. That got them into a considerable discussion, because Piers knew that Alfred had not had a good sexual relationship with Norma. Evidently that was a mistake Piers intended not to make.

Before long Carol had a problem with her job in Brattleboro, and left it. Alfred encouraged her to join them at Hilltop, and she did. Thus Genevieve got to meet her too.

That summer they did routine chores around the house and in the forest, and Piers painted the south side of the house roof, nailing a ladder there so as to be sure of staying on. Carol helped Genevieve with some baking. Alfred did not like the way Piers handled the power saw, leading to some friction between them. Genevieve said nothing; she understood about having differences with Alfred's way of doing things. Piers was protecting his identity.

In August they drove back to Philadelphia, on the way putting Carol on the bus to Keene, New Hampshire. The truck misbehaved, as it often did. Genevieve tried to take it in stride, but she simply didn't get along with the truck, which she called Joseph, after Alfred's crusty uncle. She heard her voice getting sharp as Alfred and Piers struggled with the motor and finally got it going again. Of course she did not say so, but a long trip in Joseph was like a tour of Hell.

Yet naturally she knew that to Alfred, the big city was as bad. He so much preferred the country. They needed to find a compromise.

Normal life resumed. They were in touch on occasion with Piers's friends of the summer of logging. Tall Malcolm now had a tall girlfriend, Nanna B from Sweden, and the couple visited them, and also visited Norma. Piers and Carol visited on their way to Florida for the college winter work term. Teresa also visited. Alfred seemed to find all of them more compatible when the contacts were brief. Alfred even wrote to Goddard college, interested in teaching a course in Sources of European Civilization, but nothing came of it. Meanwhile, Genevieve struggled with her weight, which tended to balloon, and managed to get it down to 146 pounds.

Then in April 1956 Piers was in Philadelphia, having been suspended from college for breaking a midnight regulation. Piers believed that the college was wrong. He played a tape recording of a student protest meeting; it seemed that the entire campus was up in arms, the students against the faculty. Alfred was cautious, not being sufficiently conversant with the situation.

But Alfred did want to help Piers, without opposing the college administration. Instead he implemented something that had been developing for twenty one years. He had sold his precious bassoon in 1935, not for the money but because his friend Anthony had wanted it for playing in the London orchestra. So Alfred put the money in a trust, and now that trust had matured the the money was available. It amounted to about $1000, and with Norma chipping in $500 it was enough to buy a small car for Piers.

What Piers wanted was a Volkswagen Bug. It was a good little German car in the right price range, with excellent reviews. He wanted it for getting and holding a job after he graduated and got married, and more immediately for getting off campus. He and Carol went shopping, and signed up for a 1962 model. Then they returned to college, the week's suspension done.

Three weeks later the car arrived at the dealer—and they had ignored the specifications of the order and had a more expensive car with unwanted options like white-wall tires. Alfred, annoyed by this breach of faith, rejected it and went shopping for an alternative. He found it: a 1955 model for $300 less.

Friday, May 25, they started off, driving the car. It was responsive, reliable, and comfortable. Genevieve certainly found it a pleasure compared to Joseph Truck. They spent the night in Albany, New York, and reached the college on Saturday, delivering the car. Alfred talked with the college president Tim Pitkin, but the man seemed to feel that unless Alfred had complete courses ready, he had nothing to offer. So much for that.

Sunday morning they drove to Burlington, Vermont, picked up Teresa, and took her to the bus station with them, showing off the new car. Then they rode the bus to Albany, and then on to New York City, thence to Philadelphia.

A month later Piers and Carol were married in Florida, having driven the car there, taking along their best man Charlie G and Teresa as Maid of Honor. The car was already serving them in good stead.

Then it was summer again. They drove north, and Piers and Carol drove south from Plainfield. They worked together to clean up Hilltop. At one point the truck had to pull the VW out of a mud hole. The little car was nice, but there were limits.

Alfred and Piers worked on the roof at Welkincroft, the house the W's had built. Alfred grumbled at Piers's lack of initiative in helping; he was amenable, but had to be told everything. Genevieve suspected that Piers was simply avoiding the risk of taking initiatives that were not in accordance with Alfred's wishes.

Hilltop secure, they set off for Europe, a trip they had long planned on. On August 9 they boarded the boat, then had a vacation for a week as it crossed the Atlantic Ocean. They had a nice little stateroom with running water and a forced air inlet. The meals were elaborate, and there were motion pictures to watch. There was even a library. They made the acquaintance of other travelers. It was all very relaxed and nice. Genevieve caught up on a dozen cards to friends. She remembered her prior journey to Europe with her friends, when she had first met Elinor's little brother Alfred.

Just about the time the limited activity and surplus of food became wearing, they arrived in England. Then they spent a busy two weeks meeting people. Alfred was plainly thrilled to be back in England, and she enjoyed it too.

At Winscombe he was reunited with Ella M, who had been such a comfort to him after her daughter Joyce's death. He recovered his British journals, the record he had kept when attending Woodbrooke and Oxford University. They had been miraculously conserved during his absence in Spain and America; he had of course never had the chance to return to England for them during the war. Delighted, he reread about Nancy M's last visit to him at Oxford. He was about to meet her again, twenty three years later. Genevieve was interested too; this was one of the girls he had known and cared about, before Norma.

Nancy arrived on Sunday, September 23, a slender dark haired woman in her early forties, with two children. She was warm and open and nice. Alfred had once considered marrying her, but hadn't done it; to Genevieve it seemed it would not have been a mistake. He might have saved himself immeasurable mischief. Ella was a wonderful person, who had suffered the double shock of losing first her husband, then her eldest daughter, yet remained supportive of others.

They went on to Woodbrooke, a very nice school. "I feel as if I might see Joyce here," Alfred said. "If I just look quickly enough."

They were in Room 39, above the side doorway. It was small but nice. It was clear that Alfred loved being here again, talking with the Warden (the head of the school) and walking through the fields and paths. They shopped in Selly Oak for groceries and washing materials.

This was the place Spencer and Alfred had wanted her to visit or attend, in 1929. Now she was here, no longer twenty three, but she surely would have liked it then. There was the aura of the quiet Quaker community, the universal friendliness and helpfulness, the common interests. This was the place for a young man to fall in love, first with the school, then with a girl in it. What would have happened, if Joyce had lived? Genevieve knew Joyce had been similar to Alfred in respects, such as her fascination with death and her love of the outdoors. She had been even more reticent about her inner feelings than he was, but surely she had them. But would the two of them have made a good marriage? What seemed right within a protected community would not necessarily be right in the harsher outside world.

Alfred was asked to give their informal Sunday talk, on a subject of his choice, falling within the purview of the school." He pondered. "I think I will base it on my own experience, not "This I believe," but "This I know."

So it was. "I know the best thing can happen," he said on Sunday. "There may be watchful waiting; there should be sincere effort not to fail in any small particular; to do all that depends on one's self, and to leave others to work out their obligations in their own way; but no good thing is denied us.

"Nothing is beyond the healing of God. There is healing of the body and a healing of situations and problems. I have come close enough to these things to know that there is no limit. Neither the process, the means or the result may be what we had expected; but the fact of healing is beyond dispute. We cannot ask it to operate in our way, in our time; but we can absolutely depend on God's vigilance for our welfare, and if we care to do so, we can watch and we can count up, in any one day, a number of instances of the invisible hand guiding us.

"A failure is nothing but an opportunity to do better. How are we to learn if we never fail? I know that no failure in my experience has been a dead loss, or has been impossible to turn to good account. My first experience of Woodbrooke, many years ago, was the result of a failure; one of my very best friends was made through a terrible loss; my failure to achieve a certain class standing in final schools at Oxford meant I failed to get a certain job and was hence available for the relief work in Spain just at the time I could be most useful. I know that with other people things may go wrong, and there may be no later redemption of the wrong; but for myself I am sure that I have received the marvelous bounty of God. I know that the best thing can happen and does happen in life. This is not faith, or creed, or hope, or reasoning. It is something I have come to know; and if it is possible for me to know it, it is possible for you, and for everybody."

Genevieve considered that. Their two failed marriages had finally brought them together. That surely wouldn't have happened if Alfred had gotten his job and stayed in England, and of course thousands of children in Spain might have starved to death if he had not been there with the food for them. It might not have been true that Alfred and Norma were the only two Spanish speaking Quakers in the British isles, but they had been the ones able and willing to do the job. Had God put them together for this purpose, then let them separate when it was done? Aspects seemed cruel, but had there been any other way? God might have to make trade-offs, considering the imperfect nature of the tools He had to work with.

The talk was straightforward and honest, and it was well received. But it did take something out of Alfred, and he spent the rest of the day recuperating in their room, except for meals. Meanwhile Genevieve felt low, and had a sore throat. Her nose started running. So she was satisfied to lie low too. She stayed in bed Monday and through Breakfast Tuesday. Alfred, exposed to her cold, fought it off with Vitamin C.

The Bourneville Brotherhood asked Alfred to speak to them the following Sunday, and of course he couldn't say no, though privately he chafed at the way things were piling up. She knew how it was; she had great difficulty saying no.

So life continued through the term; they were constantly busy with one thing or another. But overall it was a rewarding experience, and she was glad to know in this manner what she might have discovered had she agreed to attend Woodbrooke in 1929. Would she have married Spencer and remained in England? But how would it have been to be with Alfred, when the terrible shock of Joyce's death struck him? That was so difficult to understand that perhaps it was best that she had not been there. God's will, perhaps, saving their relationship for a better time.

The term ended in December. They visited Ella at Winscombe the week before Christmas. Joyce's other sister Ruth came on the 17th. Genevieve managed to repack their things to fit in three cases. The next day they took the train to Southampton, where they took the boat to France, and on to Paris. From there they took the train to Barcelona. There friends met them and took them around. Genevieve had a bad cough, and had to rest whenever she could, so was rather out of much of it. At any rate these were Alfred's Spanish friends, strangers to her, so she didn't have to be fully social.

He certainly had many friends in Spain! They traveled all around the country, including a boat trip to Palma in the Mediterranean east of Spain. Genevieve took Vitamin C and hung on. It didn't help that Alfred wasn't supposed to be in Spain; he had been banished in 1940 and was supposed to be thrown in prison if he returned. But he figured that after sixteen years, with government records as slipshod as they were, the government wouldn't notice until someone turned him in, and none of his friends would do that. That turned out to be right, but she was privately nervous the whole time.

They were there three months. Then back to France, and Germany. Now she was back in more familiar territory. Then back to England in May, and the boat to America in early June, 1957. Their nine month European adventure was over.

They stopped in Quebec, Canada, then Montreal. Then the train south to Montpelier Vermont, where Piers and Carol were waiting for them. They took them around to see their friends Herbert L and Norm and Winnie W.

And back to Hilltop Farm in Vermont, gardening and patching up the property. It was a frustrating, seemingly endless chore; there was always more to do than they could accomplish.

Later in June they went to attend Teresa's graduation from the University of Vermont, meeting Norma there. Carol came and drove them to Burlington for the hot sunny ceremony. Of course she didn't say so, but Genevieve felt some nostalgia for the children she had never had, who might have been graduating similarly and setting out on their adult lives.

In July they went to help Carol move out of the Plainfield apartment, Piers having gone to Oklahoma for the continuation of his service in the US Army. Genevieve packed, Alfred carried, and Carol packed the Volkswagen. The worst of it was the refrigerator, which the three of them finally managed to get down the stairs. Then the man in the apartment below helped them get it on the truck.

"I am impressed by how much young people have to learn," Alfred said as they drove away. "It seems that Carol is unequal to the task of moving, depending heavily on us and the neighbors for moral and physical support."

"She did what she could. She needs Piers, the way I need you."

Back at Hilltop they found a nest with three little swallows in the chimney. They tried to get them to where their parents would take care of them, away from the chimney where the heat would be, but they died. It was perhaps inevitable, but sad. The work cleaning and fixing and packing continued.

In September Alfred's right leg gave out, keeping him awake with pain until he reluctantly took an aspirin. He hated to yield to any physical malady.

At last in late November, as it was getting cold, they drove back to Philadelphia. As usual, Joseph misbehaved; the motor ran irregularly, and Alfred had to pause to clean the spark plugs. They would *have* to get another truck!

In December they returned to Hilltop for the winter. It was not easy; the cold found endless ways to get in, no matter how much they worked to seal off the drafts. The snow accumulated deeply, cutting them off from civilization. It was necessary to use snowshoes to go any distance outside.

She felt hemmed in. She could handle it for a few days, or even weeks, but this was eternal.

In March Arthur Z showed up. He was an autistic friend who had aspects of the idiot savant, being highly conversant with archaic languages, but often unable to find his way from one place to another. He would quote Greek verse while hoeing the garden. He was cheerful and would do any task requested, but ate with his mouth open, making loud smacking sounds. His presence tended to become wearing. Yet it was not in them to turn him away. Alfred gave him the Corn Crib to use. That was Alfred's well-appointed separate study, where he stored many of his papers.

On April 3 Genevieve was painting the north wall while Alfred sanded and shellacked the floor. She looked around and realized that the Corn Crib was on fire, and gave the alarm. Alfred rushed up with water and the new sprayer, but it didn't work properly—while the building burned. The Corn Crib fire progressed from the rear to the front, consuming everything while the three of them struggled vainly to stop it. They had to dump snow on it, trying to save at least one filing cabinet.

Arthur had put hot ashes in a box in the back. "I can't blame him for that," Alfred said. "I have done it myself." But Alfred was more careful. Arthur's continued presence made Genevieve nervous. They had lost a cook stove, an encyclopedia, Sabian china and cooking ware, Sabian back lessons, and bedding, table wear, chairs, and sundry books. Suppose a similar fire started in the main house? This was hardly academic; faint scorch marks remained from the fire of fifteen years before. The house was old and dry, and they used oil lamps for light and a wood stove for cooking and heating. A fire could start quickly and be devastating.

Arthur spoke of returning to Philadelphia, and they did not try to dissuade him. It seemed best that he go, and not just because of the fire. His presence put a strain on their lives.

Life continued. They learned that Carol had suffered her second miscarriage after a long siege of problems in Oklahoma. Teresa visited. Alfred applied for a teaching position at Franklin & Marshall College, but they told him to apply again next year.

Then in November Alfred received a telegram from the college: EMERGENCY, NEED SPANISH TEACHER IMMEDIATELY FOR REMAINDER OF YEAR. PLEASE CALL COLLECT IF INTERESTED.

That was it. Alfred accepted, after some complications reaching a telephone, and they set off for Lancaster, Pennsylvania, to interview for the job. Alfred got it, and they returned to Hilltop to close it up.

December 1, 1958, Alfred started. He met three classes, and two more the next day. It was difficult starting in the middle of the school year, while apartment hunting. They simply had to manage. This was certainly a change from the quiet isolation of Hilltop! But it was, as it turned out, the beginning of their new life.

In March 1959 they bought their new house. In April Piers and Carol came. He had finished his service in the Army and they were settling in Florida. They drove a rented truck to Hilltop and brought back a load of Alfred's things, including his treasured water-cooled motor cycle. Teresa visited, too.

March 12 Alfred's Aunt Louisa died. He had not had a good relationship with her, but it was another signal of the old order passing.

They settled in, but it wasn't perfect. Alfred wrapped up his classes in May, but between that and other business he was constantly busy and had no sense of free time, and got no books read. Genevieve was having trouble with glands on the left side. Alfred, amazingly, failed the driver's test. She wasn't sure how he managed to do that, but he took it again a few days later and passed with no trouble.

In June they returned to Hilltop. They saw few apples, but there was rhubarb with immense flowers, asparagus, flowering strawberries, and flourishing hedge roses.

Genevieve was delighted that the chickadee recognized her and came to her hand without hesitation. She saw a rabbit around the house, and once a fox came by. She loved wild life of all kinds, and hated to see any creature suffer. She fed any creatures that seemed to be in need. Alfred was amused once when she found mice in the house and fed them too.

In August they went back to Lancaster, then returned to Hilltop. In September classes resumed, easier for Alfred to handle now that he was starting at the beginning of the school year, and had some students continuing from the prior year.

In October he developed a problem in his right lower jaw. He was driven to take aspirin, an extreme step for him, and finally to call the dentist. The dentist couldn't tell which tooth it was, so didn't touch it.

In December the term finished, which was just as well. Alfred certainly knew Spanish, but felt increasing bewilderment at student inabilities. "They don't see what they are reading, they don't hear what they are hearing, they don't repeat what they hear, and nothing sticks in mind," he said. But of course that was true of all students in all subjects in all years, as most teachers would agree. Somehow civilization survived.

The year 1960 was routine, with teaching in winter, Hilltop in summer. But also teaching six weeks of summer class. The class was small and seemed cooperative, but it kept them busy. It squeezed out seeing movies, their reading together, and work on the house. It was nice to have a good income, but it was at the expense of their free time. For her, the housework was time consuming, and she was unable to keep it the way she would like. It was, they agreed, like being weighted down with fine garments.

They bought a new car, a Ford Anglia, making them a three car family. It felt like wicked affluence.

In 1961 Teresa joined them at Hilltop, and helped Alfred to clear out brush to make Glebe Mountain to the north more visible. She had had a job in California, but had gotten pregnant out of wedlock and had to depart. There was really nothing to do but take her in, as Norma was not in a position to do it. The situation was as difficult for Teresa as it was for Alfred, because the two of them had never gotten along well. Genevieve remembered the saying "Home is where, when you have to go there, they have to take you in."

There was political friction. Teresa objected to Alfred's criticism of United States policy toward Cuba, which he found hard to deal with. Actually when Piers visited he took a position similar to Teresa's, an oddity because the two had never gotten along well. They felt that Cuba was a Communist dictatorship; Alfred felt it was a people's republic. Genevieve stayed well out of it. She knew that Communist Russia had been the main source of supplies for those who had tried to defend Spain from General Franco's conquest, and the subsequent Franco government was no friend of Alfred's. Cuba seemed to be an echo of that, only the other side had won.

Alfred felt that Teresa's actions were those of a child. She washed the dishes and made the salad, but didn't volunteer otherwise. Genevieve wondered whether the strife between them mirrored that between Alfred and Norma in the old days. The two of them were simply moving in different channels, neither really understanding the nature of the other.

In August Teresa said they ought to consider returning to live in England. Genevieve said she wouldn't mind; she had liked England. Alfred considered it, intrigued himself. But in the end it was too complicated to embrace at this time.

Norma came early in November to see whether Teresa needed help, as it was near her time. November 7 the doctor checked her and found she was okay. Then she woke in the night and said it was time.

They took her to the hospital, and in the wee hours of Tuesday the 8th she delivered an eight pound ten ounce boy. Genevieve offered to take and keep the baby and raise it as a member of the family, but got nowhere; neither Teresa nor other members of the family wanted that. Alfred was carefully neutral; he wouldn't oppose what Genevieve wanted, but she doubted he really wanted to raise another child.

Genevieve phoned Norma and "Aunt" Caroline, and Norma said she would come right over. She stayed overnight with Alfred and Genevieve, while Teresa remained in the hospital until Saturday. Teresa's friend Sylvia came over, and Norma and Sylvia took the baby from the hospital; Teresa never saw it. Norma took the baby to a good family in Alaska. She didn't like to fly, but it was the only way. Thus, cooperatively, they took care of Teresa and her baby.

Teresa settled in again, somewhat mellowed. In January Genevieve got another cold and felt low, but carried on. Teresa helped, and later got a part-time job. In May she moved out, having been with them almost a year. That gave them the top floor for themselves, with lots of space.

It seemed that things would settle down. That was not to be the case. In Florida, Carol lost her third baby, and Piers lost his job. Genevieve had never had a baby to lose, but she felt for them.

They returned to Hilltop for the summer, then in July attended a Sabian function in Chaplin, Connecticut. They spent the night in a motel at Brattleboro on the way there. There was a bit of a problem with Alfred, because he did not seem to understand why she did not want to change clothing with the lights on and window open, so that anyone could see in. She insisted that the curtains be drawn, or the lights turned off. That bewildered him, then put him in a bad mood. She regretted that, but simply could not take the risk.

Back at Hilltop later in the month, they pondered their future. Alfred did not want to teach more than another year; the money was good, but he chafed because of the lack of time left over to do things they valued. Meanwhile, Genevieve's right knee was troubling her, and Alfred's upper left arm and the left side of his neck. "These are black days," she said, circling them on the calendar.

In two days her back felt better but her knee remained stiff. She baked a quick corn cake, which they ate for a late lunch. But Alfred's arm problem remained. This was the unpleasant part of growing older; they were now in their fifties.

In the fall they returned to Lancaster. Nocturnal anonymous phone calls kept coming in, and they had to disconnect the incoming aspect of the phone for a week. That was one of the liabilities of teaching: the students were juveniles, with juvenile values.

Alfred continued to think about New England, preferring the forest to this academic life. But Genevieve was wary of expending all their resources just to survive, as tended to be the case there. She preferred civilization. She would never say so, of course, but she could understand Norma's reluctance to remain at Hilltop. But spending all their savings to buy a house in a New England town would leave them dangerously exposed, financially.

The indecision itself was wearing. Alfred received a promotion to associate professor, which meant more prestige and more pay, but he wasn't interested. "The world is sick," he said, "and I am in search of an island of sanity."

In the summer of 1963 they bought a nice house in Chaplin, Connecticut, where Sabian friends lived, and celebrated their 34th anniversary of first coming to know each other. Alfred looked it up in his Journal for 1929, and spent an afternoon in another world, while Genevieve baked. "I saw more of Joyce that summer than I remembered," he said.

Joyce was dead for 34 years, but still he longed for her. Genevieve couldn't be jealous of a dead woman, but it made her a trifle uneasy. How long should it take to let lost love go?

Back to Lancaster in mid September. Alfred definitely wanted this to be the last year of teaching.

October first Alfred's associate at Franklin & Marshall, George E, borrowed their truck, and worked with Teresa to haul away junk. On the twenty second they had dessert at George's to celebrate Teresa's twenty eighth birthday. And in January they learned that George and Teresa were dating. George was married, but it seemed that didn't stop them. Alfred was not at all pleased.

Genevieve was more accepting. She know that marriages could fail, as both hers and Alfred's had. George was evidently unsatisfied with his. Still, it seemed that George was endowing Teresa with more qualities than she actually had, including the wish to be the mother of a family. Both George and his wife Mary-Louise talked with Genevieve. Her sympathy was with Mary-Louise, yet it did require two to maintain a marriage, and it seemed that George was no longer interested in doing so.

"We can't endow George and Teresa with maturity," Alfred said. "We just hope to be able to give them some underpinnings, some sustainment, so that wisdom can prevail."

Would it? George made good money, yet was chronically in debt; where was the wisdom in that background? It seemed a shame that such a brilliant man could allow himself to be destroyed by his sexual appetite for younger flesh.

It continued for several days. Mary-Louise spent an afternoon with Genevieve, talking it out. Genevieve tried to be supportive, but it looked bad. George seemed to be building Mary-Louise up in order to abandon her. Alfred was convinced that if they allowed George enough time, he would come to a clearer vision. Genevieve certainly hoped so, but her uneasiness about the situation made her feel low.

Her doubts turned out to be well founded. George came and told them that he planned to divorce Mary-Louise and become their son in law. This was hardly welcome news, but there was nothing they could do about it. Even Norma phoned about it, her sentiments echoing theirs. Was there irony in that?

Teresa visited, having sent George a letter she now did not want him to receive. The stress of the situation continued, and Genevieve felt low. Then she learned that her metabolism test showed low. She started taking thyroid pills, and they helped. She also rested, and that helped her sore knee. Some days she felt better, but then she would relapse.

The college administration was concerned too, as this reflected badly on it. They might have to take action against George for moral turpitude. So Alfred and Genevieve wrote to Teresa, as gently as they could, calling her attention to the likelihood that she would be dragged into whatever evolved. She was bound to lose her good name, and become known as the Other Woman in a local scandal.

Finally they acted, reluctantly. They brought George and Teresa in and informed them that they, Alfred and Genevieve, had to keep themselves out of it as much as possible, because they did not want to contribute in any way to the breakup of a marriage, an affair between a married man and a woman, a woman keeping company with a man who was not in a position to marry her, a professor risking his job and professional standing because of his extra-marital associations, the illusion that a man with a good salary was unable to keep out of debt while maintaining one family could do any better maintaining two families, or the willingness of a woman to try to get herself a man by wrecking a family including small children.

They weren't ready to hear it. Was new love ever ready to heed the complications of its realization?

Meanwhile Alfred completed the term and retired with relief from teaching. Now they were free to do what they wanted. In the summer they checked Hilltop and went several times to Chaplin, Connecticut, moving their things to their house there, which they named Woodsedge. Fortunately they were able to sell their Lancaster house for a fair price, so their finances were not strained.

They spent the summer at Hilltop, off and on, returning often to Woodsedge. Teresa wrote that she and George had set a wedding date, and they did marry. They visited, then moved to Michigan. Alfred banged his left hand on the wheelbarrow, and his fingers would no longer close or grasp properly. Genevieve was mixed; some days she felt far from well.

In 1966 Piers visited. He was now back to writing full time, and had sold a novel.

In 1967 both Teresa and Carol were pregnant. Alfred was concerned that they would not take proper care, but neither Piers nor Teresa would heed his advice. Genevieve realized that both must have been turned off by Alfred's attitude in the past. He tended to lecture, believing that his way was the only way. It was perhaps the fate of most parents, especially those involved in fractured marriages. He could not accept that they had done their own research and formed their own coping strategies.

In August Teresa gave birth to Patrick. Two months later Carol gave birth to Penelope. The first legitimate grandchildren. Meanwhile Piers's science fiction stories were appearing in print, and Alfred read them. He found his translation of *Nazarin*, by the Spanish author Benito Perez Galdós, together with the detailed critique by Stan C, and sent it on to Piers for possible adaptation. Alfred had tried to get it published, but it was rejected by American publishers. Piers wasn't sure it would be worthwhile for contemporary readers. Genevieve had seen Stan's critique, which was surely accurate, and suspected the doubt was sensible. Fiction had changed, and standards differed.

In 1968 her daughter Ruth wrote that Ella M was in severe decline. That bothered Alfred; Ella had been his best friend overseas, really a mother figure. She died November 7, 1968.

He received a copy of Piers' second published novel *Omnivore*, but it would be several years before he read it. He was, however, pleased by Piers' evident success as a writer, and found Piers' short stories well done.

Genevieve, by dint of serious dieting, got her weight down to 130 pounds. She intended to keep it there.

In January 1969 they both ran fevers with flu-like symptoms. How readily illness could make life unpleasant!

In February Stuart Dauchy made an offer for Hilltop: $30 per acre, and the assessed price for the house. That made Alfred ponder. He did not like to give Hilltop up, as it had been a significant part of his life for more than a quarter century. "But we are doing it no good now," he said. Indeed their attention to it had diminished. They decided to accept.

Then they had to go there to pack and take their belongings. This brought Alfred much nostalgia, and of course Genevieve had shared it for fifteen years. She had her own memories.

Late in the year Piers' big novel *Macroscope* was published, with a credit to Alfred for his help with the astrology. Alfred lacked reading time, but did sample it, and was impressed. Piers really was making it as a writer, with material that reflected things he had learned in life. He had rejected astrology as a science, yet treated it as such here, having researched it competently.

In May the local newspaper published an article on them, titled CHAPLIN MAN GROWS OWN FOOD, AVOIDS 'POISONS'. Alfred was bemused by the quotes around "poisons." What did they think weed and insect killers were?

Alfred also spoke messages in the Friends' Meetings now, and there were responses to his thoughts. He was becoming part of the community. But he was getting restless for change. She suggested that they plan to move when he reached age sixty five, in 1974. Perhaps to a retirement community.

They visited a friend at Somers Point, New Jersey, to see what that kind of retirement was like. They were impressed, and decided to buy a house there. But when they were ready, the man added $1,500 to the price. That was a bombshell. He thought he had told them before. He hadn't. Maybe it was a ploy, to state a lower price, then try for a higher one once the fish was hooked. They would not stand for that. Disappointed, they turned it down. Genevieve was depressed, but just kept working, trying to put it behind her. She suspected that Alfred had a visceral resistance to an urban existence.

There was something that was bothering Alfred, but she couldn't quite fathom it, as he never spoke of it. They would do work in the days, then at 6:30 she would turn on the TV news so they could watch it during supper. Then they tended to watch programs that followed, relaxing. Except that he didn't necessarily relax. Sometimes he muttered about the distraction, but wasn't more specific.

Only gradually did she fathom it, perhaps. Alfred wasn't really used to TV. It was outside his personal framework. So he watched it, interested, then resented the time it had distracted him. It was addictive in its fashion, and like addiction, it rewarded its viewers at the moment while leaving them ultimately unfulfilled. She might have turned it off after the news, had she caught on earlier. It would have helped if he had asked her to, but he tended not to ask for things; he expected others to see them and act. That could be frustrating to handle, but it wasn't in her to be openly critical.

Alfred also had difficulty saying no to requests for help by neighbors, and increasing amounts of his time were taken doing neighborly things. He didn't mind doing them individually, but in the aggregate they were squeezing out things he might have been doing for himself. One thing that suffered was reading. A complication of that was that when he did find time for it, it tended to make him sleepy.

Two more grandchildren were born: Erin to Teresa, and Cheryl to Carol. Genevieve knew Alfred was making an effort to keep his mouth shut, offering no further advice on child nutrition. He didn't understand why it was rejected. Yet the babies seemed healthy enough as they were. Meanwhile George had been dismissed from his college position, and that complicated their lives. He seemed to be unable to maintain a position for any length of time. It wasn't clear what happened, but it surely related to his wanderlust, evident in more ways than changing wives.

The routine continued, comfortable enough, but also somewhat dull. Genevieve's health was not perfect, and at times she found herself unaccountably fatigued. In the summer of 1971 she alternated between feeling draggy and feeling peppy; at one point she worried that her blood pressure was up, perhaps accounting for the way she felt heady and with her eyes burning. During the night aches developed. Finally the doctor changed her medication, and that seemed to help. It was no fun growing old; she was 65.

In June they visited Friends House at Sandy Springs, Maryland on behalf of a friend, and were impressed by that retirement community. A George School classmate of Alfred's was assistant Director; the Manager had worked in Vermont as a dairy tester, and a woman on the staff was named Guinevere, which struck Genevieve. The apartments were of medium size and fully equipped, with one door to the corridor and one to the lawn, so each person had separate access. The immediate area was rural, which pleased Alfred.

So they applied to join it, not expecting much, as there was a fair sized waiting list. They were given to understand that it was likely to to be one and a half to two years before something was available. But suddenly, three months later, they received a letter saying they were now third on the waiting list of couples, and there might be a vacancy within months. This was exciting news, though it meant they would have to scramble to get themselves sorted and moved. They judged that it would require four to six months of hard work. But if it relieved Genevieve of housework and Alfred of neighborly chores, it should be worth it.

Alfred made up a presentation for the Ministry & Counsel, tracing the sequence of events and asking to be relieved of all Meeting responsibilities so that they could focus exclusively on getting ready to go. They regretted having to take this step, but it seemed necessary.

In November Teresa phoned: their third child, Caroline, had been born on the 24th. She was an unintentional baby, as Teresa herself had been; they hadn't wanted another at this complicated time. That was something Alfred could readily understand, quite apart from his differences with Teresa.

A neighbor was convinced that her window was leaking cold air. Alfred tried to explain that the indoor air was being cooled by the frosty window and flowing down, but she refused to understand. Genevieve wondered whether that was a fair analogy of the problems of understanding and communication most people had. If a draft had to signal a leak, an alternate explanation was not welcome.

Lois S died. That was sad. Marshall S, desiring her at the outset of their acquaintance, had raped her, and she had become pregnant and in the end saw no alternative but to marry him. It was not a life she had chosen or desired, but she had carried through, a thwarted woman. Life had never given her proper satisfaction. That might be another analogy of existence for so many, hustled by circumstance into unkind situations.

Alfred's lingering toothache got worse, and at last the dentist took the tooth out. For most folk that would be routine; for Alfred it was an admission of failure. His teeth should have been perfect, considering the care he gave them.

In January they finally completed their packing and drove south to Sandy Springs. Genevieve hoped they would at last be able to relax for a while. Actually it wasn't a bad drive. Genevieve had a floating black spot in her left eye during the trip. But she wasn't jittery while driving, and not frayed on arrival.

The community was compatible. There were 120 residents, a quarter of them Quakers, and folk seemed friendly and helpful. They had no trouble fitting in.

Of course they still traveled to other places, such as Chaplin; they were not out of touch. In fact in the year 1972 they made nine or ten trips, ferrying belongings from Chaplin. Alfred also finally read Piers' 1968 novel *Omnivore*, finding its ideas and expression interesting, and noted the way Piers's forest experience showed in the novel. It had a "third kingdom" theme, featuring advanced fungus/mushroom forms, perhaps reflecting the earlier background of his grandfather "The Mushroom King."

Their several minor health complaints continued. Alfred had trouble with what the doctor called ulcerative colitis, a condition without known cause or treatment. She had trouble with her knees, occasional unpleasant colds, and once she burst into a cold sweat, knew she was going to be sick, and felt near to fainting. Apparently that was because of her thyroid imbalance; she was long past the age for hot flashes. But generally their health was satisfactory.

In August they got a Fiat station wagon. Some reviews of that make were negative, saying that it would fall apart, but it served them well enough for a number of years. Probably cars, like people, did well when treated well, regardless of their origins.

As the year turned to 1973 Alfred pondered the meaning of it all. He was concerned with meaning, interpreting events as aspects of some larger whole whose significance was difficult to grasp. "I consider the 'Why' of 1929," he said. "Why did I meet you the year I lost Joyce. Ella told me she had had a miscarriage midway between Joyce and Ruth, and then I showed up, born about that time, and she treated me like a son. I think sometimes of writing an autobiography for the five little ones, my grandchildren, so that they will know what happened. I might title it 'A Privileged Life,' because of all the travail I have been spared. It would be my way of marshaling my thoughts and trying to piece things together."

That, she thought, depended on how he saw it. By her definition he had had a fair amount of travail, including the loss of the love of his youth, a difficult early marriage, and lifelong depression.

In March, 1973, they drove to Arizona to see their friends Wes and Clara H. They saw a huge copper mine, and impressive canyons. It was a six day drive there, and six days back, but they didn't have to hurry.

Back at Sandy Springs there was a small incident. Apple rings were served at supper. They were bright red. "That's red dye #2," Alfred said. "Not healthy to eat." Indeed he did not eat his. But she, satisfied that any negative effect was bound to be very small, ate hers; she did like apple rings. Alfred wasn't pleased, yet she did have the right to choose her own risks.

That summer Alfred bought and read Piers' juvenile novel *Race Against Time*. He was becoming almost a regular reader of his son's books.

In August they went to Chicago for the Sabian Conference, always an important event. They also visited "Aunt" Caroline, Alfred's stepmother, who showed them the new Quaker retirement center then being built, Kendal at Longwood. It would cost a $25,000 initial deposit, plus $660 monthly.

In early November they drove to Florida, meeting a number of folk there, and also the grandchildren Penny and Cheryl, now aged six and three. They accepted him immediately, tugging him around, as he put it, like a rag doll. He obviously liked it, but also was frustrated by the way it prevented serious discussion. He read Piers' story "In the Barn," which was a shocker: an ordinary day in a cow barn, except that the cows here were human. That one detail entirely changed its nature.

Life continued, generally satisfactory. But Alfred's mind was also on the past. "I sometimes think of this place as I thought of Woodbrooke: where one could be happy, with no thought of leaving. I often think of Joyce, glimpses of her. But when I meet her, what shall I be able to say? In meeting I let my thoughts dwell on her. What did I talk of with her? I remember nothing. I used to read poetry to her when I could, including John Gourd Fletcher's *Irradiations*. She liked Shaw. I just don't remember any conversation. What then about the future?"

Genevieve didn't know. Joyce had become part of his being. He would always wonder how it would have been, had she lived. Yet Joyce's sister Nancy was said to resemble her strongly, at least in appearance, and she had gone her own way despite associating closely with Alfred for three years.

They visited Genevieve's sister Tem for her wedding anniversary. Alfred was disturbed because Tem did not live a healthy life, and coddled her dog Oscar mercilessly.

He wasn't completely satisfied with retirement community life either. "I think one of the dangers of living with old people is reduction to inconsequence," he remarked. "Matters of issue or import are not current, & full attention is given to trifles of weather, clouds, sun. Without the challenge of great issues, will not mental powers diminish?"

She couldn't say that wasn't the case. Yet most of the residents were here consciously for the end of their lives, so maybe it didn't make a real difference.

One day he remembered bicycles. "As a child I rode all over, and to school and high school, and to Valley Forge. Not at George School or Dartmouth. At Woodbrooke I cycled to surrounding Meetings, and I rode in to symphony rehearsals. At Oxford I cycled everywhere, and for trips as far as Stratford. At Charlbury I cycled daily to visit Norma when she was having Piers, and to the station to catch trains. What happened to these cycles afterward? I never remember disposing of one."

In March 1975 there was something wrong with her vision. "My eyes aren't right," she said.

"It's a long time since they've been exposed to natural light."

"Oh, pooh! Light is light."

That was about all there was to it, but it was in its fashion an argument, and both of them were depressed because of it.

In October he wrote a Family letter to be sent to the children and others, among other things discussing Tem's refusal to live a healthy life. Genevieve prevailed on him not to send it.

Tem's health got worse. "We have to help her," Genevieve said. They did a tarot reading on the matter, and concluded that this was best. They drove to Reading and moved in with Tem, and Genevieve assumed the running of her house. It was hardly the best situation, but there was really nothing else to do.

Alfred took over the basement, his domain, and they read lessons in their attic room. The main house remained Tem's.

Genevieve had to admit that her sister was a health disaster. But their own health was not ideal. Alfred had a problem with his colitis and his left eye, and Genevieve had sniffles, cough, fever, and a test showed her heart to be in poor shape. They had a long talk with Stan and Rusty, and Rusty read the tarot cards for them. The indication was that they had done their service and it was time to resume their own type of living. The stress was not good for Genevieve's heart. Yet how could she desert her sister? So they remained, and the stress continued.

They did make occasional trips elsewhere, and that helped relieve the tension. They decided to buy a house in the neighborhood, so that they could have their own base. They found a suitable one in Reading, and completed the purchase on Friday, June 4, 1976. It would take time to move everything in, but at least it was their own.

They went regularly to help Tem, helping her with chores like laundry and shopping, and the strain was less. Still, Genevieve had lost her diet and gained weight.

Then in August Alfred had a bad accident. He was up on a ladder, sawing off an intruding branch, but the butt hung up. He dislodged it, and it bucked into his face, butting a bloody gash under his chin and knocking out the anchor tooth for his denture. Genevieve was appalled, but took care of him and he came through all right. But after that he was unable to chew, and his food had to be liquefied in the blender. He had some bad nights from the discomfort.

Tem complained about a child crying next door. But there was no child. Genevieve hardly cared to ponder what that signaled.

In March 1977 Teresa found her life destroyed. George had found another woman, and now Teresa was the wife being frozen out. She was outraged that it should happen to her. Others, including the members of the Meeting, were fooled by George, just as she had been when she was the other woman.

They traveled to Florida in early April to visit friends and relatives, Teresa accompanying them. This was a way for her to escape her situation for a while. Piers and Carol were getting ready to move to Citrus County, about 80 miles to the north, where they had bought forest property.

In May they went to Alfred's 50th George School class reunion. One of those there was Marion G with her husband. She had been Alfred's girlfriend in high school. It seemed she had married her George School roommate's Swedish brother. Alfred had "fussed" that roommate, Linnea. Small world!

In September Tem had another stroke and was in the hospital. She had been hallucinating. Genevieve had seen her declining, and had known it would come to this, but it was painful.

On September 14 Tem died. Genevieve was relieved, because there really had been little hope and her state had been so bad.

"The reason for our being in this area is now gone," Alfred said.

It was true. But where were they to go? So they remained where they were.

In March 1978 Norma phoned that Teresa's first son Peter, who had been placed with a family in Alaska, was dead. It was listed as a shooting accident, but it was suicide. He had had a drug involvement, and was distraught over the loss of a girlfriend. He was sixteen.

In August Alfred was curious whether he had belonged to the Chamber Music Society all through his years at Oxford, as he didn't remember. He became fascinated with the year 1932, with its richness of experience. That was the year he was seeing Nancy M, whom they had met in 1956. But there were many other contacts. "The feel of it is powerful," he said. "There were times when I was aware of the presence of Joyce, who has been a living presence for me all through my life. I discovered her birthday: December 16, 1908. So she was exactly five months older than I was."

Genevieve made affirmative noises. Death seemed to cut a person off from evil, leaving only the good in memories. Alfred had not had the chance to get to know Joyce well enough to discover her negatives, so she was forever enshrined as his ideal. No living person could match that.

But Nancy remained alive. That made her qualitatively different from Joyce. Had Joyce lived, she might have looked like Nancy, but had a darker outlook on life. She had been much aware of death, just as Alfred was. Nancy was a brighter spirit. And, it seemed, no longer interested in Alfred. That made a difference.

So she encouraged Alfred to talk about it. "I did meet Nancy and her children," she reminded him. "What was your relationship with her?"

He was glad to oblige. "At first I knew her merely as Joyce's little sister, but even then the resemblance was strong enough to make me dream of her on occasion. Her sister Ruth came to attend Woodbrooke, so I saw more of her, but Nancy was really the one in my private fancy. The summer of 1932 I stopped by to see her in Switzerland, as I was on my way to Spain. She was wonderful! I could not imagine a more perfect companion." He paused. "Of course I wasn't with you then."

"I was not in the picture," she agreed.

"But somehow it never quite came to marriage. Then I met Norma, and Nancy faded out of the picture." He shook his head. "Now I have to wonder how it would have been had I stayed with Nancy. I would surely have been better off, because Norma was a disaster. Neither of us intended that way, but it was."

"Maybe you held back, because Nancy wasn't Joyce."

"I think that was the case," he agreed. "If Joyce had remained in my world, if our lives had grown gradually together, never to know separation, if my love had increased with my age and experience till it was in reality what it must have become, a love of tremendous power to draw her to me and me to her, yet leaving each free; if that love had culminated and life with it, what might not have been the result! She would have remade me, and I should have been whole and worthy of her."

Genevieve could hardly be sure of that. Real life seldom rose to the level of dream life. But dreams served as inspiration, and were worthwhile in their own right.

"At Woodbrooke I suppressed the grief," he said. "And ever since, determined not to think of her as gone, always hoping to meet her again; the Oxford exams were pressing. I could afford no time for grief. But now it has crept up on me."

"After almost fifty years," she said. "Maybe it is time to let it flow."

"I appreciate your understanding."

Genevieve wasn't sure she understood it, but she wanted to. This was a formerly suppressed part of Alfred's makeup. Whatever Joyce was to him should be explored and expiated.

He talked about it that day and the next. Then the third day he had another idea, that she appreciated. He read to her his notes on their first meetings in September, 1929.

"Actually we met before then, in July," she reminded him. "In Dresden."

"Dresden," he agreed. "I remember. Yet there is no mention of you at that time in my journal."

"There is in mine," she said. "I kept a trip diary of my summer in Europe. You were merely Elinor's little brother."

"So I was," he agreed. "Yet it seems that at that time you were merely one of Elinor's friends. My mind was on Joyce. All else was incidental."

"It was an incidental time."

"But then we met again, in September."

"The last day of August. You and Spencer arrived from Spain."

"And Spencer fell in love with you!"

"I wasn't ready for it. I'm glad he found happiness elsewhere."

"He suddenly decided to fly to England. I knew nothing. He was excited and incapable of rationality. Then on September 10 I learned that you had dismissed him with a note."

"I hated to do it. He was so gentle, and I did like him, but not in the way he liked me."

"Discovering you was total reality for him, greater than family or religion; losing you was shattering."

"I don't think it would have worked out between us. He was so intense, and I wasn't ready to leave America."

"That left me alone. I wrote in my journal that I must be all the more attentive to Elinor and you."

She made a mock pout. "And I thought you liked me."

"I did." He paged through the volume of his journal. "On September 16 I wrote of the prior day 'I spent most of the time with Guinevere.'" He looked up. "I misspelled your name!"

"How can I ever forgive you?"

He resumed. ". . . hand in hand all the way. It is surprising how fond I can be of her & how I can walk hand in hand with her and yet feel only a gentle love which appreciates & which grows more tender without demanding anything & without appealing to the body. It is the love which is content with loving.'"

"That was so sweet."

"And then you wore that stunning dress, and I couldn't think of anything to say, and you thought that meant I didn't like it."

"So you mussed up my hair."

"Then I wrote 'She draws the utmost in tenderness from me; still I love her only for her own sake, not for mine.'"

"You put me on a pedestal!"

"Where you remain today."

"You're incorrigible." She kissed him. "If only we could be in Paris again, as young as we were then, knowing what we know now."

He shook his head. "If I had known all that, then, I think I would have flown to England with Spencer and rushed to The Broads to intercept Joyce before she drank polluted water."

"So even if we could have been, we couldn't have been," she said sadly. "Fate is merciless." But it cheered her to know that she had her place in his fond memories.

Alfred continued reading his journal, sharing news of Joyce, through the middle of September. There were many details it seemed he had largely forgotten, but that were restored by the old entries. Genevieve hadn't kept a diary, apart from that one summer, and she hadn't even completed that, evidently getting too caught up in events to record them. How would she have reacted to old events, if she had kept them as rigorously as Alfred had? It was impossible to know.

September 30, 1978 they celebrated her 72$^{nd}$ birthday with driving around and shopping. Life was routine, but good, though her blood pressure was too high.

Joyce had not actually faded from Alfred's life. "When I walk, I often have her with me," he said. "We stride side by side, comfortable."

Genevieve's health and strength were not sufficient to accompany him on his long walks. She regretted that. But perhaps it was time to himself that he needed, and Joyce was certainly a worthy companion.

In June, 1979, Alfred had a private breakthrough. "The picture came to me of sighting Joyce at a distance and running, both of us running, and meeting with a warm hug in which I could feel her tousled hair against my cheek. I have never in imagination been able to touch her before, and was always fearful of any meeting in which I might be unable to venture to explain my life-long attachment to her. But now all that is unnecessary, all is understood, nothing need be explained. We are friends, if not for 300 years, at least for 50 years and more to come."

Genevieve wanted Alfred to work out his buried feelings, but this was becoming emotionally strenuous. Was she in competition with a dead girl? A living old woman could not match a vibrant girl. Reality never had the delight of fond imagination.

In February Genevieve's last contemporary Amy died. In March Marc Edmund Jones died. The old order was passing.

Alfred remembered other girls of the past. There had been Joyce's friend Connie N, an extraordinary person, and Molly M whom he had met in Sevilla and often danced with, Ricia J, and of course Ruth and Nancy M, and finally Norma S.

"But I was also highly impressed with you," he reminded her. "And a bit in love with you."

"I'm glad I was in the picture."

"What difference might it have made, if I had been able to tell you before you left Paris that I was in love with you?"

"It was important to me to have the experience of being able to share thoughts, and talk equally with a man. I still had a boy 'back home' on my mind, just as you had Joyce." She knew that wasn't a direct answer, but what was there to say about what had not and could not have happened?

"With Nancy, if I could have seen her more often, if she had been physically present at Oxford, could she have stepped in, in front of Norma? I like the thought."

"It might have been better," Genevieve agreed.

Alfred wrote to Nancy, and got an answer, with news of her family and the region. He also had a brief, nice letter from Norma, saying that no marriage could be a total loss, and that she had gained.

He transcribed and copied out his entry of June 9, 1929, when he had had all day hiking with Joyce. But the emotion of it broke him up, and Genevieve had to take over the reading while he gradually regained control. Certainly it was the high point of his association with Joyce, and Genevieve appreciated its emotional power. It was the best he would ever have of his young love. Within four months she was dead.

Alfred's reliving of his past experience continued through 1980. He took daily walks with the ghost of Joyce, to whom he could speak in a manner he had not been able to when she was alive. Genevieve encouraged him to share it with her. It was important to him, so it was important to her. "I know it was a shock to have your relationship with her cut off so abruptly, when you had every expectation it would continue," she said.

"Yes, it was like the sudden collapse overnight of the Spanish relief work we had built up," he said.

They walked to the post office to mail a birthday card to Piers's Carol, who was 43. "She may very well pass for forty three, in the dark with a light behind her," Piers wrote teasingly in his monthly Family letter, borrowing from Gilbert & Sullivan. Their children were now thirteen and ten.

At night in bed, Alfred turned to her. "I thank you for your sustainment."

"Well, I am here to provide what you need."

"You can probably see my state better than I can, because you see objectively."

She took his hand and laid it on her breast. That always transported him.

Another day he remarked on the way he and Joyce had come together. "The first I remember of her, was when she looked at me. It surprised me that any girl would have an interest in me."

"I never expected anyone to show an interest in me," Genevieve said. "That was one reason Spencer's revelation was so surprising."

"But you were an absolutely lovely creature! No one could see you and not be moved."

She was foolishly flattered. "Time does change that."

"Oh, you still are beautiful to me."

Best not to question that. "At any rate, Joyce was young."

"Yes. She may not have had the experience of being the focus of another's love. Perhaps it had to open up slowly to her that this was her situation. Until she could come to the full realization. Maybe by the end of the term she was seeing this, able to know it, able to accept it."

"She was at Woodbrooke to learn, as you were. This may have been part of it. What was her religion?"

"She was a Quaker. I explained the tarot to her. She was interested in death."

"She was borderline depressive, as you were."

"I think so. I don't know whether she believed in reincarnation. I don't think I did, until then."

"Until she died?"

"Yes. Then I had to believe, because the alternative was not acceptable. I have to know she remains with me on some plane." He brought out his journal. "Here is what I wrote three weeks after her death. 'The thought that baffles me is that Joyce was so interested in death; at first it seems so different from her. Yet if she was so interested in it, it must be like her. At any rate, if death had any stigma for me there is none now. I look for it as a welcome experience because she has done it.'"

That common interest in death had surely drawn them together. But then Joyce had died, and Alfred had not.

"But the trouble is I haven't convinced myself. For such a life to be terminated! Where is the justice? And I haven't talked myself into any real acceptance. How can such a thing be accepted?"

Genevieve didn't know. "Maybe it was necessary for the greater good. For later happiness."

"I remember just three times of happiness: Woodbrooke, Spain, and the early days of Hilltop." Then he caught himself. "And my time with you, of course."

"Of course," she agreed, smiling. But she knew that those memories were selective. Woodbrooke without Joyce had become empty for him, and there had been dark days in Spain before the end, and Hilltop soon enough become a struggle. It was the times of hope and novelty, of early accomplishment and new contacts that had turned him on. Perhaps the same applied to her: she had lost her novelty.

Alfred developed a correspondence with Nancy, and they compared old times. Of course they shared a bond, both having having loved Joyce. But Genevieve couldn't help feeling a bit left out.

Alfred picked up on this. "I can read you the account of my Paris days with you. In this period of reminiscence you should be included."

What could she say? "That's all right. I'm just waiting for you to come back from being away." Several thousand miles, and fifty years. This reminiscence had continued for two years, and she was ready to see it conclude its course. Sometimes she suspected that he really wished she were Joyce, somehow alive and his wife.

One day in August Genevieve was ill. She threw up and had continuing stomach pain through the night and into the morning. Alfred, trying to keep her company, read passages to her, but kept breaking down. She realized that he was suffering too, emotionally. "Why don't you just let yourself cry?" she asked.

He did, and that seemed to help. Thereafter they both improved.

In September he wrote Nancy a serious letter, telling her of his feelings for her in 1932 and asking whether his sudden turning away to Norma hurt her. His hope was that for Nancy it was just fellowship, not love. "What I knew of you was that it was fun to be with you."

She replied that it had seemed natural for Alfred and Ralf to be in the house. She had enjoyed his company and had no further expectations. "You did right not to express your feelings at the time, if you had I would certainly have gone shy and silent again,—or impatient,—one way or another it would have spoilt things. I had emotional upheavals of my own between the ages of 18 + 22 + wouldn't have wanted any more to cope with. That's why our relationship was a happy one for me—there were no strings, so I always felt comfortable with you. Indeed, looking back, it's remarkable how easily + gladly I accepted you + Ralf as members of the family. Your attachment to Joyce + your comfort to Mother were always the link, + also, having no brothers it felt good to me to have young male company in the home."

"That's an enormous relief," Alfred said.

But Genevieve wondered: could that have been all there was to it? The two had been close since Joyce's death, and very close in 1932. How could Alfred ponder marriage, while Nancy had no inkling? But then she remembered Spencer. He had wanted marriage, and that had astonished her. Of course their association had been only ten days, rather than two years. Still, it showed that it was possible.

But it was also possible that Nancy was being kind. There was nothing to be gained so many years later by making Alfred suffer. So she might have suffered heartbreak at the time, and covered it up. Or assumed that because Alfred hadn't asked, he hadn't been interested, as Genevieve had when he didn't comment on her special dress. Or chosen, when rejected, to believe that she had never been interested. So the real nature of her feelings for Alfred might never be known.

What did Nancy think of Genevieve, Genevieve wondered. Was there any muted resentment that Genevieve was the one who finally married Alfred?

But there was more in the letter. "You and I both took a long time to find the right ones, but we were lucky in the end. I think if Joyce had lived there would have been more confusion + complications for you, because you wouldn't have been right for each other, but because of her you didn't recognize, the first time around, that Genevieve was."

That was doubly interesting. It not only vindicated Genevieve, which she appreciated, it suggested that it wouldn't have worked out with Joyce. Nancy surely had known Joyce well; she had to have a basis for her opinion. And it was true that Alfred's attention had been riveted on Joyce, so he had noticed Genevieve not at all the first time they met, and then when they did interact, set her aside the moment he returned—he thought—to Joyce.

But Alfred was puzzled by the idea that he and Joyce wouldn't have been right for each other. So he inquired.

Nancy's response was forthright. "I just thought I'd better explain my remark about you + Joyce not being right for each other permanently.—Your second supposition was the right one,—not that you wouldn't have measured up to what she deserved, but that she wouldn't have felt comfortable on a pedestal, + real life has a way of knocking them out from under us anyway! Secondly there was the fact that you met + were attracted to Genevieve at that time, + that lasted all those years of other diversions—so there's proof for you!"

It was easy to like Nancy.

By the end of the year, Alfred said "In morning walks I have gradually released Joyce, hoping this is right."

Genevieve hoped so too.

In June 1981 Alfred's eldest brother John died at age 78. His wife had died two months earlier.

In July the doctor diagnosed the swelling in Alfred's abdomen as an inguinal hernia, and laid out three possible treatments: an operation, a pressure pad, or exercise to strengthen the relevant muscles. Naturally Alfred chose the third alternative, but he did also wear a special low belt.

In October he wrote to Piers to ask advice about the prospect of having a dental root canal performed. Piers had had more than one, and responded in reassuring detail. In December Alfred had it done.

In February 1982 Alfred read Chapter 10 of Piers' Xanth novel *Centaur Aisle* to her, wherein the protagonists Dor and Irene were imprisoned in adjacent cells, and could only touch each other through the wall. They spoke the reverse of their true meanings, to hide their plans to escape from their captors. It got into their demeaning each other, which actually meant affection or love. Alfred found it charming.

In May, on his birthday, Granddaughter Penny phoned him. She was now coming up on fifteen, a teenager. How swiftly time fled!

Genevieve had trouble walking through the year. It seemed to be another penalty of age.

In April 1983 there was an unfortunate episode. Alfred disliked seeing people touch their faces in public; he called it face fingering. Many people did it, often to partially conceal their mouths; it was unconscious defensiveness. Alfred took note when he observed that Piers did not do it. Genevieve did her best to avoid it.

They were watching TV at the kitchen table when Alfred started shielding his eyes. "Is there a problem?" she inquired. Then she learned that he did not like her rubbing her arm. She had thought his restriction applied only to the face. This distressed her; she did not like the idea of unconsciously turning him off.

Then in the morning she complained about discomfort in her right knee. "I do not feel free to make suggestions about such things," he said. "Because you know my thinking, and would be inclined to greet my comment as 'there he goes again.'" This she didn't like. All she had done was remark on a problem she had, and he had made it into a rebuke.

She did know his thinking: she was exercising too little, and carried too much weight. This put a strain on her weakened knees. She needed to exercise more and keep her weight down. And he was right, but it was difficult to do, and she lacked the willpower for such things that he had.

In May her breathing was uncomfortable, and she had to get up. That breathing problem was to continue.

Scott Nearing died in August, aged 100. He had been a neighbor near Hilltop Farm, a political radical and vegetarian, giving weekly talks on social and economic subjects, and was the author of many books on what he called the good life of self sufficiency. When Piers had met him at age eight they had discovered they had the same birthday, 51 years apart. Scott had been a good friend, and to an extent a mentor for Alfred. His death was intentional: he had decided that he had lived long enough, and stopped eating, gradually fading out. He had ended his life as he had lived it, in his own fashion. Genevieve knew that Alfred felt the loss; a considerable presence was gone.

Alfred continued to be disturbed by the "face fingering" of the people around him, including Genevieve. She tried her best to stop it, but an unconscious action was difficult to prevent.

"Am I too critical?" he asked rhetorically. "Should I seek to remove from my attitude and speech all detraction, disparagement, censure, depreciation, condemnation, contempt, censoriousness & disdain? Have I not done too much of that? Nothing in my life with you invites it."

What could she say? His critical attitude was as hard for others to handle as their mannerisms were for him to handle. She tried to reassure him, but her words lacked force. It was getting more difficult for her to manage emotional conflict; she lacked the energy.

Piers sent them his novel *On A Pale Horse*, and they immediately began to read it. It was a fantasy with Death as the main character, which Alfred of course appreciated. It made the bestseller lists, showing that many people were reading it.

Life continued through winter and into 1984 with slowly declining health. Alfred took walks, but Genevieve had trouble. An April they walked to the bank together, but she had to pause repeatedly to recover her breath. She was weakening. They planned another trip to Florida, but she had increasing doubt about this.

They managed it, however—a twelve day trip, spaced out to allow them time to rest along the way. They traveled with Lillian, who was recovering from knee surgery, and divided the tasks between them. The worst of it was getting caught in rush-hour traffic in Charlotte, and Alfred also developed a stomach ache so that he had to rest for two hours before resuming activity. Palm Beach was fine. Then they drove up to Inverness, where Alfred and Lillian were amazed by Piers' computer with its typing appearing on a television-like screen, then super-fast printing to paper. Granddaughter Penny was away, but fourteen year old Cheryl was there. She was interested in archaeology, and they hoped to be involved with the excavation of an untouched Indian burial mound. Four days driving home, and they were very glad to get there.

Genevieve knew she couldn't handle another such excursion. She had to rest more frequently, even at home, continuing weak and short of breath. She lacked appetite. Alfred wanted to help, but she simply needed to rest. He read to her often. Dr. Williams was close-mouthed, which was not a good sign. And so they finished the year.

In March 1985 Dr. Shippen observed fluid in Genevieve's legs, an enlarged heart, water in the lungs, and some constriction in the neck. He prescribed a number of pills, but she lacked the will take most of her tablets. She knew she was fading.

It continued. She was not inclined to read, because laser work had left her only one good eye. Dr. Shippen's diuretics were helping to clear the excess fluid from her body, but she was losing track, making misjudgments. She knew it bothered Alfred when she ate junk food, but it was easier to handle and she preferred to go out in her own fashion.

And she was going out. She knew it. She was at peace with it. Some people fought death; she preferred to coast.

Piers started writing his autobiography, titled *Bio of an Ogre*. It seemed he had been accused of being an ogre at conventions, before he had attended any, so he was making something of it. Alfred found the material fascinating, as it arrived chapter by chapter. He shared it with her, and sent back careful critiques. Piers' early memories were intense, and his perspectives on England, Spain, and America were quite different from Alfred's. Alfred, of course, had his Journal records of all those times, but the children hardly appeared in them; this was the other side. The chapters affected Norma, too: she wrote of her memories of the experience in Spain.

In July Teresa visited with her son Patrick, and Piers' children Penny and Cheryl, all teenagers now. Alfred was highly impressed with them. "How did such wonderful young people come into the family?" he asked. Dark-haired Cheryl, now a lovely girl, reminded him a little of Joyce.

Nancy wrote from England that she had found Piers' novel *Omnivore* there. She found it compelling reading. "What an amazing imagination . . . the mind boggles." Alfred was thrilled to see one of Piers's other books on the B DALTON bestseller list.

Life was continuing, but Genevieve found herself increasingly removed from it. She hoped that Alfred would carry on successfully after she was gone.

"What do you think about going to Lancaster for Quarterly Meeting?" she asked on the last day of the year.

"I am undecided," he said.

"I am willing to go, if you want to."

But he demurred, and she knew why: he was concerned for her weakness. It was true that any traveling was hard on her now, but she did not want to hold him back.

They stayed up for midnight, ringing in the new year. She had bought champagne, but didn't bring it out. She simply wasn't sure she could handle it.

On January first she was coughing a good deal. Then she lost her voice and couldn't speak. Fortunately that passed, and on the fourth they walked around the block.

So it continued through the month: coughing, resting, sorting mail, taking care of the cat, watching TV, shopping, resting. She had very little appetite, and simply tided through.

Teresa visited in May, helping with garden work, and Alfred offered to contribute $2,000 a year to enable her to take work at Westtown School. "I have the feeling she has become a friend, not just a daughter," he said. That was a significant and positive change.

Alfred spent a good deal of time reviewing his earlier journal entries, reliving the 1930s and 1940s. Genevieve could understand that; she surely wasn't much company these days, with her inactivity. But he put a different slant on it: "I never told Joyce I loved her. Then it was too late. That experience helped me advance to the ability to tell you that I love you. I did not want to make the same mistake again. I want you to be sure of my love."

She was. Alfred never really let go of his women. He cherished his memories of Joyce, and surely his memories of Genevieve.

In July he remarked "As I drove to Lillian's I passed a young woman brightly dressed. Surely a woman should be like a flower in some man's life. And when I remember how I was uplifted in the presence of Joyce, and in yours, does not everyone need an uplifting presence?"

Like a flower. She had been that, once. But now her season was finishing.

In August Penny wrote that she was working at a forest camp, and reading *The Meaning of a Liberal Education*. Alfred replied that that book had changed the whole course of his own education. That month, also, they made the journey to the Sabian Conference in Chicago. She knew that Alfred was very pleased to have her with him there once more, and she was determined to accomplish it. She suspected it was her last.

1986 passed, and she was hardly aware of where the time had gone. She was definitely not well. The doctor had mentioned congestive heart failure and the possibility of a small stroke. In practical terms this meant that her body was losing aspects of itself, mentally and physically.

In February 1987 she was coughing a lot and breathing with very short gasps. Alfred rubbed her back a little, and she gradually settled down. He kissed her and told her that he loved her. She appreciated that, knowing that such an expression was not easy for him.

March first he found her sprawled across the bed, her legs hanging over the edge. He gradually straightened her out. He encouraged her to walk to the bathroom, but she couldn't stand.

Alfred had to go answer the phone. She tried again, but wound up kneeling on the floor. Friends came and heaved her back onto the bed, washed her, and put a clean nightie on her. She would have preferred to do such things for herself, but simply lacked the strength.

As the day ended, she relaxed on the bed and drifted off to sleep. At midnight she finally let her body go, starting the new day with her transition to the spirit domain. She remained for a while as she was, relaxing, adjusting to her recovery of senses and personal vigor. She felt young again, newly born but not a baby.

Alfred woke at 1 AM with a cramp in his left foot. He jumped out of bed to stand on it and squeeze the cramp out. It was almost comical.

Then he looked at her body and saw that it was not breathing. Incredulously he touched her with his hand, and put his cheek against hers. She was not animate. She was sorry to leave him this way, but her body had simply worn out. He would have to carry on without her.

She watched and listened as he telephoned Teresa, then Anna, to tell them of her death. Then he lay down beside her. She knew he did not want to see her go, any more than he had wanted to see Joyce go. But he was restless, understandably, so he got up and wrote some letters to friends about what had happened. At 4 he returned to lie beside her and slept for two and a half hours.

In the day a number of friends came, and had a circle of healing with prayers of faith and thanksgiving. Curtis, Charmoine, Anna, Alfred, and Genevieve's body made the ceremony. Alfred opened it with praise of her, and the others spoke similarly. Then Alfred said "Dear Lord, behold thy handmaiden Genevieve. We deliver her into thy loving care." He could hardly get the words out, as he was weeping.

She wished she could speak aloud, to reassure him. But that was not possible directly. For now all she could do was watch.

Later in the day he read to her, and she did hear. Then Teresa came and joined him for supper, comforting him to the degree she was able.

After Teresa left, he brought out the typewriter and wrote about the events of the day, from his discovery of her body on. Then he wrote to Elinor, and phoned Piers, talking with him for half an hour. The day was done.

He slept beside her body again, then woke before 5 AM, cold and shivering. It was more than physical. He felt three waves of grief for her and broke into sobs. "But please don't be distressed," he said to her. "Help me if you can."

She touched him with her spirit substance. He could not feel it physically, but he did calm. "I love you so much," he said. "I shall miss you so much."

Others visited that day, including Stan and Rusty. Rusty was psychic; she sensed Genevieve's floating presence. "Tell him that he should not give special emphasis to the hours between now and the funeral van's departure," Genevieve said, and Rusty received the essence and told Alfred. "Avoid farewells, because I will continue to be here. I am interested in your conversation and am participating in my fashion."

On March 4 friends took Alfred out for a walk, while other friends supervised the appearance of the undertaker, who took her body. The cremation of that finally freed her to roam more widely, and to commence her exploration of the universe beyond.

She did not separate from Alfred. He talked to her every morning, and she heard him. But she was no longer limited to him. An aspect of her remained in touch, wishing him well. The rest of her being ranged out to meet the others who inhabited this realm. One she was eager to meet was Joyce. She knew Joyce, from Alfred's old journal entries. But also, she now recognized, from a contact they had had just before Joyce's death. Alfred had dreamed of her, Genevieve, and Joyce had joined that dream, kissing him in an ardent manner she had never broached in life. The two young women had been together, in Alfred's dream, and now she recognized that and knew Joyce's identity. It should be easy to find her. They should have much in common.

# CONCLUSION

The 50th Reunion of the George School Class of 1927 was a big event. Marion had been active in its organization, writing to the class members whose addresses the school retained and encouraging them to participate. Among these was Alfred, whom she had seen only once in the interval. They had corresponded for several years after graduating, but had slowly disappeared into other relationships. She had seen him and his then-wife Norma in 1940 when she visited Pendle Hill, and not since.

Then May 14, 1977, it happened. She encountered dozens of classmates she had hardly thought about in the interim, and several she was really glad to see again, however briefly. And Alfred. It was really quite routine on the surface.

"Hello Alfred! Marion G S, and this is my husband Eric. And this is Genevieve, of course."

*Ah, Alfred, you were my high school crush, and you've hardly changed, just older. Are similar memories coursing through your mind? We were so very close, once.*

They continued the banal chatter, then went on to other contacts. But Marion was shaken; even after all this time, Alfred still meant more to her than she had thought. If only he hadn't had this fool idea about not monopolizing her time, giving her freedom—a freedom she had finally exercised, breaking up their romance. From this distant vantage, that seemed foolish. But Alfred, at least, seemed happy.

In fact that high school breakup had led to Alfred dating her Swedish roommate, Linnea, a great girl. That relationship had not lasted beyond graduation, but Marion's friendship with her roommate had, and eventually she had married Linnea's brother Eric. A storybook romance—but the reality had turned out to be somewhat less than ideal.

Five years later she hoped to meet him again, at the 55th Reunion. But then he changed his mind, and she had to remove his name from the list. "I am especially disappointed that you will not be with us," she wrote. "At our fiftieth reunion I was so happy to meet your wife and enjoyed the brief time we had together. I was looking forward to seeing her again and to seeing you as well. After all, how many people are still around who shared experiences with you from seventh grade onward?"

But he did plan to attend the 60th reunion. His wife Genevieve died in March, just two months before it, leaving him alone. She was sorry to learn of that, appreciating how lonely he must be. But there was also a current of something else. There had been a tremendous erosion of classmates, with death and health decimating the planned attendance.

On May 9, 1987, they met again. Only three attended: the two of them, and Catherine T. What a difference a decade made! More than eighty had attended the 50th. Alfred came to Normandy Farms Estates, the retirement community where she and Eric lived, and she drove him to George School. They wandered over the campus together, catching up on old times and on the intervening years and experiences. Alfred was far more forthcoming now; perhaps it was because there were now so few of them. He had never liked crowds. But mainly, she suspected, because he had no companion at home. He had been cruelly cut loose by Genevieve's death, and he had much to say about his lost wife.

Alfred joined her for supper with Eric. Time had matured Alfred considerably, and he was better able to handle a social event like this than she remembered him to have been in youth. He still had his different way of looking at things; the details had changed, but his odd, interesting nature became familiar again.

"You are the only person I can talk to," she told him as they parted that evening. Even so, there was so much she couldn't say at this time. She wanted to meet him again, and suggested Skippack.

When she was alone, she thought about his sad eyes, and even cried a bit. He was in grief for Genevieve, and it showed. That became him.

On Thursday May 28 they did that, meeting at Evansburg Park just after 10 AM. He greeted her with a brief impulsive hug; then they walked about half a mile through woods and along a brook, talking as they went. The park was vacant, except for a ranger named Kevin. They returned to her car for picnic supplies she had brought, then to a picnic area among tall limbless trees. They sat and ate, with leisurely conversation, filling in their lives. She told him of the way her marriage to Eric, at first so promising, had become sterile. He was wealthy, but was an alcoholic, with little time for anything but his bottle and the TV. It was truly frustrating.

He in turn told her about his current interests of astrology and spirit communication. She was familiar with the daily newspaper astrology columns; she didn't take them seriously, but had nothing against them, and they could be entertaining. She didn't know about spirits either, but was willing to discover more. If she had lost her beloved, she would want to stay in touch that way too.

He had two grown children, and his granddaughter Penny had recently telephoned him.

"We have a cottage in Avalon, on the coast of New Jersey," she said. "We'll be there all summer."

"Please let me knew if another open day appears," he said.

"I will," she promised.

A few days later she received a card from him, "Thanks for a memorable day." That was thoughtful of him. She wrote a letter in answer, and they developed a correspondence.

In July she wrote to him: "I have been puzzling for hours and days and I have only a theory that must be tested with you before I can make any sense of it. Such surprising things . . ." She suggested that they meet at her house next time.

In her next letter she wrote that she believed their meeting was not by chance, but in answer to her prayer.

Then in August, back from Avalon, she met Alfred again. They hugged. Truly it seemed like the answer to her prayer for relief, because she felt so confined in her marriage to Eric. "Piers refers to living with an alcoholic as a subdivision of hell," Alfred remarked. "He has readers who tell him things." His son was a successful novelist. The description seemed apt.

Their time together was a delight. They made a breakfast of mushrooms and side dishes—Alfred was now a vegetarian—and talked about anything. Their early knowledge of each other was returning with full force, and sometimes it seemed as if they were seventeen again. It was like magic.

In the afternoon he took a nap—they were after all *not* seventeen—then joined her, alone. "Once, before, you allowed me to lay my hand on your breast," he said. "This I long for."

She remembered. She considered. Alfred was clearly interested in her in a way that Eric was not. That thrilled her. She unbuttoned her blouse a little, baring a portion of one breast. Her heart was racing; this was wild adventure, for these times.

He touched the flesh of her breast. She could see how it thrilled him, and that thrilled her. She was being daring, like a teenager. "This is just so—so—I lack words," he said. "Wonderful doesn't do it justice."

She opened her blouse further, allowing him to peer inside. It was so nice to be appreciated! They were both in their mid seventies, yet it was indeed reminiscent of that time six decades ago. They were—petting.

They talked, ever more intimately, interspersing it with further touches and peeks. It was such an exhilarating experience. Then supper, a final full long hug, and kissing. They were doing it all, up to a point.

Next day she wrote him an impassioned note. "I had just put my feelings to sleep, until you came and gently woke them." But that didn't suffice, and she wrote another: "I learned more about you yesterday; I wonder what you learned about me?" Of course he had verified the shape of her breast, by touch and sight, but that was only the merest portion of the experience. *The man desires the woman*, she remembered. *The woman desires the desire of the man.* She thought she had gained as much joy of the occasion as he had. How long had it been since Eric last touched her like that? It felt like decades. Alfred was interested and excited, and that made all the difference. He made her feel as if she had treasures in her blouse. She needed so much to be wanted, and he did want her.

She planned to be in Avalon the first week of October; she had to go there every so often to maintain it. Eric would not be there; travel disrupted his TV watching. She hatched a wonderfully naughty notion: could Alfred be there with her, this time?

She phoned him: how about it? To her wicked delight, he agreed.

He did drive out to join her at Avalon. They had a great time together, reading, talking, walking, sight-seeing, eating dinner out, and some togetherness with music in the evening. It was like dating, like courtship, picking up where they had left off so long ago. Mind and body, a superlative time of closeness, really dissolving any barriers there might have been. They had a tremendous sense of contact, communication, and communion beyond anything she could remember. She was overwhelmed, floating on air, and knew he felt the same. It was such a marvelous discovery, and revelation, a feeling of no barriers, complete acceptance, full confidence, total fulfillment, and the blessing of God over all.

Back home, he phoned her. "There seemed to be a moment Wednesday night when you, of your own volition, accepted me into your heart."

She remembered. It was when he removed his pajama coat, which was getting in the way of the touch of her hands, and he was gilding her with his hands and getting under her nightgown so that there should be no intervening substance. "Let me get rid of this," she said, and tossed the nightgown away. What a difference that made! Now no barrier remained. She opened her whole

form for him to see. He embraced her, so their bodies were in full contact
with each other, except for his pajama bottoms. But as he pulled his thigh up
between her legs nothing was concealed. To be virtually naked together—that
seemed to bare not only their bodies but also their souls to each other.

It felt like love.

There was one almost humorous incidental incident. They visited a
bookstore in Avalon, where it was discovered that Alfred was the father of
Piers Anthony. That made him a celebrity, and they asked to shake his hand.
Alfred had earned a Ph.D in Spanish Literature, done relief work in Spain that
saved many lives, written learned articles—yet what he was suddenly known
for was being the father of a popular fantasy writer. Well, it *was* a bookstore.

She wrote to him. "There is a sense of serene happiness and a feeling of
total commitment which I have not experienced ever before." Certainly not
in her marriage; that was the problem. Alfred had made a better marriage in
Genevieve than she had in Eric. She continued, saying that the two of them
had begun a new chapter, all fresh and new. Could she help it if she wondered
about the next page? Whatever it was, it would be glorious and good. His
hands had told her so.

Yet it wasn't enough. She wrote another note and posted it. "I can think
of little else except Avalon." Surely he realized that she had made the deepest
commitment of her life on that night. "You asked for nothing, but the die
is cast." Her prayer for relief from the locked-in sterility of her marriage had
certainly been answered. Who could be better than Alfred, her friend from
high school? She knew she could trust him.

Yet she remained unsatisfied with her expression, so she wrote still another
note. "The feelings that I have are completely new." She had never experienced
them before—ever. She was completely overwhelmed by her own feelings.
But what if she had missed this glorious experience? Her reserves seemed to
have disappeared completely and she returned to the original thought: with
him every word, thought and touch seemed natural—like breathing.

His letters were crossing with hers, saying much the same thing. They
had loved each other as teenagers; now they were there again. Something was
going on that was greater than they expected. The purity, the refinement,
the trust, the willingness, the understanding, the beauty—Alfred suggested
that they might have their roots in some other existence that they were now
continuing. Maybe he was right; how else were they to explain it?

On Friday the 16th they had breakfast together at Skippak. Their dialogue
was lively, affectionate and communicative. It was so nice to have someone
to talk to!

Then they went to the park and walked the previous route with great joy, reliving those now-remote moments. Time flew. Alfred explained his letter, and they reviewed hers. Such wonderful things to read and clarify. She spoke again of the commitment she made during their Avalon experience, but didn't spell it out. To her, allowing a man to see her and touch her naked was near the ultimate. He seemed to understand. "To me, the moment you voluntarily removed your nightie took it to a new level. That was overwhelmingly important to me."

"It was entirely new to me," she said. "Part of my new being."

"I am glad for that. I can't properly express the beauty and impressiveness of that moment, engraved on my consciousness."

Oh, it was fun reacting like teens, rediscovering themselves.

The following week they breakfasted together again, in great harmony and sharing. She told Alfred more about her intervening life. "I have lost feeling for Erik," she confessed.

"As I did for Norma in 1946," he agreed. "I realized that marriage was a mistake almost from the outset, but thought that somehow it could be worked out. Eventually I gave up."

"I hate his constant drinking," she said. "But that's only part of it. I took him for a drive recently, but lost the way, and he hounded me mercilessly for it. He is verbally abusive."

They continued to talk. She was reluctant to part; it was so nice having compatible company after so long with incompatible company.

They exchanged further letters. They planned to get together again at Avalon. Meanwhile Erik caught on to her interest in Alfred, and of course was not pleased. "What does he do for you?" he demanded.

She thought seriously about it, the gave him a straight answer. "Everything I have always needed and wanted from you, and you never gave me."

"I disagree."

"You think money is enough? It isn't."

Evidently that made an impression, because thereafter he was more considerate. They even had a discussion without hostility.

Saturday the 31$^{st}$ she had a happy day with Alfred, breakfasting on French Toast at Skippak, then driving to Green Hill for a nostalgic visit to the scene of many happy times. They took a walk down the lane to his father's house, and along the old route to Maple Avenue. So many ancient memories! They visited his daughter Teresa, who showed them around and let Alfred drive her new Honda car. Teresa seemed compatible, apparently not resenting her father keeping company with another woman. They visited Alfred's brother John the house-builder's estate, and the quarry he had used.

Finally they returned to the parking lot, where they talked further, not wanting to separate. She bought liquors for Erik; that was most of what it took to keep him happy. She told Alfred about her recent dialogue with her husband, and he appreciated it. Then at last, at 4:40 PM they separated.

The first weekend in November they got together at Avalon. It was great to be alone with Alfred again, and they took full advantage of it. They had dinner with her son Rick, now in his late 40s. They watched some TV, then went early to bed.

That was when the real action began. Alfred quietly joined her. She was in her nightgown, he in his pajamas, but they hardly got in the way. He gilded her body with his hands. That was all they did, but it was so good to be together. The quiet sharing of bodies and feelings was something she hadn't had with Erik for decades, if ever.

In the morning he was up before she was. Rick came and took them all over the town, and to see a house he was interested in, the last one on a little boardwalk. Meanwhile she got a call offering $800,000 for her house. She turned it down. She made oyster and fish for supper.

They retired early again, and again Alfred joined her, putting on music: *Concierto de Aranjuez.* This time he took off his pajamas, and her nightgown. How delicious, to feel their two bodies close together! He played with her breasts, and all over her, calling this a true garden of delight. How nice to have a man appreciate her body as if it were seventeen! He listened to her heartbeat. They snuggled and kissed. They lay full length against each other. It exceeded all description.

It got late, and he thought he should go. She stretched her arms out to him. Neither of them wanted to break the enchantment; it was a whole other world. But eventually, after many relapses, he got her tucked in, affectionately bid her good night, and went to his room.

She lay there, smiling. Had he chosen to go all the way, she would have let him. But it was not something she cared to initiate. She was after all a married woman. And that act had never been all that much for her. It was the tender touching, the togetherness, that was most rewarding. It was evident that Alfred valued the experience similarly, and was not looking for quick sex.

Superstition would have it that Friday the thirteenth was an unlucky day, but that was not the case for her. She met Alfred before 9, filled with the same excitement, cherishing the same memories of Avalon, marveling at the closeness they had discovered, and greedy for more. He gave her a little glass bell he had bought, and she received it with delight. It was like getting a ring, only that was of course impossible. The symbolism was there.

It took a while to get into breakfast, because of a different waitress. They had cheese omelet. They didn't get out until noon, then went to the Presbyterian Church at Wyncote, which she explained to him in detail. Then she showed him the house where she had raised her family. Finally they returned to Skippak. They had the usual difficulty getting away, with much outpouring of love.

"This is all so new to me," she said. "I always held back before, being on guard. Never before have I flowed into it, with it, giving myself gladly and willingly." She had had hope at first, with Erik, but that happiness had never been realized. She had been a good wife to him, and borne his children, but never had true love. "I thought I was happy then, because I didn't know there was more. Now there is more." But what a prior waste of a life!

He left at four in the afternoon, after they agreed to meet again in a week. Between times they exchanged letters.

Erik was doing better now, and even gave her some words of praise. If only he had thought of that three decades ago!

Friday the 20th they got together again at Skippak for a breakfast of French toast and much coffee. They read the Daily Word, hugged in the open, and had lively discussion. They went to Evansburg Park and around the trail, marveling at the quiet beauty of the woods and river, with opportune hugs. Alfred couldn't seem to get enough of her, and she loved it. He told her of his Woodbrooke love, Joyce, and showed pictures of her. They played George Ritner's songs. They went to the state liquor store for bottles of hard liquor for Erik. She always made sure Erik had what he wanted; it simplified her life. Before they parted, she listed Alfred's attributes that she appreciated. It was a litany of what Erik lacked.

The following week they went to the Gypsy Rose Inn. They had wine, and Alfred had swordfish. She was glad he didn't take his vegetarianism too seriously. When she was back home she phoned him, to let him know of her happiness.

It became regular as they met for meals and talk. Once they toured the marvelous Longwood Gardens.

Then she had a bright idea: why not have Alfred move to Normandy Farms estates? That would really make things convenient! She broached it, and he was interested but uncertain.

Other members of his family, it turned out, went to Kendal at Longwood, an excellent Quaker retirement community. His brother Edward and his wife were there, and his stepmother Caroline. And his ex wife Norma.

He suggested seeing one of the Normandy rooms. She phoned him noon the day after Christmas, excited. "You need to make application early," she said. "There's a fair waiting list."

There was an irony about her home life: the only time Erik behaved well was when Alfred was there. She took refuge with her friends Susan and Courtney. Courtney wanted Alfred to talk with her father, who had read Alfred's son's books.

On the 30th Alfred went to Normandy and talked with Janice M about entering as a resident. He viewed sample rooms and other parts of the complex. Later that day they got together. He was definitely interested; there was no more talk of Kendal.

A friend of hers named Charles died. Erik said "I suppose you would like me to go and join Charles." Distressed, she phoned Alfred and told him about it.

John and Courtney had a party, and invited Marion and Erik, but Erik didn't want to go, so she had to stay home too. This was all too typical. He stifled what little social life they might have had by refusing to be part of it.

Next week Alfred made the application. It might take two years for his number to come up, but at least now it was in the works. Meanwhile they kept company often.

In March Alfred read to her from his Journal entry of May 22, 1925, expressing the depth and intensity of his love for her. Overwhelmed, she suddenly stopped the car and hugged him.

Erik was not pleased with their relationship. He referred to Alfred as his "husband-in-law."

They traveled together to Cape May, where he enjoyed, as he put it, her endlessly fascinating bare breasts.

In May, 1988, Alfred read to them from his son's autobiography, *Bio of an Ogre*. He supplemented Piers' memory with his own, viewing all the anomalies of that period from his present distance. When Piers described the place at Seaside Park as a "cabin," Alfred tried to correct the word but got twisted up. He meant to say it was a cottage, but what came out was "Not a cabin but a cabbage." They all burst into peals of laugher.

In June she gave Alfred a yellow rose. She also learned how Alfred was annoyed by the way other people kept touching their faces in public; he called it "face fingering." She understood how that could be annoying, and was careful not to do it herself.

They drove again to Avalon. She was sleepy, and once swerved as she started to nod off. Perhaps for that reason Alfred became more talkative. They talked freely, repressing nothing. "I hope there will be opportunity to get out of our clothing and lie close," he said.

"I have the same idea," she said. She had lived a loveless life, and discovered love only late in life: now. "I had no sex life or sex enjoyment. Any feeling I had for Erik has been dead for years."

In October she confessed that if she had known on the first day of their first visit to the park how this love would overwhelm her, she might not have risked it. It remained so new, never a part of her life before. She had mistaken Erik's silence for strength. But she did not condemn the experience; it was part of what made her what she was.

In January 1989, Alfred took a walk, as he often did, but slipped on the ice and fell sliding down the slope. He hit his shoulder against a jutting building. After that his shoulder was half out of commission, making it hard to change clothing.

He carried on as usual, though when his car had a flat tire he had trouble changing it with the sore shoulder. Finally she prevailed on him to call a doctor, and he consented to check with his chiropractor. Dr. Lombardi said a rib had been driven into the spine between the vertebrae, and set about extracting it. That helped. Marion was bemused; an injury like that, and he had tried to ignore it. He didn't like admitting to any physical liability. His mother had been a Christian Scientist, and had evidently influenced him to distrust doctors.

Next day they drove together to Avalon. She told him about the frustration of her life, Eric's constant needling. The man was alcoholic, but he retained a sinister wit and knew exactly how to get to her. With Alfred it was so different!

Avalon was in satisfactory order. They exchanged some good hugs, then drove back. Alfred read to her as they traveled. That was one of his pleasant little ways; he shared things when it was convenient.

She consented to be his Valentine when that day came. It was another quaint, fond signal of their memories of the distant past.

In April they drove again to Avalon—and were stopped by police for speeding and not wearing seat belts. Her own fault; she was under a cloud, having had words with Eric the day before, but she didn't want to go into it with Alfred. So she had been neglectful, and gotten caught. But they thoroughly enjoyed the house, had some hugs, lunched upstairs viewing the sea, walked on the beach, and saw new houses under construction. Maybe not all of that was romantic *per se*, but the pleasant company made all the difference.

Along the way he read from his journals of 1924 and 1926. She remembered his journal; on rare occasion back then he had lent it to her, and even allowed her to make a few entries in it herself. That had been such a thrill! Now, over sixty years later, he still had those notes. That was remarkable.

"I have a feeling that my Normandy time is fast approaching," he said.

"I hope so. It will be so much more convenient."

Three days later her son Carl Eric married Jean. It was a great family gathering, with Marion being honored as the oldest family member. In the course of the day she got Alfred to talk about the treatment he had had with Dr. Hadfield, and his early life with Norma, which had been about as dysfunctional as her own life with Eric. Maybe that was one reason he understood so well. She knew that those early memories, good and bad, were still with him. He would walk with the ghost of Joyce, his lost love. It was charming.

In May Alfred learned that he had a great grandchild. Unfortunately the boy was illegitimate. Teresa's younger daughter Carrie had had a boy, Ian. Marion suspected that left Alfred with rather mixed feelings.

In June they went to Avalon again, and planted geraniums Alfred had saved and rooted. She was stopped for speeding on the way back when doing 71 miles per hour, though at other times she had done 85. They stopped at a flower stand. Of such things were a pleasant encounter made.

Then it was time for her to go with Eric to Avalon for the summer, which meant she wouldn't be seeing Alfred. She regretted that, but the forms had to be honored. She stayed in touch with Alfred by mail, of course.

On the 29th Eric suggested that she phone Alfred, as it was Thursday, the day they had so often breakfasted together. She had once told Alfred "I need our Thursdays, and six other days of the week." Erik was of course being ironic. So she called his bluff and did call Alfred, surprising and pleasing him.

She called again in July, cautioning him not to address her as Marion J S when they were in public, and saying she had a plan she would put in a letter. She did, and they got together Tuesday at Normandy. Great was the joy thereof! She was wearing a white shirt with a front button. He undid the button and roamed over what he called her precious magic garden. She loved his appreciation.

Meanwhile Erik was depressed, a non-participant in life, but he no longer pressed to sell the house, even at $1,650,000, twice what had been offered before.

July 26 Alfred read her a passage in his son's fantasy novel *Being a Green Mother* that he found apt, and she agreed.

> They lay together, not making love, just simply holding each
> other. Mym had, he confessed, known many women in sexual
> detail; it was expected of a prince, and concubines were a rupee a
> dozen. But he had never been in love. Orb admitted that she had
> no experience in either love or sex, and had never felt the lack,
> until now.
> "The touch of your hand is melody to me," he told her.
> "That's just my magic!" she reproved him. He laughed, and
> they kissed and kissed again.
> On other nights they did make love, many times and with
> abandon, but it was only an affirmation of their love, not an end
> in itself. She just wanted to be with him as closely as she could.

That led them into a discussion of whether and when to have full sex. He opened her shirt and could see and sometimes touch the top of the twins. He also stroked her back and legs; it was hard for him to keep his hands off her, and she loved that difficulty.

"Yet I should not transgress Erik's rights as long as you are married," he said.

"Sex has not been a function of our marriage for many years."

But they needed time and uninterrupted privacy. It could happen only at Avalon.

In October they were together at Avalon, and were in bed together naked, doing everything short of intercourse. She had resolved to do it if he chose it, but still was unwilling to initiate it herself.

Later in the month they were driving together and ran out of gas. She called Triple A without result, but kind neighbors helped. Alfred stayed that evening to watch *60 Minutes* on TV, then was about to go, but Erik urged him not to drive back at night. So he stayed the night. Erik still surprised her on occasion. Was it possible that she treated him better when Alfred was there, just as Eric did with her? Alfred might be a catalyst for their good behavior.

In March 1990 they were having a breakfast of pizza omelet, and she told him of her reaction when he had read to her of his love for her in 1925. It was very strong, but held within herself. She did not externalize things.

Then she had an attack of angina. Alfred seemed to think he could fix it just by laying his hands on her. Quaint belief, but she had to take nitroglycerin. She sat in a chair with her feet up and waited for it to take effect. It had been three years since her last attack; that time she had been driving alone. It passed, and she was all right. She always kept her medicine near. It was a stern reminder that life was not eternal.

In April Alfred's granddaughter Penny visited with two friends. She was, as he described her, a young woman of twenty two with blond hair to her waist. Alfred was charmed. "I was just entering Oxford University, when I was her age."

In June they sold the house at Avalon. It was for a good price, but Marion was broken up over it. That house held so many memories, good and bad. Later that month, going there with Alfred to start the moving out process, she told him of the rip-rearing fight she had had with Erik, fortunately in their son Rick's presence, which had left them not speaking to each other. It wasn't really about the sale, as he had always wanted to sell, and now she agreed. It was really an accumulation from the past, not expressed until it overflowed at this point.

Alfred helped her clean Avalon up, but the process depressed her. Then they looked at the Cornell Harbor condominium development, a unit of which could be had for $375,000, and that cheered her. In September Erik offered $350,000 with a deadline of Sunday. Three days later they bought it for $355,000. He still knew how to do business.

Then Normandy Farms had a room for Alfred, after a two and a half year wait, with a $56,000 entry fee. He took it. The long wait for them both was finally almost over.

Alfred had the required physical exam, on which he did very well, selected light colored carpet, and got his date for entry: December 12.

Meanwhile in October he drove to Avalon to help them move to Cornell Harbor. Erik welcomed him. Erik was practical: Alfred's help would make the move considerably easier.

On December 13 Alfred's daughter Teresa and granddaughter Carrie came and packed and loaded for him, drove two loaded cars to Normandy, unloaded and arranged the room, and stayed for supper with Erik, who was well behaved in company.

Meanwhile Marion had so much to do it was hard to make time to be with Alfred. He tried to walk around the great circle daily for exercise. Other residents didn't know what to make of this; exercise wasn't in their lexicon.

1991 came and progressed. It was ironic: now that Alfred was convenient, Marion was finding him less interesting. He had little habits that she found annoyed her, such as his inability to make small talk. The innocent greeting "How are you?" could bring a rebuke. He tended to go into little set speeches about the unhealthiness of things like cornflakes that were awkward when that was what she was eating. Erik was also zeroing in on Alfred with increasing finesse, seeking ways to put him in the wrong or to set him off. She knew how irksome Erik's needling could be, but Alfred didn't seem to know how to handle it.

They still had some breakfasts together, just not as regularly as before.

Late in April Teresa phoned Alfred with the news that her mother Norma was in Bryn Mawr hospital with heart surgery. It was supposed to be a routine bypass operation, as several of her blood vessels were 80% to 90% obstructed. He visited Norma the next day, but apparently she brushed him off, not ready for visitors at this time.

Norma came through the surgery satisfactorily and was recovering. Then suddenly, on May 3, she died of a pulmonary embolism. It seemed a clot had formed in her leg and made its way to her heart, blocking it. She was 81. It was a shock to her children and grandchildren, and to Alfred too; he had had nineteen difficult years with her.

But ten days later, breakfasting with Marion, Alfred was criticizing America. This made her impatient, and she reproved him for it.

Near the end of the month the family gathered for Norma's memorial service at Kendal. Alfred told her about it later. Piers read the selected verse from Rupert Brooke, "The Soldier," Teresa's ex-husband George spoke, others expressed appropriate sentiments, and Piers said: "This is a station, and Norma is beginning her journey to eternity." It seemed that Norma had always preferred to travel by train, so perhaps was touring the Afterlife by rail.

That evening the family had a dinner at the China Royal. Alfred found it a moving occasion. He sat next to Granddaughter Penny, who was considerate and helpful.

Still, "The cloud of Norma's memorial hangs over me," he said later. "Her life, my life—what does it all mean?"

Marion found no mystery there. It meant that Norma had once been a significant part of his life, and he felt her loss, as anyone would.

June 1 he went to the Buick agency with Teresa's daughter Carrie, short for Caroline, where Carrie bought a new Geo Storm with all the trimmings. Alfred used his credit card to provide a $2,000 deposit, and co-signed the loan. Then, after the fact, he learned from Teresa that he had done wrong; Carrie had no responsibility or reliability. Indeed it proved to be a disaster; the girl never made a payment on the car, and Alfred took a considerable loss when they returned it. Marion would have warned him about the severe risk in co-signing anything, but she had been away.

Three weeks after Norma's memorial, Alfred's stepmother Caroline died. (Piers called her Caroline the Elder, to distinguish her from Caroline the Younger.) She was 99, a considerable figure in Quaker circles, but had been fading for some time. Her memorial was the 22$^{nd}$, and her family members attended. Granddaughter Penny came too, and brought Alfred mementos from Caroline's room. It was a time of disturbed musing for him. She had been his father's third wife, but had had significant and beneficial effect on the whole family.

On the 27$^{th}$ Marion had to travel. "What am I to do without you?" Alfred asked.

This annoyed her. "You always talk about you, but what about me?" she retorted. He didn't understand.

But she wrote him in July: "I *do* miss you."

Penny visited him again, and sorted through his clothing, discarding much, and taking him shopping for new shirts and shorts. She was with him to see Marion off to Avalon. She was a pleasant, pretty young woman, and surely did Alfred some good. Marion offered her the use of her guest room, so saw her fairly often in this period. For once Alfred's companionship was better than Marion's, as she had a difficult and stormy return trip to Avalon.

In August one Sheila B from an ElderCare agency came to see Alfred, and they talked for five hours. This was arranged by Penny's father Piers, feeling that Alfred needed assistance. Sheila would look for someone who could help organize Alfred's papers and help him handle problems.

"I don't know who pays for this," Alfred said, bemused.

"Piers will," she assured him. She knew the way of such things, and Alfred did need some help. For example, he didn't phone people. She urged him to make calls, but he had developed some kind of phobia about it, and was able only to receive calls, not initiate them. So his family was now taking steps to support him. That was just as well.

She also wanted him to be more social, inviting people to his room and entertaining them, but what was easy for her was difficult for him. He was growing more limited. She hadn't been aware of that before; now it could become burdensome.

Penny went home, but Sheila took up the slack. Alfred needed to talk with people, and she now saw to that. Marion gathered that Piers was quietly becoming more actively supportive elsewhere in the family, as needed. It was a fairly fragmented family.

In October Alfred's friend Lillian died of a massive brain hemorrhage. Teresa's ex husband George died of cancer. He had not been kind to her and their separation had been rancorous, but it was another shock to the family. It seemed to be a time of death.

The year finished, and 1992 appeared. Breakfast was not to her liking, nor was Alfred's boiled egg, which she found revolting to look at. "It isn't a matter of liking, but of whether it will do the job it's supposed to do, to nourish my body," he explained annoyingly. Another time she simply left the meal before he had finished, not caring to argue about his mannerisms. "I don't want to talk about it."

Piers sent out a joint letter to all the members of his family at the end of each month, catching up on his news, as he had been doing for 30 years. Sometimes Alfred shared those letters with her. In January 1993 he enclosed memorial essays on their horse and dog, who had both died, and Alfred was much moved. Death was still in the air. Alfred tended to dwell on death, as did his son.

Alfred seemed to lose initiative, and no longer exercised on a regular basis. He also could not seem to get around to sorting his voluminous papers unless someone was helping or doing it for him. Penny visited for a few days in August. She cheered his life and set him up with soups he would be able to use later. She was a vegetarian, another trait that had traveled down through the generations.

Marion still saw him often, before she left for a week in Sweden later in August, and after. He told her that he loved her, and she responded, but for her the edge was gone. She could see Alfred fading; he was not as he had been. He was gaining weight. He had developed a tendency to fall forward, which could be dangerous if not corrected. He tended to get lost when driving or walking. He seemed to be in denial about encroaching liabilities. She knew he wanted to be with her more, but he was becoming too dependent, and she had had more than enough of that with Erik. What could she do except gradually withdraw from him? The future she had anticipated with him when Erik died was dissipating.

In May she came down with something. She carried on, hoping it would pass. Erik mentioned antibiotics, but she thought she could manage. Her coughing got worse, and she had bronchitis. Finally she collapsed, and the ambulance took her to the hospital, where they put her on oxygen. The treatment helped, and she felt much better. She had many visitors, and of course Alfred came. She went home after a week, still feeling droopy.

Alfred accompanied her to church in December. He couldn't see the words and notes well enough to sing the hymns. Afterwards she queried him about another thing: "Why didn't you speak to the minister?"

"I don't volunteer to speak to people I don't know. I don't know what to say."

"Well, you have to have heart."

But he didn't understand. How was it she had not noticed this asocial tendency earlier?

There was the matter of the pills. Alfred believed in vitamin and mineral supplements, along with who knew what herbal nostrums, and made sure to take them regularly. In fact he had about a five years supply of some. One day when they were at the dining room table, about to have a late breakfast, he brought them out in their various containers, laid them on the table in a line, then proceeded to take them methodically one by one, with a drink of water for each. The whole process seemed to take about fifteen minutes, though that was probably her subjectivity. The fact was, he was making a production of it, interrupting dialogue until all of it was accomplished. That was a turnoff. She tried to explain, but he could be very slow to understand what he did not want to understand. She finally said, simply, that it was not polite to take private pills in a public place. Of course he didn't understand that either. It seemed there were many social things he was doomed not to understand.

Then Erik was taken to the hospital. He had cancer, and would have to have chemotherapy and radiation.

Alfred saw the movie *Shadowland*, about the late love interest of the writer C S Lewis, and was deeply moved. Lewis was English, and fell in love with an American woman, who then died of cancer. Again, death seemed to be lurking.

Alfred's gait was worsening. Sometimes he had to stop in the hall to rest. In May he took a walk and fell on his face, making his nose bleed. How different from the man who had walked miles daily for routine exercise!

Later that month Piers introduced him, via correspondence, to a Florida woman, Frances. Sheila also came with a new helper, Maureen, a registered nurse, who turned out to be compatible. She helped him organize his papers, and talked with him, cleaned up his room, made phone calls for him, and helped organize his life.

Meanwhile Erik was given two months to live. Two months later, August 14 1994, he died. It was a shock, but an expected one.

Then on August 25 her son Rick was flying in his tiny airplane, which scraped some treetops and nose dived into the ground, killing him. This was an unexpected shock, and was much worse. Rick had been her bad boy, her most troublesome child, but somehow his untimely death at age 51 hit her worse than another might have. This made her aware of mortality with brutal efficiency. Everything seemed changed. What should be her future course?

Then early in October Alfred fell and fractured his hip. Maureen found him, and Sheila came and talked him into going to the hospital. There really wasn't much choice; he had been on the floor thirteen hours before they found him, and would have needed to use the bathroom. Marion and members of his family visited him in the hospital. After the surgery, when Sheila was absent and unable to intervene, they were going to ship him off to a different place for recovery, brushing aside Teresa's objection. Piers got on the phone and harassed them, and ElderCare finally called and forbade them to move him. That did it, and he had a good recovery at a local facility, and returned to Normandy Farms by the end of the month.

In early November Piers and Penny visited. Alfred thought very well of each of them, and together they had considerable import: his highly successful son and highly social granddaughter. Penny shopped for shirts for Alfred, while Piers talked with him. Marion joined them for dinner at a restaurant, which Piers paid for. Marion was surprised; she had become used to paying for things, having the money. But Piers was wealthy in his own right. Physically he resembled Alfred, a quarter century younger, and bolder.

After four active days Piers and Penny left for Florida, and things returned to normal, with Sheila, Maurine, and Teresa running Alfred's life. Piers later sent his trip report, titled "Dreams and Bones" after a Pete Seeger song he and Penny liked. Years later Penny set up a personal Internet Web site with the same name.

In March, 1995, Alfred traveled to Florida, visiting Penny, Piers, and Frances. He was quite impressed with Frances, who had been an excellent hostess. He returned in good order, and rested.

Marion wasn't certain what she thought about this development. Alfred had evidently become quite interested in Frances—yet why should Marion object? Her romantic interest in Alfred had faded. Still, she was not entirely easy with the change.

Alfred visited Frances again in April for another week, and was highly satisfied. But thereafter she did not answer his letters for some time. That was surely a signal of mischief. Frances had evidently discovered things about Alfred that made him less desirable, as Marion had.

At the end of April he traveled a third time to Florida, for Penny's wedding. It was a pagan ceremony, with family members participating, and Alfred read a selection. It was another whirlwind adventure. Piers' younger daughter Cheryl had bought a Saturn car, and other family members were impressed. Piers bought one himself, and Alfred decided to buy one for Teresa.

When he returned, he finally received a letter from Frances clarifying her situation. She remained interested, but twice a week correspondence was simply too much. He was much relieved.

In May Alfred forgot that Marion had a breakfast date with him for his birthday, and missed it. She was annoyed, and let him know. But a few days later they did breakfast together, and talked, and he was clearly delighted.

Frances wrote again, discussing Alfred's happiness with Genevieve and unhappiness with Norma. Her thesis was that his encounter with Norma produced Piers Anthony, and that was more important than his personal happiness. She and thousands of others had been moved by his son's books. Well, that was one way of looking at it.

Alfred lost his driving license, thanks to the concern of his children and ElderCare. He didn't understand. He had driven since 1924, he said. But Marion understood: Alfred could no longer see the road signs. The others were afraid he would kill himself and someone else in a crash, so they saw to it that he could be taken wherever he needed to go. He also needed a walker to help him stay upright when he walked; a wheelchair would have been better. But he was in denial about that too.

In September his granddaughter Erin, Teresa's daughter, married. Piers and Carol came from Florida, and Teresa, mother of the bride, handled it. It was a lovely wedding, by all accounts.

Three days later he was off again to Jacksonville Florida to see Frances for another week.

Sheila and her current assistant Bella saw to Alfred most days of the week, organizing his life. It was clear that he would get nothing done otherwise. He didn't even read any more; he gave his library to Penny's friend Alan.

Frances invited him again for Christmas, but Bella advised against it, because of the difficulty of traveling during the crowded season, and he declined.

In November he considered it again. Bella called Marion, and Marion said Alfred should stay in Florida for the winter. In January 1996 he was considering it again, but it seemed that the weight of Sheila's and Bella's

opinion dissuaded him. Marion would have been satisfied to see him go and
be happy in Florida.

In February Piers had a blowout with his publisher, threatening it with a
high-priced lawyer, and made it honor the agreement it had originally made
but then reneged on. In April he bought a compound bow he saw on sale in a
catalog, then had to set about learning to use it. Alfred kept Marion informed,
still sharing his son's monthly letters. They also talked in the middle of each
month, when Piers phoned.

In May Teresa's younger daughter Caroline got married. Piers and Penny
came up from Florida once again to attend with Alfred, and stayed for his
87th birthday. Thus Alfred's family was interacting with him increasingly,
lending support. Piers later wrote a six page report on the trip, making it
seem like an adventure.

In October a new helper appeared for Alfred, Ardene. She stayed with
him for eight hour days, drove him around, talked with him, and became a
good friend. She efficiently packed and sent many of his remaining papers to
designated relatives, including his voluminous Journal to Piers, as he was no
longer making entries in it. But as time passed this became problematical. She
was paid an hourly rate for her time, but wasn't satisfied. Alfred let her use
his credit card, and wrote her frequent checks for fifty, a hundred, or more
dollars. She was draining down his account, and his children were getting
alarmed. Teresa got records from the bank, showing how much money was
disappearing, and Piers finally had it out with ElderCare for not curbing this.
It wasn't any concern about inheritance, as Piers already had more money than
he could use, but the outrage of seeing Alfred being illicitly milked like an old
fool. This led to a rift between Piers and Penny, who took Ardene's side. The
situation didn't abate until finally Ardene moved on and a new helper appeared.

Meanwhile Teresa was frustrated because she felt Alfred needed more
monitoring of his diet, more exercise, and more awareness of his physical
condition. She wanted him to move to the assisted living wing where the
personnel would see to such things, but he didn't want to go, and ElderCare
seemed to prefer the present expensive arrangement. She was right; there was
an odor in Alfred's room, the floor was sticky with spilled food, and he was
in denial about being in any need. His sense of identity was tied in with his
perceived independence. He didn't understand why Marion was turned off.

And so the year ended with no change where it counted.

Early in 1997 Piers' wife Carol took over Alfred's income tax return, as
he wasn't going to get it done himself. Teresa took over his finances, using the
power of attorney he had signed earlier, though he didn't see the need. But the

family did not bruit such news about. Piers' March Family letter reported a humorous ad he had seen for a new stamp honoring the fire ant: lick it, and it left stinging red welts on your tongue.

In May Granddaughter Cheryl moved from Sarasota to Piers and Carol's old house near Inverness, Florida, returning home, as it were. Alfred had his 88th birthday. Life continued. Piers paid for the Eldercare and Teresa visited Alfred every week or so, making sure things were in order. The children he had not really wanted were taking care of him.

Marion lent Alfred a wheelchair she had, and that helped him get to meals in less than the half an hour per trip he required with the walker. People had been alarmed that he would fall over; he pooh-poohed the notion, but it was a real concern, so she had to do something.

Then in June there was real mischief. Alfred had been active for most of his life in the Sabian Society, which seemed to be a kind of astrology group founded by Marc Edmund Jones. Mr. Jones had set up two residual trusts related to his books which they had been selling. Someone had forgotten to renew the copyright on the main book in 1981, so that the title entered the public domain. The American publisher had been paying royalties for the past fifteen years, and sub-licensed it to German and French publishers who had also paid royalties. Now that it turned out that the copyright had lapsed, they might legally demand that money back. It could amount to a hundred thousand dollars, while all that remained in the trust was about $7,000. Stan had resigned his co-trusteeship and put the matter into Alfred's hands, but Alfred had little idea how to handle it. He couldn't handle his own finances, after all.

Alarmed, Piers hired a lawyer to protect Alfred's interest. The lawyer investigated and queried relevant folk, and the matter finally died out. It seemed that no one much cared about the technicality of a lapsed copyright. The American publisher did not alert the foreign publishers, who might be more interested in money than fairness, but this bothered Piers and his lawyer as unethical. Alfred met with the lawyer, and agreed to let the lawyer handle it. That did seem best.

In August Granddaughter Cheryl got a job with her local newspaper, THE CITRUS COUNTY CHRONICLE. That enabled her to remain in that locale, which pleased Piers and Carol. She wasn't a reporter; she handled things like subscriber accounts and printing classified ads, and determined how many copies of each edition to print.

Alfred, in contrast, had to move: to the assisted living facility. Marion was sure it was best; he simply was unable to handle his life competently, and the assisted living folk were trained for it.

Piers reported that Penny was having a number of babies. This was more of his humor: she was a licensed doula, assisting at the births of babies. In September she visited Alfred again for three days.

In June 1998 Alfred visited Penny in Florida, and Piers, Carol, and Cheryl visited with him there. Penny was playing an increasingly large part in his life. That helped make it easier for Marion, who preferred to stay somewhat clear. Alfred was no longer the same person he had been; he had become forgetful and in denial about his declining situation. She had seen more than enough of that sort of thing with Eric, and it turned her off.

In October Piers went to his college reunion, 42 years from his graduation, but the 60th for the formation of the college. Alfred remarked on that: 60th anniversaries had become important to him.

In January 1999 Alfred's step-uncle Francis, approaching a hundred years in age, had some questions about the Sabian problem, concerned that Alfred's bequests to the Sabians could be complicated. Piers and the lawyer advised him that the bequests were legitimate; there was no quarrel with the Sabian Assembly. Alfred did not follow the financial details, but was satisfied that things were in order. He was a trusting soul—perhaps too trusting.

In fact, Alfred was beginning to lose track of some old names. Losing new names was understandable, being common enough as people aged, but old ones tended to be pretty firm. When those started going, it was a signal of deterioration of the brain. When Teresa visited him, she was disturbed because he sometimes confused her with her mother Norma, and had no memory of his several falls. He thought the assisted living personnel were making it up. He saw no reason for him to be in the medical wing. Penny phoned him every week, and Piers every month, but he didn't remember the calls. He tended to forget Marion's visits, too. He was existing in the present tense, losing it as it passed. He was generally lucid enough when talking, but still didn't understand why he couldn't drive. He no longer read his books or magazines. She suspected that cataracts made it difficult or impossible for him to read much, but that he was in denial about that too. There was TV, but he had contempt for its usual fare. He was supposed to exercise, but he didn't, seeing no reason. Sometimes his speech was slurred.

Penny moved to Oregon, and sent pictures of their five acre forest property there. Having been born and raised in warm Florida, she preferred the colder climate. But first she visited Alfred, in March, meeting him daily for several days. He really appreciated seeing her; he had told the staff of her incipient arrival for several days. He was evidently more with-it in her presence. There was some friction between Penny and Teresa, who didn't get along too well.

Alfred of course was not released from the assisted living facility. But he remained in denial about it. The head nurse tried to explain why he should not move back to his private room. For one thing, he was falling. He said indignantly that he was used to falling, as he had been a soccer player in school. Everyone chuckled, but the falls were serious matters, because of his weight and frailty; he could do himself real damage. He felt he was trapped here, as if in jail.

As the meeting drew to a close, the nurse said that they would like to hear him make just one positive statement about being in the unit. There ensued a long, painful silence. He was getting paranoid about the personnel, thinking they could not be trusted.

They got him a motorized wheelchair, paid for by Medicare, but it had a short circuit that caused the fuses to blow, when plugged in for recharging, so he wasn't supposed to use it. It was a fabulously expensive device, largely wasted. Apparently the government didn't care.

Ardene left, and a new helper came: Bonnie. She was good, helping Alfred considerably. She helped Alfred argue his case for vitamins with the staff. But there was no avoiding the fact that he was largely helpless. Probably he had suffered small strokes that didn't show physically, but took out aspects of his personality. Had he been able to look ahead when younger, and see himself as he was now, he would have been appalled.

Marion could have married him, after Erik died. But his deterioration had already begun, subtly at first, then more obviously. Why should she have substituted one dependent, declining man for another? It made more sense to retain the freedom she had found. Yet it seemed too bad. Alfred had had so much to recommend him, once.

Bonnie and Teresa labored to get Alfred's remaining things boxed and organized, as it was clear to everyone but him that he wouldn't be leaving assisted living. Yet he was, gradually, getting more into the social life at Normandy Farms. He ate in the dining room, and watched the movies they put on, and sometimes talked with residents who had become familiar. He joined the "Lunch Bunch" group that went out to eat together and socialized.

However, family members were having increasing difficulty reaching him by phone. He was forgetting to be there to receive scheduled calls.

Marion visited him through 2000 and 2001, and he was lucid as they talked, remembering their times together, early and late, and sometimes very sweet. But by 2002 it was more than apparent that he did not remember her prior visits; each time it was new for him. She went regardless, but it was clear from his physical and mental degeneration that his end was approaching. He had really left most of his life behind.

He died December 14. That triggered a flurry of activity with his family and friends. Piers came up alone from Florida, Penny brought her husband and child from Oregon, and of course Teresa was close by. They got together with Teresa's daughters and friends and held a small informal memorial. They did the things people did when there was a death in the family, concluding Alfred's affairs, speaking well of him, and going home. She did not join them; her feelings were mixed, and it seemed best simply to stay clear.

What of Marion herself, who had known him early and late? She had been his first and last love, yet not his most intense love, and not the one who had generated his children. The other women died before him; only she was left. What was her role in his finished life? She pondered, but was able to come to no fair answer. She needed some kind of closure, but was having trouble finding it.

She slept, and dreamed, and the answer spread out before her. There was a scene, perhaps of England. Yes, she recognized it from Alfred's fond description: the Clee Hills.

And there he came, climbing the gentle slope to the forest. He was shedding years as he walked, as if the elevation thinned age. He became sixty, then forty, then a breathlessly handsome twenty as he reached a lovely dark forest glade.

There was a dark haired young woman standing in the glade. She turned to smile at him as she heard his approach. This was his second love and his most intense. "How long has it been, Alfred?" she asked, as if this were routine.

"Seventy three years, Joyce," he replied. "I wanted to tell you—"

"There is no need to explain," she said. "I have been watching you. I know what to do now, as I did not in life."

He hesitated. "I'm not sure I understand."

"Just say the words, Alfred. The ones you could not say in life. You can say them now."

He tried, and discovered it was true. "I love you, Joyce. I never ceased loving you."

"Thank you." She stepped into him and kissed him. There was a burst of radiance.

Then she drew back a little. "But we are not alone, beloved," she said. "We must not exclude the others."

"The others?"

"See." She gestured to the edge of the glade, where another woman stood, perhaps two years older and breathtakingly lovely.

"Genevieve!" he exclaimed.

"I love you too," Genevieve said. "I came here because I know you would, when you could. Joyce welcomed me, and I joined her, fifteen years ago. There is no rivalry in eternity."

"She did for you what I could not," Joyce said. "Kiss her, Alfred."

He went to Genevieve, embraced her, and kissed her. "I am doubly blessed," he said.

"But we must not forget the others," Genevieve said.

"Others?" he repeated, perplexed.

She indicated another young woman. "Norma!" he exclaimed.

"Please, no, no fuss," Norma said. "I am merely passing through. I finished with Alfred in life; I wanted only to be sure he made a successful transition. I am satisfied that he has done so." She waved, and walked on through the forest, disappearing.

"That leaves only one more, of the major ones," Joyce said. "But she can't join us yet."

The three of them turned to face Marion, who had thought herself invisible. Shocked, she vaulted from the dream.

And yet didn't it make sense? Could there be better company for her, when her time came?

# AUTHOR'S NOTE

I am Alfred's son, the one to whom Norma gave all the names, who did indeed become an author and use the first two as his literary pen name. When I received Alfred's lifelong Journal in September 1997, five years before he died, Alfred suggested that I adapt his description of the best day of his life, when he walked the Clee Hills with Joyce, to a story or scene in one of my novels. I thought about it, and in the end decided on a more ambitious project: a biography of Alfred with that sequence included. This is that biography. I have used first names only, other than for publicly known figures, to protect relatives from possible embarrassment.

I started by making a reference file to key in his voluminous Journal. By the time that was done, that file had expanded to about 170,000 words. The Journal itself is much longer. It is penned in ink, in many lined notebooks; only the later volumes were typed. A few volumes were damaged; one was so badly chewed that only a fraction of the pages remain. I can only roughly estimate the full Journal's length: perhaps three million words. It begins when he is 15 and ends when he is 86: three quarters of a century of his life. He died at 93, so it covers the great central portion of his existence on this plane.

Apart from its length and condition, it was a challenge to read, let alone index. Concerned with privacy, for many years he alternated paragraphs between regular English, Spanish, German, and shorthand. Sometimes there are amendments or inserts, and on occasion the pages are not in order. Some may have been lost. Sometimes letters are included: copies of his to other folk, the originals of theirs to him. At the end of some years he would have a summary of the year, and lists of the letters he wrote and received, the meals he ate together with their prices, and other bits of statistical information. My father was a methodical man; he liked to keep records. This is something I understand, for I am similar, and my own journals and records may exceed his in volume and detail, despite being broadly intermittent. This is apart

from my published writing; I am likely to be one of the best documented
writers extant. Perhaps it runs in the family. Alfred knew I would understand
and respect his private Journal, and I do. He regarded his Journal as his most
precious possession, from its earliest years on, and I regard it as an invaluable
record of his life. (I am also similar to him in having bad teeth no matter
how well I take care of them, and in being made sleepy by reading. We were
of similar height and build, and once when I telephoned my mother she
almost mistook my voice for Alfred's. She told me that when a friend first
saw me as a baby, I looked so much like Alfred he burst out laughing. So I
am indeed my father's son, and hope I have a basis to understand him in a
way others did not.)

The journal was not my only source for this biography. I have some
material from my mother, Norma, and a 1929 trip diary by Genevieve. My
sister Teresa did several booklets based on interviews with Alfred and papers
she acquired, covering his life as a boy and his tenure at Oxford University.
I also have my own personal memories of him. From these scattered sources
I tried to compile an authentic record of his life. Alfred did not get to write
his autobiography for the grandchildren, *A Privileged Life*, but perhaps these
other records will substitute.

But I am a fiction writer. I like what I write to be interesting, in the
manner of a novel. There was an enormous amount of dull detail. How could
I make his life read like a story while remaining true to its nature? That was
how I thought of showing him from the perspective of others: the several
significant women in his life. It was a special challenge, because I knew Marion
and Genevieve only in their later lives, and Norma as my mother. (There
is a painting of Genevieve as she was in youth; she was a hauntingly lovely
woman.) I never knew Joyce, of course, and don't remember Nancy, though
it is possible I met her when I was a baby, when her mother Ella took care of
me for a while. I have very little that any of them had written; I know them
mainly through the Journal. I translated the material there to their likely views
as well as I could. Thus this is a fictionalized biography, as I put impressions
and thoughts into the minds of women who may or may not have had them.
The facts are as accurate as I could research them, but the feelings of the
women are largely conjectural. One thing I struggled with was the identity
of Elinor's and Genevieve's friend and traveling companion Marion; I believe
this was a different person than the one Alfred dated, because he showed no
reaction to her in Germany.

In some cases I departed entirely from the record, as with Joyce's thoughts
and dreams as she died, and Genevieve's after she died. I do not regard this

as fantasy. Alfred believed in the Afterlife, and was sure he would meet Joyce and Genevieve again there. So I made literal what he believed, though it is not my belief. I differ from him in having no belief in the supernatural, but I try to respect his belief in it. It is my hope that if he was correct, and there is an afterlife, and he is able to see what I have done here, he approves.

This is one of the things I tried to fathom: at what point did Alfred change from his skeptical, virtually atheistic doubt as a teenager, to passionate belief the supernatural ranging from astrology to Afterlife in his later years? When did he become religious? My conclusion is that there were two major events that forced the change. The first was the death of his mother Edith when he was a teen. The second was the sudden death of Joyce. I have a notion of the sort of shock such things can be. When I was sixteen my first cousin Teddy died of cancer of the bone. This is mentioned only passingly in the biography, as it wasn't important to Alfred, but it was one of the defining elements of my life. I can't say Teddy and I were close, but we were only a year apart in age and attending the same school. He was seemingly a happy boy, with a unified and increasingly wealthy family so that he was in no material need and had many friends. I was more depressive, not at all sure I valued my life, from a fractured family, and used to doing without material advantages most other boys had. He was typically in the middle of a happy crowd; I was more of a loner. I never believed in God, but it seemed to me that if there could be a God, making conscious decisions of merit and needing to sacrifice one boy from this larger family, surely I was the logical one to go. Instead it had been Teddy. It was a double shock: the death itself, and the seeming wrongness of the choice. It took me time to work it out in my mind and emotion, but in the end I was more aware of mortality than I had been, and I became a vegetarian so as not to contribute to death in any way I didn't have to. That gradual decision had the force of religion and complicated my existence in college and the US Army and as a professional writer, but it remains a fundamental tenet of my existence.

Okay: I know its origin, from the ugly shock of my cousin's death. Surely the shocks of Alfred's loss of his mother at a similar age, followed by the death of his beloved, had greater impact. He came to believe in the Afterlife because it was the only way he could recover Joyce. The timing seems to be there also: after Joyce he wrote of her existing in the Afterlife. So I believe that was the point of transition, though as in my case, it was not an overnight thing. It was the trigger, whose conclusion might have taken years to realize. To save Joyce he had to believe, and that enabled the belief in other manifestations of the supernatural. I do not mean for this to seem superficial or simple; there are many threads in a person's outlook, which is more like an intricate tapestry than a linear cause and effect. But there are underlying imperatives, and this is the way I see Alfred's.

Another example might be his younger brother Philip: if their mother's early death had impact on Alfred, surely it was greater on Phil. So did Phil develop an interest in the supernatural? Indeed he did. He was a handsome, athletic, intelligent man who once saved the life of another passenger when an airplane they were in crashed in water. Phil was a strong swimmer, having set records at his high school, the same one I attended later. But it was difficult to talk to Phil for more than one sentence without God entering the picture. If a person wondered why a friend suffered misfortune, Phil would say "I don't know the answer, but I know the one who does." From that point on it was all about God. God completely dominated his life; indeed, he joined a religious cult and largely disappeared from societal view, perhaps destroying his immediate family in the process. Enough said; I have savagely negative impressions of the whole business, and it is one of several reasons I never joined any religion. I did not know my uncle well enough to be sure that it was his mother's death that started him on that course, but it is my suspicion.

I learned things as I went through the Journal. It is not necessarily pleasant to discover, for example, a parent's true judgment of yourself as a child, or violence between parents. I dare say that at such time one of my daughters goes through my own private records of thoughts there will be some wincing. We try to protect our children's innocence, and to the extent we succeed, there is potential disillusion later. But some things are simply surprising. I do have an example.

When I wrote my novel of Death, *On a Pale Horse*, I had my father in mind, because of all the people I knew, he was the only one for whom death was a more constant presence than it was for me. I put in one sequence that concerned Alfred. It was family lore that he was close to his mother as a teen, and that as she lay dying in the hospital, her Christian Science faith wavering, she asked him to read the words on the door to the ward she was in and tell her what they were. He went out and looked, but the words were in Latin and he did not understand them. So he spelled them out for her, and she thanked him. Next morning she was dead, having given up her effort to survive. He learned that the Latin was the designation for the ward for the incurable: those doomed. He had inadvertently given her the information that deprived her of hope. He was to live the rest of his life with the lurking belief that he had in effect killed her. That was the story I put into the novel, of course explaining there that the messenger was not to blame for the situation. I did not identify it for Alfred, as I thought he would instantly recognize it. And he did not react. He knew there was something in the novel that related to him, but he was unable to identify it specifically. I marveled at this, and let the subject lapse; maybe it was simply too sensitive. Only with the Journal did I discover that it had not occurred. His mother did not die in a hospital, and Alfred knew Latin and several other languages, so would hardly have been deceived. I think it must have been an embroidered version of the telegram he took to her, which may indeed have contained the news of her hopeless condition, and the way her husband and sister in law violated her privacy by reading it, making Alfred an inadvertent accomplice. He was disgusted, of course, but that was the extent of it. So my little mystery had been solved. Why should Alfred react to an episode that had never happened?

While I fictionalized where I needed to, I did base it on reality as much as possible. Obviously I was not partial to Joyce's dreams as she died, but Alfred did dream of Genevieve at that time; I simply made Joyce a silent participant in that dream. With Nancy it was more complicated. 1932 was the Year of Nancy, Alfred wrote, and indeed it seemed to be true. He did seriously consider asking her to marry him. But he felt he needed advice, and the main person he trusted for this was Ella. How could he ask Ella whether he should marry her daughter? That balked him, and he did not make the decision. Then he encountered Norma, and Nancy and all other young woman simply faded from his romantic awareness. I saw it in the Journal; the references to Nancy stopped. I was sorry to see this, as I feel that Nancy would have been much better for him than Norma. Ugly as it may be for me to say it, I nevertheless believe it: the marriage of my parents was a disaster from the start. Both would have been better off had they never gotten serious about each other. Of course then I would not have come into existence, which puts me in an awkward position. Had I the power to travel back in time and warn Alfred of the magnitude of the mistake he was about to make, and to persuade him to avoid it, would I do so? I am relieved that this is not a decision I have to make.

Actually I can't be sure that Nancy would have been right either. I concluded that she must have changed her mind, and departed from his life, leaving him free to encounter Norma, but that was not quite the case. For one thing, he had already met Norma before Nancy's final visit, and that process was fairly started. For another, Nancy herself denied that she had any romantic designs on him. I discovered that when I was in the Genevieve section, after (I thought) concluding the Joyce/Nancy section. He corresponded with Nancy in the 1980s, long after their separate lives had parted, and asked her: suppose he had gotten up the nerve to express his amorous interest in her? Had he caused her grief by abruptly dropping her? She replied that it was surely just as well that he had not expressed himself at that time, because she would not have known how to handle it. She had regarded him as a friend whose company she much enjoyed, but not as a romantic prospect.

That could certainly be so. But it could also be that she, a nice person, was loath to cause him discomfort at such a late date. She might have been hurt, and chosen not to tell him later, as it was far too late to change. What would be the point? Or she might have been hurt, gotten over it, and preferred to believe that it had never been that serious with Alfred. Or if it was, that she, rather than he, had broken it off. So I left my fanciful scene in place. It is, after all, more romantic, and there could have been at least an element of truth therein.

Alfred was an unusual man. He could make an excellent impression, and be very outgoing and considerate. He could also be withdrawn and hostile. Sometimes he was maddening, and sometimes, when balked or defied, violent. This can be said of almost anyone; we all have our limits and we all make our mistakes. But there was a subtle consistency of pattern underlying his nature that intrigued me, and I wanted to understand it. For one thing, I do have significant points of similarity to him, surely by no coincidence, and it is often easier to fathom a syndrome in another person than in oneself. What was the mystery of Alfred?

The answer, I think, is the Asperger's syndrome. This is a diagnosis that has come into popular awareness relatively recently, and there have been a number of articles about it, replete with conjectures of its existence in historical figures such as Albert Einstein. It is a high-end facet of autism. Most autistics are barely functional in normal human society; they have extreme trouble relating competently to others. Asperger's is less extreme, and its sufferers generally can relate, and sometimes do very well. Einstein is known as the father of the theory of relativity that helped usher in the modern age. Yet as a person he could be quite insensitive. It was as though his brain was wired for special physics rather than for social relations. But the diagnosis is uncertain. Asperger's victims are said to have little sense of humor, and to be unable to make small talk. Einstein had a sense of humor, and so did Alfred. Still, there is a case to be made. Alfred could not make small talk; it drove him crazy. He saw no point in it and was baffled by the way others practiced it. It is also partly in the sometimes startling examples of insensitivity he recorded in the Journal without embarrassment. More than once I murmured to myself "How *could* he!" He was merely perplexed by the reactions of others. Few examples are in this biography, not because I sought to spare him—some involved me, and made me angry at the time—but because they were not observed by the women whose viewpoints I adapted. The women were not in a position to see the complete Alfred, and neither was I. The Journal could be eye-opening in this respect.

Here is one example that is in the text: when Genevieve was loath to change her clothing in front of an open window with the light on, so that anyone might see in. Here is the entry directly from the Journal, for Tuesday, July 10, 1962, referring to Brattleboro Vermont: "Very tired there and close to cantankerous, because of bewilderment at G's notion that people are standing outside the window gazing at her and so having to have lights off or doors closed or curtains down or something like that." That strikes me as pretty clear. What woman of any age wants to risk naked exposure before strangers? Yet Alfred was bewildered and annoyed by what he took as her unreasonableness. Logically he may have been correct: the chances of anyone passing outside at that moment might have been small, and what would it matter anyway? How would it harm her to have someone escape with a secret peek? But this is a consideration of feeling more than logic; of propriety rather than convenience. Most people *don't* like inadvertent private exposure; it can be horribly embarrassing. I believe any normal person appreciates Genevieve's position. Why didn't Alfred?

The key as I see it is empathy. This is a word Alfred did not understand. He believed it was a laboratory phenomenon that could help a scientist understand aspects of the reactions of laboratory animals. He believed it was a misuse to apply it to ordinary life as if it were a synonym for sympathy. This was one of a number of spot mini-lectures he had on various subjects. "It is," he said, "a technical psychological term that only trained psychologists understand." When I said that the dictionary did not agree with him, he was so upset that it took him some time to recover. Now this is interesting. When I differ with a person on the meaning of a word, I go to the dictionary, and when I am wrong, I modify my definition, as the proper usage of every word is important to me. I earn my living by the nuances of words; they fascinate me. I have a fair collection of big dictionaries: the original 1913 Funk & Wagnalls I received on my tenth birthday, the Webster's Unabridged Second Edition of 1945 I inherited from my father-in-law, the Random House Dictionary, and the Compact Edition of the Oxford English Dictionary (OED). (Hmm—should that be abbreviated COED?) That latter is not an abridged edition; it is the full encyclopedia-sized work with print squeezed down so far you must use a magnifying glass to read it. They are all laid out on a shelf and I go to them daily; I have the dictionary habit with a vengeance. Why didn't Alfred go to the dictionary? I suspect it was because he suspected it would give his definition the lie, and he couldn't handle that. There is an aspect of denial here; denial shuts out reality and protects itself from knowing it has done so. Denial is, as the theoretically humorous saying goes, not a river in Africa.

So what is the dictionary definition of empathy? The OED says "The power of entering into the experience of or understanding objects or emotions outside ourselves." The Random House says "The intellectual identification with or vicarious experiencing of the feelings, thoughts, or attitudes of another. The imaginative ascribing to an object, as a natural object or work of art, feelings or attitudes present in oneself." And it says for synonyms to see sympathy, which is "harmony of or agreement in feeling as between persons or on the part of one person with respect to another." Also compassion, commiseration. That seems clear enough to me. The fact is, empathy is large in my life; it is one of the things that enable me to be an effective writer. I can put myself into the place of others, including those of the opposite gender or even alien creatures, feeling their feelings. I am not unusual in this respect; I believe that empathy is one of the defining conditions of being human. I believe I have it and understand it—and Alfred did not.

I conjecture that what is called Asperger's may be to a considerable extent a lack of empathy. That is, the inability to feel what others are feeling. A person short on empathy does not hate others or wish them ill; he merely does not automatically pick up on how they feel. He may not be entirely lacking in it, merely with reduced capacity for it. When another person accidentally cuts himself, most of us wince, almost feeling the pain. That's empathy. When a young couple falls in love, and women cry at their wedding, overwhelmed by emotion, I believe that's empathy. Opposition to the death penalty, however clothed in logic, is fundamentally empathy: no one wants to die. And yes, those promoting the death penalty may be short on empathy, or long on the empathy of vengeance.

As I see it, this lack of empathy was a crucial limitation that handicapped Alfred throughout life, isolating him from others. He could not feel their feelings, only his own. His Journal is marvelously feeling, but it is all *his* feeling; he seldom even wonders how others might feel, and hardly seems to care. When his feelings changed, he forgot what it was like before. When he was young at times he hated his father for not letting him use the car, but as an adult he did not understand the imperatives of children or teenagers. He condemned my sister and me endlessly, calling us infants, alienating us. We were supposed to be little adults and got the message: as children we were simply in the way. As I put it once to my mother, who of course had her own problems with Alfred: "If you can't be young when you're young, when can you be?" As a child I had severe emotional problems. When I figured out that the stress on me derived from my parents rather than myself, I resolved to distance myself emotionally from my family. My empathy may have been destroying me, just as my vivid imagination could terrify me. That was my turning point; I trace the beginning of my slow recovery to that decision. That actually alienated my mother more than my father, as she also lacked empathy, and thereafter she worked to get me packed off to boarding school. The tone of this discussion demonstrates that I retain it to this day: I do not accept the illusions of my parents, and am militantly my own man. But unlike my parents, I have a basis for understanding, and this volume is an example of that effort.

Put two people who lack empathy together and you invite disaster. That was the marriage of my parents. They both meant well, but they couldn't understand or get along with each other, and they simply didn't know how to handle children. They were not cut out to be *parents*. We children were not abused, we did not go hungry, but I do not remember either of them ever kissing or hugging my sister or me as children, or using the word "love" with respect to us. My fondest memory of childhood is the earliest, when I was cared for by a Scottish "nanny" evidently hired by my British grandparents. After that it was pretty much downhill. When at age about ten I spent three hours struggling hunt-and-peck to type out the rules to a game I had invented, and showed it to my mother, she said "Very nice. And here is your spelling list," handing me a list of the words I had misspelled. That was it. When I sent her a copy of *With a Tangled Skein*, the novel wherein a woman with regret left her son to be raised elsewhere, as my mother did by leaving the children in England while she worked in Spain, she said "I don't know why I don't like fantasy." That was all she ever said on that subject. Evidently that concept connected with her no better than the missing episode of inadvertently dooming his mother did with my father. It simply wasn't on her radar. My father was far more responsive about my career as a novelist, and to me in general, while my mother was closer to my sister. For what it's worth, I read somewhere that effective writers are made by having happy lives that then suffer serious disruption in childhood. I do fit the pattern.

So as I see it, my father was unable to appreciate the full meaning of the term "empathy" because he hardly experienced it himself, and therefore had to believe it was invalid. To make a crude parallel, there seem to be some feminists who do not like sex, don't understand how anyone else could like it, and therefore consider all sexual appetite to be abusive. They think men demand it simply to be mean to women. They have to find an explanation for what is otherwise mystifying. Similarly my father sought a reason for the way so many other people used a term he deemed to be meaningless in human relations. He concluded that these people were simply ignorant, and were misusing it. And when I challenged that, he had a problem, because by that time I had established my command of the English language and my ability to document my statements about it. It left him with no recourse except to suffer, and to put the matter from his mind. I was not trying to torment him; it was that incident that set me on the track of the problem, and it took me years to fathom it. It had not occurred to me that he could lack such a basic human quality. Only as I went through the Journal did that pattern start to appear. Again, I want to clarify that he did not wish anyone ill; he simply was often unable to see that others had a special ability he largely lacked. I say largely because of course such things are seldom absolutes; there is a continuum ranging from near total to near absence. On a scale of 10, his empathy might have been a 3. There were times when he did show understanding and sympathy, but these were relatively rare, and tended to be on an intellectual plane. Only someone extremely accommodating to his wishes could really get along with him at close range. That person was definitely not Norma; it was Genevieve.

Even there, there could be occasional problems. Alfred was annoyed with me because I did not do chores he wanted done. He did not spell them out; he expected me to fathom them on my own and do them unasked. I of course had learned not to volunteer, having been rebuked for not doing things his way; I kept peace by letting him set the agenda. But there was an occasion when he was riding with Genevieve, and it was hot, and he knew she would prefer to have the window open, and that it was too stiff for her to open herself. But he did not open it for her, because she did not ask him to. Genevieve, an extremely obliging woman, preferred to suffer rather than put him to the inconvenience. So his own rule of fathoming and volunteering did not apply to himself. I am reminded of a science fiction story I read, about a doctor who did not treat a dying patient because the patient did not request treatment. The patient was comatose, unable to ask, and doctor knew this, but still did not act. Why? Because the doctor was a machine, programmed to obey, not to initiate. The moral: A MACHINE DOES NOT *CARE*. Alfred could be like that. He did care, but could not necessarily translate that to relevant action.

Another thing that shows in the Journal is the obsession Alfred had with what he called "face fingering." Normal people, when they interact with others, tend to cover their mouths or mask their faces to a degree with their hands. They may rub or scratch absentmindedly. It is a largely unconscious way to ease discomfort or nervousness, and it often is a habit. You can see it when people are interacting on television, or at meetings. It is practically universal. But it drove Alfred up the wall. He couldn't stand to see it, and would avert his gaze or depart. Evidently his lack of empathy prevented him from appreciating how this, like the use of interjections like "er" or "um" when speaking, was actually a social lubricant. It seemed to him like an unclean demonstration. It was something he mentioned to me because he observed that I did not do it. That's because I have had my own awkward experiences, and learned to keep my hands away from my face in public; I regard it as discipline rather than a positive state. It was ironic that it became a small point of accord between us. But my question is, what business of his was it if other people rubbed their noses or covered their mouths? I never even noticed it in others until Alfred mentioned it, and it doesn't matter to me if they do. I can understand why they do it, as my empathy is not thwarted, only my emulation. So I wonder if Alfred simply found a need to be critical, as he was of my sister and me when we were children, lacking the ability to relate.

The Journal largely skipped the Spanish years, not because Alfred lacked interest, I think, but because he was simply too busy. For that I filled in from Norma's discussion of Spain, which was published as an appendix in my autobiography *Bio of an Ogre*. I remember some, of course, but had no knowledge of the Spanish Civil War or the relief work my parents were doing. My sister and I were taken care of mainly by Spanish staff; we were beginning to learn Spanish, but lost that when we came to America.

I was curious when Alfred became a vegetarian. My own vegetarianism I decided for myself in college; of course I knew of Alfred's, and had his example, but that was not my reason. When did he change, and what was his reason? I found no point of decision. I believe it happened during his time in England, and could have related to the death of Joyce, but I have no evidence.

The portion of the Journal that affected me the most was the copy of his letter to Ella, Joyce's mother, after Joyce died. I quoted most of it in the main text. I find it painful yet absolutely beautiful in its poignant memory and its love.

It is no wonder, then, that every glance from my window,
every touch of the cold wind, every curve of the silhouetted skyline

brings with it the thought of her whose heart was in these things. As I sat just now on a snowy mound on the side of a wooded hill, watching the clouds above the black trees across the valley, I thought and thought.

And so do I, thinking of my father, half-longing for what it seemed could never be for him. I fault him, perhaps, for lacking the ability to feel what others felt, but it can not be denied that his own feeling was relevant.